Creating the Desire for Change in Higher Education

Also Available from Bloomsbury

Community-Based Transformational Learning, *edited by Christian Winterbottom, Jody S. Nicholson and F. Dan Richard*
Scholarly Leadership in Higher Education, *Wayne J. Urban*
Dominant Discourses in Higher Education, *Ian M. Kinchin and Karen Gravett*
Pursuing Teaching Excellence in Higher Education, *Margaret Wood and Feng Su*
Changing Higher Education for a Changing World, *edited by Claire Callender, William Locke and Simon Marginson*
Decolonizing University Teaching and Learning, *D. Tran*
Leadership for Sustainability in Higher Education, *Janet Haddock-Fraser, Peter Rands and Stephen Scoffham*

Creating the Desire for Change in Higher Education

The Amsterdam Path to the Research–Teaching Nexus

edited by Didi M. E. Griffioen

BLOOMSBURY ACADEMIC
LONDON • NEW YORK • OXFORD • NEW DELHI • SYDNEY

BLOOMSBURY ACADEMIC
Bloomsbury Publishing Plc
50 Bedford Square, London, WC1B 3DP, UK
1385 Broadway, New York, NY 10018, USA
29 Earlsfort Terrace, Dublin 2, Ireland

BLOOMSBURY, BLOOMSBURY ACADEMIC and the Diana logo are
trademarks of Bloomsbury Publishing Plc

First published in Great Britain 2023
Paperback edition published 2024

Copyright © Didi M. E. Griffioen and contributors, 2023

Didi M. E. Griffioen and contributors have asserted their right under the Copyright,
Designs and Patents Act, 1988, to be identified as Author of this work.

For legal purposes the Acknowledgements on pp. xii–xiii constitute
an extension of this copyright page.

Cover image © courtneyk/Getty Images

This work is published open access subject to a Creative Commons
Attribution-NonCommercial-NoDerivatives 3.0 licence (CC BY-NC-ND 3.0,
https://creativecommons.org/licenses/by-nc-nd/3.0/). You may re-use, distribute,
and reproduce this work in any medium for non-commercial purposes,
provided you give attribution to the copyright holder and the publisher
and provide a link to the Creative Commons licence.

Bloomsbury Publishing Plc does not have any control over, or responsibility for,
any third-party websites referred to or in this book. All internet addresses given
in this book were correct at the time of going to press. The author and publisher
regret any inconvenience caused if addresses have changed or sites have ceased
to exist, but can accept no responsibility for any such changes.

A catalogue record for this book is available from the British Library.

A catalog record for this book is available from the Library of Congress.

ISBN:	HB:	978-1-3502-4479-5
	PB:	978-1-3502-4481-8
	ePDF:	978-1-3502-4477-1
	eBook:	978-1-3502-4478-8

Typeset by Integra Software Services Pvt. Ltd.

To find out more about our authors and books visit www.bloomsbury.com
and sign up for our newsletters.

Contents

List of figures	vi
List of tables	vii
List of contributors	viii
Foreword	x
Acknowledgements	xii

	Introduction: Creating Desire to Change Research–Education Connections *Didi M. E. Griffioen*	1
1	The Origin, Content and Context of Changing Research–Education Connections *Didi M. E. Griffioen*	21
2	Mechanisms for Change *Didi M. E. Griffioen*	43
3	Instruments to Debate Change *Didi M. E. Griffioen*	63
4	Changes in Perceptions of Research Integration *Mette Bruinsma and Didi M. E. Griffioen*	95
5	Changes in Curriculum Rationales *Linda van Ooijen-van der Linden, Indira N. Z. Day, Jolieke Timmermans and Didi M. E. Griffioen*	123
6	Changes in Curriculum Learning Goals *Linda van Ooijen-van der Linden, Natalie Pareja Roblin, Jason Nak, Iris Jong and Didi M. E. Griffioen*	149
7	Changes in Academics' Job Profiles *Sanne R. Daas, Didi M. E. Griffioen, Chevy M. van Dorresteijn and Indira N. Z. Day*	175
8	Reflections on the Multiple Layers of Organisational Change *Didi M. E. Griffioen*	199

Index	209

Figures

1.1	Overview of the combined layers and perspectives of research–education connections	30
2.1	Overview of change approach based on projects	48
3.1	The Strategy Mapping Instrument to be used at the university-, faculty- or department-level debates on research–education connections	67
3.2	The String Instrument with sorted beads on the type of planning in the left-hand model and functionally stringed beads for implementation in the right-hand model. This instrument was previously published in Dutch in Griffioen, Visser-Wijnveen and Willems (2013)	69
3.3	Landscape Overview Instrument	70
3.4	The perspectives of research instrument	73
3.5	Levels of certainty and risk model: What is research in the educational programme for?	76
3.6	The research phases model: short version	78
3.7	The phases of research instrument	79
3.8	Research level and content instrument, example comparison	84
3.9	Routine versus innovative professional action	87
5.1	Percentage of appearance of the four types of argumentation on including research in the curricula	134

Tables

3.1	Overview of the Research Autonomy and Complexity Tool (RAC-T)	81
3.2	Elements of professional routine and professional innovation	86
5.1	Overview of included self-reports in both time periods	132
7.1	Overview of all tasks and competencies including example quotes	184
7.2	Relative occurrence of research- and teaching-related competences and tasks (percentage of profile totals)	186
7.3	Frequencies of four most occurring job profiles. Relative occurrence between brackets	193

Contributors

Mette Bruinsma is lecturer in Cultural History at Utrecht University, the Netherlands. She obtained her PhD in Human Geography at the University of Glasgow, Scotland, in 2021. Her research interests focus on the history of knowledge and the history of academic education.

Sanne Daas is a researcher at the Department of Higher Education, Research and Innovation at the Amsterdam University of Applied Sciences, the Netherlands. Her research interests focus on the strategic policy of applied universities and employee behaviour in regard to connecting research and education. She is completing a PhD dissertation on this subject under the supervision of Prof. Dr. Jeroen Huisman (Ghent University) and Dr. Didi M. E. Griffioen (AUAS).

Indira Day is a postdoctoral researcher at the Department of Education at Utrecht University, the Netherlands, where she studies the professional development of teachers in higher education during educational innovations in a project funded by the Netherlands Initiative for Education Research. Additionally, she is a researcher at the University of Applied Sciences Leiden, the Netherlands's Faculty of Health, where she studies student well-being. Her previous work includes research into feedback and assessment in higher education.

Chevy van Dorresteijn is a researcher at the Research Institute of Child Development and Education at the University of Amsterdam, the Netherlands. His most recent publications focused on the transition to online education following the Covid-19 pandemic. He is working on research concerned with how legal students are prepared to work as legal practitioners and the effects of experiential legal education.

Didi M. E. Griffioen works as a university-wide Professor and Head of the Department of Higher Education Research and Education at Amsterdam University of Applied Sciences, the Netherlands. She specialises in the enhancement of interactions between research, education and professional fields, with a holistic focus ranging from curriculum and organisational development, to student education, to collaborations at the micro-level. She has published nationally and internationally for scientific and professional audiences.

Iris Jong is a third-year Liberal Arts & Sciences student at Amsterdam University College, the Netherlands. Sociology and international relations are the fields she explored during her bachelor's. Her research interests focus on migratory experiences, biopolitics and community formation in times of polarisation.

Jason Nak works as a tutor at the Department of Psychology at the University of Amsterdam, the Netherlands. His research focuses on educational development and psychological methods. He has published on curriculum development and is working on developing measures to monitor student learning.

Linda van Ooijen-van der Linden is senior researcher at the Department of Higher Education, Research, and Innovation, Amsterdam University of Applied Sciences, the Netherlands. She is an all-round researcher with human learning and development as main topics. Since she wrote her PhD thesis *Prediction of Study Success – Creation of Magic Zones* (2018), she focuses on learning and innovation in higher education.

Natalie Pareja Roblin is an educational researcher, instructional designer and teacher educator. She works as Policy Researcher for the Teaching and Learning Centre of the University of Amsterdam, the Netherlands. Her research focuses on curriculum design, educational innovation and teacher professional development, and on how these may be supported by research-practice partnerships.

Jolieke Timmermans was a student assistant at the Higher Education Research and Innovation research department, Amsterdam University of Applied Sciences, the Netherlands. During this time she contributed on two different projects: 'To create tomorrow together' and a monitoring study on 'visions of research in the curriculum'. With also being a student herself while working on these projects, she was driven by wanting to make a difference for other students at her university. She is busy with writing her thesis to get her Bachelor of Science, and studying Communication and Multimedia Design.

Foreword

Bringing about successful changes in higher education requires not only a clear vision of the desired change, but also a depth of understanding of the processes of change and the range of options that are appropriate to the local and national context and culture that may help deliver the vision.

Much has been written over the last twenty years on promoting closer linkages between research and education (teaching) within higher education. There is also a growing literature on change management in higher education. This book provides a detailed and nuanced discussion of how the insights about the process of change may be applied to developing research–education connections within one institution, the Amsterdam University of Applied Sciences (Hogeschool van Amsterdam) over a five-year period.

The insights provided by Didi M. E. Griffioen, the architect of the 'research into education strategic programme', and her team, bring the book alive. As participant researchers, they cleverly integrate the literature on change management with that on linking research and education and show the importance of adopting a nuanced approach to navigating the local context, the wide range of views on the desirability of undertaking these changes, and the different perceptions of what is meant by research and connecting it to education. Importantly they recognise that not all change is for the better. The picture that emerges is that for change to be successful, many conversations between stakeholders are essential, but these need to take place within a clear framework and sense of direction provided by senior management. They present a wide range of instruments that they used in stimulating the process of change, which others charged with bringing about closer integration between research and education in their contexts should find most helpful. There are separate chapters exploring the rationales for bringing about curriculum changes, changes in curriculum learning goals and, importantly, the changes needed in academic job profiles.

I can thoroughly recommend this book to readers interested not only in the promotion of research–education linkages, but as a case study of successful change management within higher education. They eschew a cook-book approach and present us with a clear framework embedded in the culture of their institution and the Dutch higher education system. Prof. Griffioen and her team have done us a service by their detailed analysis and thoughtful reflections on their experiences in bringing about change in research–education connections in their context.

Mick Healey
Healey HE Consultants
Howden, UK
December 2021

Acknowledgements

It is necessary that change processes have many mothers and fathers. It is the same for a book as this one. First, I would like to thank the authors of contributions to this volume, as authors, but even more as researchers, co-creators, debaters and advocates of the Research into Education change programme that underpins its content. The change programme was a collective effort, and so was writing this book.

The change programme itself had many prominent actors in different phases of its development: Huib de Jong as president of our university who, already in his first week of office, asked for a more integrated approach for research–education connections, and has remained an active advocate of the topic ever since. Dymph van Outersterp as senior policy officer, who kindly commented on every twist and turn of this programme in the preparatory phase, and who provided me with the initial time and space to take on the programme leader role.

The change programme was shaped as an evidence-driven and continuously evaluated path, based on the argument that as higher education professionals we should be willing to work evidence-based, especially if that is what we aim to train our students to do as future professionals. We walked the talk, also when it was not easy. As the managerial programme owner, Jean Tillie embraced this perspective and was our spokesperson for this approach among university management, to make sure we could apply our own complex metrics and not singular university metrics throughout the five years. Without Jean taking this stance, this book would not have been possible. The particular metrics provided the foundation for Chapters 4, 5, 6 and 7. The many debates Jean and I had about the strategy and content of university-wide change are very visible in the content of this volume.

The content of this book has been provided by many of our seventy-plus Amsterdam University of Applied Sciences (AUAS) educational programmes, who provided us insight into their developments, the choices that were made for research integration, and the difficulties they perceived along the way. We thank them for their participation and honesty.

During different phases of the change programme, Heleen Wellner and Linda van Ooijen-van der Linden served as executive co-programme leaders, several others played their parts as colleagues or student-assistants in the change programme team. And finally, very many colleagues were actively part of the debate sessions, surveys or interview. Several colleagues from other institutions came over to our university to provide keynotes or workshops, sometimes even across continents. The national network of policy officers connecting research and teaching, as well as the network of faculty representatives were important reference groups to test and enhance ideas for strategy and content of the change.

The Higher Education, Research and Innovation (HERI) team pulled together to create the work underpinning this book, as well as to ensure the quality of the final manuscript. It is wonderful to see how a group of colleagues can work together to create a collective piece of work. The collective desire to do so is a great joy to experience.

And finally we would like to thank our reviewer and our editor for their kind support and enthusiasm about this book. It is great to know that others can feel as passionate about a project as we do.

Thank you all.
Didi M. E. Griffioen
Amsterdam
24 January 2022

Introduction: Creating Desire to Change Research–Education Connections

Didi M. E. Griffioen

Introduction

Many governments view the connections between research and education as important for the proper education of future citizens (Griffioen, Ashwin, & Scholkmann, 2021). Additionally, these connections are considered foundational for the innovative force that is higher education. Many international scholars have confirmed this importance (Barnett, 2012; Heggen, Karseth, & Kyvik, 2010). However, this positivity about research–education connections, which we later on in this chapter call 'the romantic notion', following Robertson (2007), does not make them uniform or easy to establish.

Research–education connections can have many different shapes and forms related to different levels in the university organisation, such as in modules, curricula or departments. In current research and education universities, these connections are in all cases foundational for the university set-up. Many state that the co-existing of education and research makes a university a university, although others disagree (for the debate e.g. Rosowsky, 2020). With the presence of research and education in a single organisation, one can at least argue that the type and intensity of their relatedness – or connection – characterise the university as a viable hybrid organisation. The organisational necessity of research–education connections is an addition to the current scholarship of research–teaching nexus.

This book focuses on the change approaches needed to alter research–education connections in university organisations. Research–education connections are a wider perspective than the research–teaching nexus. 'Teaching' here is seen as part of 'education', which also includes 'learning', 'the curriculum' and the many organisational characteristics needed to provide education, such as strategy, policy, structures and procedures in the organisational context (derived from Buller, 2015). Changing research–education connections therefore focuses not only on changing actions of academics in teaching, but also the multiple layers of organisational change that need to be altered when changing research–education connections as such. Therefore, this book explores the organisational perspective of micro-level and meso-level change, instead of the macro-level policy alterations on which many studies about change are focused (Kondakci & Van den Broeck). University organisations are here defined as: 'a structured system in which individuals come together as a group in order to achieve a common goal' (Buller, 2015, p. 11) and where the individuals recognise their relationship with that system and its commonly understood purpose (Griseri, 2013). University organisations are here therefore defined through their structures and membership.

The presumption is that collectives of individuals make organisations, and to change organisations implies changing the actions of its collectives of individuals. This perspective follows from the need for individual actions for research–education connections to exist in university practice. As argued in Chapter 2, for research–education connections to change, individual academics need to reinvent their individual and collective practices. Studies have shown that individual academics can indeed change their own actions and therefore their own research–education connections (e.g. Åkerlind, 2011; Brew, 2010; Visser-Wijnveen, 2009). Similar studies indicate that the potential of these changes are related closely to academics' values and perceptions, and are not experienced as easy while organisational structures often hinder intended changes (e.g. Durning & Jenkins, 2005; Lopes, Boyd, Andrew, & Pereira, 2014; Schouteden, Verburgh, & Elen, 2014).

The field of the research–teaching nexus generally focuses on *what* stakeholders involved believe the research–education connection is or should be. The field mainly provides suggestions, perceptions and ideals about the content of the potential connections between research and education, which are generally normative in nature (Trowler & Wareham, 2008). The answers are multiple and often conceptual or normative, whether in the curriculum (Fung, 2017; Griffioen, Groen, & Nak, 2019), in didactical approaches (Elsen, Visser-Wijnveen, Van der Rijst, & Van Driel, 2008; Healey, 2005) or in the wider organisation (Jenkins & Healey, 2005; Jenkins, Healey, & Zetter, 2007). Studies alternatively focus on the connection between research and education in the stakeholders' activities: of students (Pitcher, 2011; Pitcher & Åkerlind, 2009), of academics (Griffioen & De Jong, 2015; Visser-Wijnveen, Van Driel, Van der Rijst, Verloop, & Visser, 2009), or of administrators (Boerma, Griffioen, & De Jong, 2013; Griffioen & De Jong, 2017; Neumann, 1993). Studies focusing more generically on educational change mostly consider the changes in a curriculum as such, without including the curriculum's organisational context (e.g. Potter & Devecchi, 2020; Trowler, 2020). Where the *what* of educational change receives attention, the *how* or the *why* is not focused on as much.

The *how* of change is a topic that expectantly appears in change management literature. Those authors focusing on change in higher education have detailed attention for how changes can be achieved, as well as why change processes should be embraced generally. The content of the change receives much less, if any, attention, presuming that the change process on different topics can be similar (e.g. Bess & Dee, 2008; Buller, 2015; Kezar, 2018). Buller illustrates this (2015, p. 55), suggesting that 'it isn't whether we should change but how'. Bess and Dee (2008, p. 796) state that change can be defined as 'an alteration in the structures, processes, and/or behaviours in a system or as the introduction of something new in an organisation'. Content is implied in the last definition, but nothing more than that. The presumption for writing this book was that change processes are not generic in their execution and that the content in which the change takes place matters for its sensibility, planning, execution and results. Considering the change process is content related, we also define change processes as purposeful. A certain aim for direction is intended when a change process begins, even when the outcome cannot be defined yet, and even when the changes followed from grassroots changes before they were formalised. When we consider 'change' in this book, it is about an alternation that needs to be done purposefully in which someone or a larger group of people had decided at some point to start achieving some changes. Others have suggested that change can be seen as continuous change for improvement (Kondakci & Van den Broeck, 2009). While we acknowledge the importance of continuous improvement in universities, the notion of 'change' is here framed as a purposeful and systematic process. Thus, for the authors in this book, a change process is longer than a few incidents and at some point includes a purposefully added mechanism intended to change the current status quo. Change in this sense can emerge from continuous improvement, as is elaborated on in Chapter 2, but purpose and sense of direction are needed to define it as 'change' (see also Kezar, 2018).

This book provides the conceptual knowledge for creating situational change mechanisms to alter research–education connections with a specific focus on one or more organisational levels in a particular university. The concept of the mechanism for change is here founded in both the current body of knowledge of the field of the research–teaching nexus and the field of organisational change as well as in the case of a five-year university change programme called 'Research into Education' at Amsterdam University of Applied Sciences (Amsterdam UAS), the largest university in the Netherlands (48,000 students; 5,000 employees). This book's main argument is partly derived from theory and partly illustrated by this large case study, which was also empirically researched during its five-year existence. The full case study is introduced in Chapter 2. Throughout the Amsterdam UAS change programme, conceptual principles and practical tools from the two disciplinary fields were combined, resulting in a new mechanism for change that is both conceptually rich and very hands-on in that multiple tools were developed for changing elements of research–education practices across the university, as needed for substantial change processes. Therefore, this book provides an important insight for colleagues around the world eager to increase the connection between research and education.

This chapter first introduces a more conceptual perspective to university change, considering what proposed and purposeful change is viable in terms of higher education's societal responsibilities (Section 1.2). Then we elaborate on the characteristics relevant for changing research–education connections (Section 1.3). Combined, these sections set the scenery for changing research–education connections in universities. At the end of the chapter, the full outline of the book is described.

Sensible Reasons for Higher Education Change

This book addresses change and change mechanisms, while all too often a university would have been better off if change had never been proposed. Changing the processes of higher education is inevitably a costly endeavour in time, money and energy, and should therefore be initiated for the right purposes. As Kezar (2018, p. xiii) states: 'Change is too disruptive a process to engage in with these high failure rates, and poor change efforts can lead to poor morale, disengagement by employees, and wasted time and productivity'. While Kezar (2018) argues for research-informed change processes, as was the Amsterdam programme, Buller (2015) provides several examples of higher management (himself included) starting change processes for the wrong reasons. He illustrates the importance for top leaders not to fall in the naive action bias, which wrongly suggests that any action is better than no action. We are all familiar with examples of unfortunate organisational change processes, yielding that every change agent at the start of a change process should actively wonder out loud whether the proposed changes are needed.

Higher Education's Responsibility to Society as a Frame of Reference

One approach to weighing the sensibility of an organisational change proposal is to consider whether they contribute to higher educations' core responsibilities. Often, the narrative of a change process is more operational, for instance when aiming to implement a new pedagogy, new ICT system or a new governance model. Factors considered are therefore budget, time and politics. Without disregarding operational variables, truly changing the processes in a higher education institution has a large impact on everyone and everything involved and should not be started without knowing its impact on higher education's societal purpose. Higher education institutes are not only organisational units, but also fulfil a particular role in society and have societal responsibilities (Griffioen, 2021). Most universities have formulated mission statements, which can alter over time and are often intended to differ between universities in a single region. However, the responsibilities that society addresses to universities have a much longer duration and generally only differ between universities in their interpretation. Following Bourdieu (1986), the responsibilities of the university system, and therefore (the collective of) higher education institutions, are threefold: to ensure *embodied capital*, to create and guard *institutionalised capital* and to provide for *objectified knowledge* (Griffioen, 2019).

Embodied capital relates to the learning of individuals and groups of people. Universities have the societal responsibility to provide people access to the knowledge present in society through providing pedagogical and didactical learning instruments. This access results in the highest level of learning systematically provided in our societies, next to the possibilities for learning in other school types. Historically, this responsibility for high level learning focused on the society's male elites. Since the 1960s, this responsibility was expanded to all citizens of society, although more focus is still given to the younger ones. There is a large international debate about the equality in citizens' access opportunities, which also differs between countries and parts of the world. We acknowledge the importance of this debate, as well as the importance of access to education independent from funding, ethnicity and social status; however, this is not a central argument in this chapter.

Higher educations' responsibility to institutionalised capital focuses on certification, through which citizens who have shown competency at the highest level of learning receive a formal degree with civil effects in society. This responsibility to institutionalise shown ability via certificates, yields higher educations' responsibility for selecting certain roles in society (Pels, 2009), although there is increasing debate about the function of degrees in job application (Gallagher, 2016; Wheelahan & Moodie, 2021). Higher education's role in institutionalised capital is often combined with its responsibility to help people learn, but can also be mutually distinguished. People can intend to learn without aiming for a degree or develop their competencies elsewhere and then later qualify for a certificate at a higher-education institution.

Finally, higher education institutes are responsible for systematised knowledge. They are society's keepers of knowledge developed in society, as well as through the methodology needed to systematise new knowledge into bodies of knowledge. With this responsibility, higher education promises to provide society with powerful, declarative knowledge that is considered true (Griffioen, 2019; Nowotny, 2016; Rupp, 1997). Recently, this responsibility has been extended from mostly disciplinary knowledge only – including the traditional university-educated 'professions' of medicine, law, theology, architecture and teaching – to including professional knowledge at the highest level, such as commercial economics, physical therapy and nursing, by implementing research at applied universities.

Hence, by wondering whether the proposed organisational changes relate to learning, certifying or systematising disciplinary or professional knowledge, one gives oneself a frame of reference for the proposed changes' sensibility.

Two Types of Change Sensibility

Thus, the first question to answer in a change process is if the change is needed. This can be addressed through considering its impact on higher educations' three societal responsibilities and by asking *why* the change is important. Answers that indicate the change is indeed needed, come in two forms: the interpretation of one or more societal responsibilities has changed, or the interpretation of how this can best be achieved has altered. To unpack these two, first the notion of 'interpretation' needs to be acknowledged. It is important to realise these three societal responsibilities are not as clear cut as they seem; people, and organisations as collectives of people differ in how they interpret or perceive learning, certifying and systematising knowledge. These interpretations depend on many variables, such as higher education's public or private role as well as financing university research (Teixeira, Kim, Landoni, & Gilani, 2017), the role of students as part of a community or as consumers (Tomlinson, 2017), the importance of equal access and who is in/excluded in that notion (Ilie & Rose, 2016) and individual beliefs in the scientific method and its limitations (Gibbons et al., 1994; Nowotny, Scott, & Gibbons, 2001), to state just a few relevant topics. Depending on one's beliefs, interpreting higher education's core responsibilities can be different between individuals and groups of people. A proper insight in the beliefs of core stakeholders is 'need to know' information in a change process. However, this information is fluent. The interpretations of the three societal responsibilities also change over time within the same group, as discourses, ideas and contexts alter – which again influences their relationship to a proposed change process. Therefore, to consider the relationship between a proposed change process and higher educations' societal responsibilities is to first consider the current, local and contextual interpretations of these responsibilities.

The first cause for a change programme follows from altered interpretations of one or more of higher education's societal responsibilities. An example of this changed definition is the returning strive for inclusiveness in higher education, which occurs over time and with changing definitions. Just after the Second World War, Dutch higher education requested for more students because they were needed to rebuild society, as the then Minister of education explained (Koppen, 1990). In the 1960s, higher education organisations needed to adapt to the active influx of students of non-elite groups, in particular of women, through the teacher-education route (Griffioen, 2013). Over time, the introduction of study tuition has provided opportunities for students of lower income families (Marchand, 2014). Currently the strive for diversity and inclusion (Salmi & D'Addio, 2021) is again an effect of the changed definition of who should benefit from higher education's responsibility in society. With society redefining higher education's responsibility to include a more diverse group, new changes need to be made to higher education to re-become successful according to the new interpretations, which provides a serious and important challenge.

Another example of redefining societal responsibilities can be seen in the aforementioned changed definition of the responsibility for objectified knowledge. Higher education adapted its processes to a changing definition of knowledge at the end of the nineteenth century when the scientific turn in higher education positioned principles from the natural sciences on central stage. To empirically test phenomena became of increased importance (Ruegg,

2004). In the last decades, another shift in interpretations of objectified knowledge occurred, from 'testing to discover true knowledge' to 'usable knowing for practice and society'. Applied universities are the frontrunners in this change. Their new research activities yield for and extend the responsibility for objectified disciplinary knowledge from being mainly about disciplinary knowledge, to now including professional knowledge, which consists of new artefacts, methodologies and quality criteria (Griffioen, 2019; Young & Muller, 2014). Embracing professional knowledge in this responsibility will not only extend higher educations' responsibility, but also change its knowledge beliefs and knowledge processes (Gibbons et al., 1994; Nowotny et al., 2001) due to the multifaceted structure of professional knowledge. With its need for applicability, professional knowledge integrates procedural knowledge (know how), embodied knowledge (feel how to do) and evaluative knowledge (know how to evaluate), next to the more declarative or disciplinary types of knowledge (know that) (Griffioen, 2019). Therefore, the changed definition of higher educations' responsibility for objectified knowledge will further request for changes in relevant activities, perceptions and methodologies, which relates to the core higher education change topic in this book.

The second reason for higher education change related to its societal responsibility is more instrumental: Change is needed if new approaches can provide better results on the same interpretation of responsibilities. Sometimes context infuses these approaches. The Covid-19 pandemic requested for a new fully online or hybrid approach to education as well as to academic working in general. Implementing ICT applications was not based on a changed idea of learning; it was merely implemented because learning as it is interpreted would otherwise no longer be possible. Thus, new ways of teaching and learning were invented and executed, except in those programmes where online working had already been the basic standard due to previous existing different interpretations of learning and/or accessibility, for instance in programmes that included students from across a larger region.

A second example of better approaches is elaborated on in Chapter 2. In the Amsterdam UAS case, the responsibility for implementing research in the curriculum changed from the research professors' responsibility to the educational managers' responsibility. Here, the interpretation of learning and what educational provision should look like did not change; the changes were made to create such educational programmes.

Starting a change programme thus also implies wondering why the changes are needed. Did the interpretations of higher education's societal responsibilities shift? Is there a better way to achieve the same goals? There should be a visible connection. If not, one should seriously wonder if the higher-education institute, its students and academics will indeed benefit from the proposed changes.

Universities as hybrid organisations of research and education

In addition to the reasons for higher education change, the context of higher-education organisations is relevant. There are many perspectives on what constitutes the workings of an organisation such as universities. When one aims to change aspects of an organisation, it is important to first consider these workings because these are the ones that need to be changed to result in changed practices; therefore, the precise mechanisms of higher-education institutes need to be considered. In Chapter 2, we unpack ways to influence that mechanism.

In general, organisations are a mechanism, or way of working, consisting of more fixed and more fluent elements. Thornton et al. (2012, p. 14) explain that 'mechanisms have two sets of distinct abstract elements, the specification of actors and the specification in which the actors are assumed to operate'. The more fixed context in which the actors operate is the organisational architecture, which is the fabric or the playing field that makes an organisation what it is. This organisational architecture consists of all formalised decisions, such as formalised roles in research, teaching, administration and in support; formalised hierarchies; formalising delegated responsibilities; the assigned budgets and the wages paid for certain roles. When these combined decisions are made, they create the basic structure or architecture of the organisation that directs who is allowed or stimulated to act in a certain way.

The organisation's fluent elements can be witnessed in the ways its people individually or collectively interact with the organisation's architecture. This way of interacting can differ between individuals and groups, resulting in a university organisation of multiple realities. Trowler (2020, p. 97) states: 'Universities do not have a single organisational culture but a dynamic multiple cultural configuration'. As is known from implementing policy at the national level, stakeholders within universities – academics, policy officers, students and others – also have their own perceptions, interests, goals and values that play a role in their daily functioning. They likely do not consider themselves as willing executors of university strategy (Duivenboden, Van Hout, Van Montfort, & Vermaas, 2009). This fluency results in the multiple organisational realities within which change agents need to work. This fluency makes organisations generally resistant to change, even more so with large numbers of highly qualified professionals, as universities are (Buller, 2015). A better understanding of the set-up of university organisations can assist in designing a functional change mechanism, as is further explained in Chapter 2. First, we need to elaborate on the nature of universities that is built on education *and* research.

The Hybridity of Universities

In addition to the fixed and fluent characteristics of any organisation, the university organisation incorporates research and education as two primary processes, which makes it a hybrid organisation. Research-intensive universities have started to transform – *avant la letter* – into hybrid organisations since the scientific turn in the nineteenth century. The increasing dominance of the natural sciences resulted in a deviation between 'learning and teaching' on the one hand and 'researching' on the other. This new duality raised the wish to achieve a 'connection' between both. Even though some time has passed, the connection between research and education remains a challenge for research-intensive universities (Fung, 2017).

European applied universities have started to become hybrids following the Lisbon Treaty (EUA, 2007), which still makes the responsibility of 'research' relatively new for applied universities. Since the 1990s the *Polytechnics*, *Fachhochschulen* and *Hogescholen* have functionally (and some formally) transformed into universities of both research and education (Griffioen & Van Ooijen-van der Linden, 2021). Different national systems have so far resulted in different types of ambitions for applied universities, ranging from being research-driven, to education-driven, to professional practice-driven strategies (Ellis, McNicholl, & Pendry, 2012; Griffioen & De Jong, 2017; Hales & Clarke, 2016).

Both research-intensive universities and applied universities are in some way aware of needed to tune their organisational research–education connections because their organisation's complexity follows from these two primary processes. Some national governments actively stimulate this connection between research and education, as does the European Union (2015), while other countries leave that responsibility to the higher-education sector or to the separate universities (Griffioen et al., 2021).

When organisations are considered as a 'structured system of individuals' (Buller, 2015), the hybridity creates increasingly complex universities. They include the active presence of more than one primary process, culture and/or logic (Skelcher & Smith, 2015), not only between but also within groups of people. A single university department can consist of people working as lecturer, while others mainly work in research. Applied universities show this division more often. Other universities' departments focused on research, are separated from those with a thick focus on teaching and only few research activities, making them thoroughly different. While many refer to Von Humboldt's university as a unity of research and education with its ideal of 'learning in a research mode', his idea has not been realised as such (Robertson, 2007; Simons & Elen, 2007). The primary process of education comes with other activities, another culture and another pace than the primary process of research. Academics more involved in research are expected to have another pattern of basic assumptions and other ways of working that are considered more valid than the academics more involved in teaching. Some even show that the same people feel they need to handle different cultures, discourse or norms in research activities and in teaching activities (Boyd & Smith, 2011; Santos, Pereira, & Lopes, 2021; Winkel, Van der Rijst, Poel, & Van Driel, 2016). These differences frame people's identities through how they act and think and what they consider viable results of their work, as well as what is important in the process to achieve goals (Hermansen, 2020).

Education and research are founded in different logics (Thornton, Ocasio, & Lounsbury, 2012), with the activities in the primary process of research framed by the logics of science (Greenwood, Raynard, Kodeih, Micelotta, & Lounsbury, 2011), with its own notions of truth, ways of working and types of output. In turn, the logics of pedagogy influence the activities in the primary process of education (Meyer, 1977), which differs from that of science. Logics influence human behaviour because they can be defined as 'the socially constructed historical patterns of cultural symbols and material practices, assumptions, values and beliefs by which individuals produce and reproduce their material subsistence, organise time and space, and provide meaning to their daily activity' (Thornton et al., 2012, p. 51). For instance, research activities follow free academic inquiry or funded problem solving, while educational activities follow scheduled learning with increased student numbers (Robertson, 2007). More in general, '[L]ogics are often in conflict – that is, their respective systems of meaning and normative understandings, built into rituals and practices, provide inconsistent expectations' (Greenwood et al., 2011, p. 321). Although others emphasise the potential benefits of two logics in a single organisation, such as an increase of organisational legitimacy and an increase of creativity and innovation (Johansen, Olsen, Solstad, & Torsteinsen, 2015; Smith & Besharov, 2019), as – one could argue – did Von Humboldt.

Still, many aim for a better connection between research and education following Von Humboldt's ethos of a symbiotic relationship. However, it could also be argued that based on Trowler and Wareham's (2008) analysis, this is merely

> a 'romantic preference' in the minds and hearts of academics worldwide, and remains evident in much of the institutional rhetoric surrounding the nexus [of research and education].
>
> (Robertson, 2007, p. 542)

However, from an organisational perspective, the connection between research and education needs to become more than a romantic notion. Hybrid organisations show increased organisational complexity (Brown & Duguid, 1998) and organisational instability (Johansen et al., 2015), which needs to be justified by achieving something more with having two primary processes in a single organisation. After all, separating them into two different organisations would be much easier. Hence, synergy between both processes is needed to justify the organisational set-up's increased complexity (Brown & Duguid, 1998). Achieving synergy is not easy: '[…] [O]rganisations must evolve over the long term to sustain hybridity' (Smith & Besharov, 2019, p. 1), but a higher change of organisational success can occur when sufficient balance has been achieved (D'Aunno, Sutton, & Rice, 1991), although this balance most often is temporary (Johansen et al., 2015).

Most universities still are in the process of becoming hybrids in which research and education are practically and conceptually connected. In these emerging situations, often the two processes and their logics still are sharply contested on-and-off. This is different from more mature fields of hybridity, although the balance between logics is never definitively settled (Greenwood et al., 2011). Also within universities there is the expectation that the research–teaching connection needs to be reinvented from time to time. The research and education balance is still emerging in most universities, because it is not only recent and each setting requests its own situation specific connection, but also the conceptual and empirical knowledge about what connections are possible, beneficial and for what purpose, still is underdeveloped (Trowler & Wareham, 2008). Additionally, changing the connections between research and education requires knowledge about the connection as such, about hybrid segments in organisations and about the mechanisms to achieve that change; three fields in which the body of knowledge is relatively limited.

This book aims to assist those who intend to change the research and education connection in their university by presenting what is known as well as what knowledge has been gained through a long-term change programme. Most change agents can be expected to intend to increase the research–education connection. However, some countries have had national debates about separating research and education into research universities and teaching universities, 'reflecting global economic imperatives and accountability demands' (Robertson, 2007, p. 542). This book does not intend to take a position in that debate and merely intends to assist those who aim to change the connections between research and education. This often implies intensifying that connection, but the same principles to design a mechanism for change can be applied to decrease the intensity of the connection between research and education.

This Book, All Chapters

This book balances theoretical notions underpinning organisational development with hands-on instruments for organisational change that arose from an extensive, five-year case study in an institute for higher education with 48,000 students. The first section of this book is more conceptual and hands-on by providing practical insights and instruments based on thick concepts and practical experience. The second part of the book presents the four scientifically based instruments to monitor the changes in the Amsterdam case as well as the actual changes seen. The second part also is illustrative for how a change programme can be research informed.

Chapter 1 provides the first elements of a mechanism for change. Didi M. E. Griffioen provides a more detailed consideration of a particular future research–education connection, its historical origin and particularities in its internal and external contexts provide the framework for choosing the proper change mechanism. This chapter begins with a focus on the importance of historical perspectives to change topics, provides an instrumentation for deciding on a more detailed content and shows how internal and external contexts are important to consider when choosing a mechanism for change.

In Chapter 2, Didi M. E. Griffioen introduces an institution-wide mechanism for multi-layered university change over time. Multiple informal conversations with higher-education senior management in many countries have shown that leaders of institutional change programmes can often envision the final result of institutional change, although they find it very difficult to design the *path* to achieve that change. Therefore, Chapter 2 presents the principles underpinning mechanisms for change as gathered by integrating the mechanisms applied in published higher education change projects as the international body of knowledge. These are then conceptually expanded to create a comprehensive overview of choices change leaders need to create sustainable hybrid universities of research and teaching, as illustrated by the Amsterdam UAS case.

To practically achieve change, tools are needed to shape the multiple debates throughout the process. Previous scholarly work presents many instruments and models for integrating research and education. However, very few have included the change process needed to achieve these aims at particular layers, for example, within the lesson, curriculum, educational programme, department or full institution. In Chapter 3, Didi M. E. Griffioen presents several new tools developed to discuss aspects of the proposed changes for changing research–education connections with stakeholders at different levels of higher-education institutes. These tools are intended to be adapted for use in future higher education change programmes.

Chapters 4 to 7 each present a scientifically based instrument to monitoring an aspect of the organisational change over time and across the university or even nation-wide. These are the monitoring instruments as applied in the Amsterdam 'Research into Education' programme, their relevance for the university-wide change programme as well as their findings.

Chapter 4 focuses on the changes in university's students and employees. In this chapter, Mette Bruinsma and Didi M. E. Griffioen address the changing perceptions of both lecturers and students on the role of research in higher professional education. This chapter's content is threefold: first, there is a short discussion of the value of perceptions in higher-education change processes, based on international literature. Second, the findings show how perceptions changed over time as well between lecturers and students in the Amsterdam setting. Third, this chapter shows how the empirical study on perceptions on the current situation and the ideal situation can assist in setting future directions for change between what is perceived about what that is and what that should be.

As part of the organisational change process, curriculum characteristics are central in Chapters 5 and 6. In Chapter 5, Linda van Ooijen-Van der Linden, Indira Day, Jolieke Timmermans and Didi M. E. Griffioen present the importance of the rationale of a curriculum as a core element to achieve coherence in curriculum design and curriculum change, following Van den Akker's (2003) model. Changing the rationale can be an important impetus for change, while a changed rationale can in hindsight be an illustration of a changed curriculum.

This chapter presents the current body of knowledge on implementing research into the higher education curriculum. This line of reasoning is illustrated by an empirical comparison of the rationales of all Amsterdam bachelor's programmes from the period 2011–2015 to those in 2016–2018.

In Chapter 6, the changes in learning goals are central. Linda van Ooijen- Van der Linden, Natalie Pareja-Roblin, Jason Nak, Iris Jong and Didi M. E. Griffioen explain how developing research competences is increasingly regarded as key in preparing future professionals. This has led higher-education institutions worldwide to make various efforts to integrate research throughout the undergraduate programs' curriculum. Learning goals are an important carrier of curriculum content, following from the notion that what is aimed for will also be examined. This chapter integrates current international knowledge on the role of learning goals in curriculum design. It illustrates the role of learning goals in curriculum change by reporting on the results of a longitudinal study on the changed intended curricula of all undergraduate programmes at Amsterdam UAS between 2015 and 2018, which was based on Verburgh et al.'s (2013) measurement instruments. Differences between disciplines are presented to show how higher-educational change needs to be fit for disciplinary purpose.

Academics working in higher professional education play a significant role in integrating research in bachelor's curricula and in establishing an organisational research culture. Sanne Daas, Didi M. E. Griffioen, Chevy van Dorresteijn and Indira Day argue in Chapter 7 that a change in competences and tasks of academics is key in further integrating research and education. This chapter discusses the importance of the role of academics in connecting research and education within higher professional education based on current international literature. Furthermore, the chapter addresses the changes in competences and tasks of prospective academics, as illuminated by a longitudinal data set of job openings for academics in Dutch applied universities, collected annually between 2016 and 2019. For this study a new measurement model for academics' tasks and competences of research and education was developed based on Pitt and Mewburn's (2016) concepts and the Vitae (2010) researcher development framework.

The purpose of concluding Chapter 8 by Didi M. E. Griffioen is to draw together the insights from the previous chapters. This is achieved in three ways: first, the chapters in part 2 of the book are considered for their combined content of the institutional change across the layers of the Amsterdam institute to learn how developing these layers might be a mutual influence. Second, the chapter reflects on the conclusions in the context of the conceptual model as presented in Chapter 1 and the mechanism for change as presented in Chapter 2. Finally, the implications for future (research about) higher education institutional change are discussed.

This book provides the first effort to bring together both the fields of the research–teaching nexus and change management in higher education, and rich theory with hands-on organisational change. Readers are invited to create their own insights and change practices based on ours. We sincerely hope that you – as we – will make time to write down your insights in this regard to benefit our future university organisations, their students and academics, with the intention to benefit society as a whole.

References

Åkerlind, G. S. (2011). Separating the 'teaching' from the 'academic': Possible unintended consequences. *Teaching in Higher Education*, 16(2), 183–95.

Barnett, R. (2012). Learning for an unknown future. *Higher Education Research & Development*, 31(1), 65–77.

Bess, J. L., & Dee, J. R. (2008). *Understanding college and university organisation* (Vol. II Dynamics of the System). Sterling: Stylus Publishing.

Boerma, K., Griffioen, D. M. E., & De Jong, U. (2013). Het belang dat managers hechten aan onderzoeksvaardigheden van docenten in het hoger onderwijs. *Tijdschrift voor Hoger Onderwijs*, 31(1&2), 59–72.

Bourdieu, P. (1986). The forms of capital. In J. Richardson (Ed.), *Handbook of theory and research for the sociology of education* (pp. 241–58). Westport: Greenwood.

Boyd, P., & Smith, C. (2011). *Being a university lecturer in a professional field: Tensions within boundary-crossing workplace contexts*. Paper presented at the Society for Research into Higher Education, Newport.

Brew, A. (2010). Transforming academic practice through scholarship. *International Journal for Academic Development*, 15(2), 105–16.

Brown, J. S., & Duguid, P. (1998). Organizing knowledge. *California Management Review*, 40(3), 90–111.

Buller, J. L. (2015). *Change leadership in higher education*. San Francisco: Jossey-Bass.

D'Aunno, T., Sutton, R. I., & Rice, R. H. (1991). Isomorphism and external support in conflicting institutional environments. *Academy of Management Journal*, 34(4), 636–61.

Duivenboden, H. P. M., Van Hout, E. J. T., Van Montfort, C. J., & Vermaas, J. C. (2009). *Verbonden verantwoordelijkheden in het publieke domein*. Den Haag: Lemma.

Durning, B., & Jenkins, A. (2005). Teaching-research relations in departments: The perspectives of built environment academics. *Studies in Higher Education*, 30(4), 407–26.

Ellis, V., McNicholl, J., & Pendry, A. (2012). Institutional conceptualisations of teacher education as academic work in England. *Teaching and Teacher Education*, 28, 685–93.

Elsen, M., Visser-Wijnveen, G. J., Van der Rijst, R. M., & Van Driel, J. H. (2008). How to strengthen the connection between research and teaching in Undergraduate University Education. *Higher Education Quarterly*, 63(1), 64–85.

Estes, R. J., & Sirgy, M. J. (Eds.). (2017). *The pursuit of human well-being: The untold global history*. Zurich: Springer.

EUA. (2007). *Lisbon Declaration*. Retrieved from Brussels: https://www.lisbondeclaration.eu/

European Higher Education Area. (2015). *Yerevan Communique*. Retrieved from http://bologna-yerevan2015.ehea.info/files/YerevanCommuniqueFinal.pdf

Fung, D. (2017). *A connected curriculum for higher education*. London: UCL.

Gallagher, S. R. (2016). *The future of university credentials: New developments at the intersection of higher education and hiring*. Cambridge: Harvard Education Press.

Gibbons, M., Limoges, C., Nowotny, H., Schwartzman, S., Scott, P., & Trow, M. (1994). *The new production of knowledge. The dynamics of science and research in contemporary societies*. London: Sage.

Greenwood, R., Raynard, M., Kodeih, F., Micelotta, E. R., & Lounsbury, M. (2011). Institutional complexity and organizational responses. *The Academy of Management Annals*, 5(1), 317–71.

Griffioen, D. M. E. (2013). Research in traditional universities and higher professional education: Not in its genes. In D. M. E. Griffioen (Ed.), *Research in higher professional education: A staff perspective* (Vol. PhD). Amsterdam: University of Amsterdam.

Griffioen, D. M. E. (2019). *Higher education's responsibility for balanced professionalism. Methodology beyond research*. (Inaugural lecture). Amsterdam University of Applied Sciences, Amsterdam. Retrieved from https://www.hva.nl/content/evenementen/oraties/2019/10/didi-griffioen.html

Griffioen, D. M. E. (2021). *Veranderingen vragen inzicht in het mechanisme*. The Hague: Nationaal Regieorgaan Onderzoek.

Griffioen, D. M. E., & De Jong, U. (2015). Mapping Dutch higher education lecturers' discourse on research at times of academic drift. *Scottish Journal for Arts, Social Sciences, and Scientific Studies*, 26(1), 81–94.

Griffioen, D. M. E., & De Jong, U. (2017). The influence of direct executive managers on lecturers' perceptions on new organizational aims in times of academic drift. *International Journal of Leadership in Education*, 20(4), 451–67.

Griffioen, D. M. E., & Van Ooijen-van der Linden, L. (2021). Awareness and desire as strategy for change. The Integration of Research and Education at Amsterdam University of Applied Sciences In I. Huet, T. Pessoa, & F. Sol Murta (Eds.), *Excellence in teaching and learning in higher education: Institutional policies and practices in Europe* (pp. 217–44). Coimbra: Coimbra University Press.

Griffioen, D. M. E., Groen, A., & Nak, J. (2019). The integration of research in the higher education curriculum: A systematic review. *The Higher Education Journal of Learning and Teaching*, 10(1).

Griffioen, D. M. E., Ashwin, P., & Scholkmann, A. (2021). Who ensures that society has the professionals it needs? Differences in the policy directions of three European countries. *Policy Reviews in Higher Education*. doi:https://doi.org/10.1080/23322969.2021.1880290

Griseri, P. (2013). What are organisations? In *An introduction to the philosophy of management* (pp. 9–22). London: SAGE.

Hales, A., & Clarke, A. (2016). So you want to be a teacher educator? The job advertisement as a construction of teacher education in Canada. *Asia-Pacific Journal of Teacher Education, 44*(4), 320–32.

Healey, M. (2005). Linking research and teaching to benefit student learning. *Journal of Geography in Higher Education, 29*(2), 183–201.

Heggen, K., Karseth, B., & Kyvik, S. (2010). The relevance of research for the improvement of education and professional practice. In *The research mission of higher education institutions outside the University Sector* (pp. 45–60). London: Springer.

Hermansen, H. (2020). Knowledge discourses and coherence in professional education. *Professions & Professionalism, 10*(3).

Ilie, S., & Rose, P. (2016). Is equal access to higher education in South Asia and sub-Saharan Africa achievable by 2030? *Higher Education, 72*, 435–55.

Jenkins, A., & Healey, M. (2005). *Institutional strategies to link teaching and research*. Retrieved from York: http://www.heacademy.ac.uk/assets/York/documents/resources/resourcedatabase/id585_institutional_strategies_to_link_teaching_and_research.pdf

Jenkins, A., Healey, M., & Zetter, R. (2007). *Linking teaching and research in disciplines and departments*. Retrieved from York: http://www.heacademy.ac.uk/assets/York/documents/LinkingTeachingAndResearch_April07.pdf

Johansen, S. T., Olsen, T. H., Solstad, E., & Torsteinsen, H. (2015). An insider view of the hybrid organisation: How managers respond to challenges of efficiency, legitimacy and meaning. *Journal of Management & Organization, 21*(6), 725–40. doi:10.1017/jmo.2015.1

Kezar, A. (2018). *How colleges change. Understanding, leading and enacting change*. London: Routledge.

Kondakci, Y., & Van den Broeck, H. (2009). Institutional imperatives versus emergent dynamics: A case study on continuous change in higher education. *Higher Education, 58*, 439–64. doi:10.1007/s10734-009-9204-2

Koppen, J. K. (1990). Het wetenschappelijk onderwijs: Egalitair of utilitair? De externe democratisering en verschuivende legitimaties in het beleid. *Mens en Maatschappij, 65*(2).

Lopes, A., Boyd, P., Andrew, N., & Pereira, F. (2014). The research-teaching nexus in nurse and teacher education: Contributions of an ecological approach to academic identities in professional fields. *Higher Education, 68*, 167–83.

Marchand, W. (2014). *Onderwijs mogelijk maken: Twee eeuwen invloed van studiefinanciering op de toegankelijkheid van het onderwijs in Nederland (1815–2015)*. (PhD). Groningen University, Groningen.

Meyer, J. W. (1977). The effects of education as an institution. *The American Journal of Sociology, 83*(1).

Neumann, R. (1993). Research and scholarship: Perceptions of senior academic administrators. *Higher Education, 25*(2), 97–110.

Nowotny, H. (2016). *The cunning of uncertainty*. Malden: Polity Press.

Nowotny, H., Scott, P., & Gibbons, M. (2001). *Re-Thinking science. Knowledge and the public in an age of uncertainty*. Cambridge: Polity Press.

Pels, D. (2009). Mixing metaphors: Politics or economics of knowledge? In N. Stehr & V. Meja (Eds.), *Society & knowledge. Contemporary perspectives in the sociology of knowledge & science* (pp. 269–98). New Jersey: Transaction Publishers.

Pitcher, R. (2011). Doctoral students' conceptions of research. *The Qualitative Report, 16*(4), 971–83.

Pitcher, R., & Åkerlind, G. S. (2009). Post-doctoral researchers' conceptions of research: A metaphor analysis. *International Journal for Researcher Development, 1*(2), 160–72.

Pitt, R., & Mewburn, I. (2016). Academic superheroes? A critical analysis of academic job descriptions. *Journal of Higher Education Policy and Management, 38*(1), 88–101.

Potter, J., & Devecchi, C. (Eds.). (2020). *Delivering educational change in higher education. A transformative approach for leaders and practitioners*. London: Routledge.

Robertson, J. (2007). Beyond the 'research/teaching nexus': Exploring the complexity of academic experience. *Studies in Higher Education, 32*(4), 541–56.

Rosowsky, D. (2020). *The teaching and research balancing act: Are universities teetering?* Retrieved from https://www.forbes.com/sites/davidrosowsky/2020/06/11/the-teaching-and-research-balancing-act-are-universities-teetering/?sh=1836d4592ed8

Ruegg, W. (2004). *A history of the university in Europe. Universities in the nineteenth and early twentieth century* (Vol. 3). Cambridge: Cambridge University Press.

Rupp, J. C. C. (1997). *Van oude en nieuwe universiteiten. De verdringing van Duitse door Amerikaanse invloeden op de wetenschapsbeoefening en het hoger onderwijs in Nederland, 1945-1995*. Den Haag: Sdu Uitgevers.

Salmi, J., & D'Addio, A. (2021). Policies for achieving inclusion in higher education. *Policy Reviews in Higher Education, 5*(1), 47–72. doi:10.1080/23322969.2020.1835529

Santos, C., Pereira, F., & Lopes, A. (2021). Research, teaching and publication: The challenges of academic work. In I. Huet, T. Pessoa, & F. Sol Murta (Eds.), *Excellence in teaching and learning in higher education: Institutional policies and practices in Europe* (pp. 199–216). Coimbra: Coimbra University Press.

Schouteden, W., Verburgh, A. L., & Elen, J. (2014). Teachers' general and contextualised research conceptions. *Studies in Higher Education, 41*(1), 79–94. doi:10.1080/03075079.2014.914915

Simons, M., & Elen, J. (2007). The 'research-teaching nexus' and 'education through research': And exploration of ambivalences. *Studies in Higher Education, 32*(5), 617–31.

Skelcher, C., & Smith, S. R. (2015). Theorizing hybridity: Institutional logics, complex organizations, and actor identities: The case of nonprofits. *Public Administration, 93*(2), 433–48.

Smith, W. K., & Besharov, M. L. (2019). Bowing before Dual Gods: How structured flexibility sustains organizational hybridity. *Administrative Science Quarterly, 64*(1), 1–44.

Teixeira, P., Kim, S., Landoni, P., & Gilani, Z. (2017). *Rethinking the public-private mix in higher education: Global trends and national policy changes*. Rotterdam: Sense.

Thornton, P. H., Ocasio, W., & Lounsbury, M. (2012). *The institutional logics perspective. A new approach to structure, culture, and process*. Oxford: Oxford University Press.

Tomlinson, M. (2017). Student perceptions of themselves as 'consumers' of higher education. *British Journal of Sociology of Education, 38*, 450–67. doi:10.1080/01425692.2015.1113856

Trowler, P. (2020). *Accomplishing change in teaching and learning regimes. Higher education and the practice sensibility*. Oxford: Oxford University Press.

Trowler, P., & Wareham, T. (2008). *Tribes, territories, research and teaching: Enhancing the teaching research nexus*. Retrieved from York: https://www.heacademy.ac.uk/resource/tribes-territories-research-and-teaching-enhancing-teaching-research-nexus-literature#sthash.5NK7FyDy.dpuf

Visser-Wijnveen, G. J. (2009). *The research-teaching nexus in the humanities: Variations among academics*. (PhD). Leiden University, Leiden.

Visser-Wijnveen, G. J., Van Driel, J. H., Van der Rijst, R. M., Verloop, N., & Visser, A. (2009). The relationship between academics' conceptions of knowledge, research and teaching–a metaphor study. *Teaching in Higher Education, 14*(6), 673–86.

Wheelahan, L., & Moodie, G. (2021). Gig qualifications for the gig economy: Microcredentials and the 'hungry mile'. *Higher Education*. doi:https://doi.org/10.1007/s10734-021-00742-3

Winkel, M., Van der Rijst, R. M., Poel, R., & Van Driel, J. H. (2016). Identities of research-active academics in new universities: Towards a complete academic profession cross-cutting different worlds of practice. *Journal of Further & Higher Education, 42*(4), 539–55. doi:10.1080/0309877X.2017.1301407

Young, M., & Muller, J. (2014). *Knowledge, expertise, and the professions*. London: Routledge.

1

The Origin, Content and Context of Changing Research–Education Connections

Didi M. E. Griffioen

Introduction

Universities' hybrid set-up is a complex environment to formulate and execute a mechanism for change. While many initiate and lead change programmes in higher education, 'it is certainly true that there is no well-developed theory of change in the practice-literature, particularly in relation to higher education contexts' (Trowler, 2020, p. 71). Still, searching for a 'well-developed theory of change' implies the possibility of such a theory. However, following Buller (2015) and Kezar (2018), this chapter argues that every change process in a university requests its own change mechanism, based on its own combination of existing theories, depending on the origin, content and context of change. Existing theories and practices for change are important to inform change agents about their options for approaching change and phases the change are expected to go through. The origin, content, context, approach and phases combined all characterise the change mechanism. This chapter elaborates the origin, content and context of changing research–education connections in higher education. The following chapter focuses on the change approaches, the phases of change and how they care combined results in a change mechanism.

The current chapter first focuses on the importance of knowing the origin of change as a starting point for a change mechanism. The Amsterdam UAS Strategic Programme 'Research into Education' is introduced by explaining its origin. Throughout this chapter and the remainder of the book, different elements of the Amsterdam case are further explained by providing theoretical lenses from both the body of knowledge of the research–teaching nexus, as from the change management literature.

As is likely for all current efforts to change research–education connections, the strategic programme was not the first effort to alter higher-education practices and it is not the last. Understanding the history of a setting increases the chances of achieving the intended changes. Second, the content of change matters. Changing research–education connections in a department, module or across multiple universities requires substantially different knowledge than implementing a new ICT support application or merging two departments. All intend substantial change, all require a mechanism for change, but all also require different content knowledge. Therefore, Section 1.3 focuses on the characteristics of the content that comes with changing research–education connections. Finally, every change programme has a particular context. In all three mentioned examples, the general context is the higher-education organisation. However, depending on the content and origin, a different view on that organisational context is needed to design a fitting mechanism for change. In Section 1.4, the notion of hybridity discussed in the introduction is positioned as context for a change mechanism. Also explained here is how external developments and incidents need to be recognised as potentially important context for organisational change.

Before the Change: The Origin of Change

In this section, the Amsterdam strategic programme is introduced, along with its origin and preamble. It is important for change agents to have a detailed understanding of the route a university organisation took to execute a change programme. The Amsterdam case is illustrative of the types of information that can aid the change agent's work.

Chapter 1 argues that viable reasons for change are related to the three societal responsibilities of higher education: to embody knowledge, to certify learning and to systematise knowledge. Viable change should follow from a changed interpretation of one or more of these responsibilities and/or a new insight into how these responsibilities can be fulfilled (see also Introduction). Scholars provide different models to consider the origin of organisational change. Generally, indications for change can come from feedback within the organisation, generated from assessment and programme evaluations as well as from environmental changes, such as changes in student population, competition, resources or public policy changes to which the university needs to respond (Bess & Dee, 2008). Buller (2015) labels the externally induced change as 'received change' in which timeliness matters: changes can be forced upon an organisation right now, or can be anticipated because they would eventually be forced on them. Internal changes are labelled as 'intentional change' (p. 29). Saarinen and Valimaa (2013) present an even more detailed model based on their analysis of higher-education policy research in which four types of research are defined by two axes: Change can be either external or internal, juxtaposed with it to be either conflicted/discontinuous or balanced/continuous. The combination of external and balanced results in change as reform while internal and balanced is labelled as evolution. External and conflicted results in an intervention change and internal and conflict is labelled as revolution.

Based on these labels, the origin of the Amsterdam change programme is hereafter described to show how origins of change can be considered. The Amsterdam case also illustrates that even though it is important to know the factual developments that have led to a change proposal (internal/external), it is essential for a change mechanism to understand how different stakeholders involved characterise the origin of the proposed change. The proposed changes intend to increase the role of research in educational bachelor's programmes, which are further explained in Chapter 2. However, this direction for change came into full swing fifteen years prior.

The Origin of the Amsterdam Change Programme

In 2015, the board of Amsterdam University of Applied Sciences formalised the strategic programme 'Research into Education' to help further implement research into the educational programmes, particularly the bachelor's programmes. This strategic programme was part of a total of seven strategic programmes, collectively used as instruments to implement the new five-year strategic agenda throughout the university. Other strategic programmes aimed, for instance, to personalise educational trajectories, create more embedded honours programmes or tighten the university's administrative system for research funding. The 'Research into Education' strategic programme (from now on the strategic programme) was under the supervision of one of the faculty deans with a university-wide mandate the university board handed out, similar to the other strategic programmes. The faculty dean was assisted by a programme leader (this book's editor) who was responsible for designing, executing and monitoring the strategic programme.

This strategic programme was formalised when research activities had been part of Dutch applied universities for fifteen years. The binary higher education system of the Netherlands includes research-intensive universities and applied universities. As part of the national and international governments' reform to create universities out of, for instance, teaching-only *polytechnics* in the UK, *hogescholen* in the Netherlands and *fachhochschulen* in Germany (Kyvik & Lepori, 2010; Kyvik & Skodvin, 2003), and in line with the 1999 Bologna declaration, Dutch applied universities nationally received research funding in 2001. However, in the Netherlands, the obligation to do research had been part of the educational law since 1986 (Kickert, 1986) and applied universities had been part of the higher education system since 1992 (Griffioen, 2013).

Over time, the Dutch national government framed research at the core of professional abilities, similar but differently to research as the core of academic abilities in research-intensive universities. In 2001, a treaty between the Dutch Minister of Education and the collective UASs resulted in funding applied research professors (Dutch: *lectoren*) with three generic responsibilities (De Weert & Leijnse, 2010: 1) to raise the quality of educational programmes by raising the quality of the teaching staff through research; 2) to add to the theoretical body of knowledge of professional fields, which would also make professional higher education curricula up to date; and 3) to help the professional fields innovate. These research professors would become the first to conduct research structurally in the former mainly teaching-only universities.

Originally, among the university's administrators, it differed between applied universities whether implementing research was wished for or forced upon the organisation. Some high-level administrators considered 'research' to be a welcome contribution to the organisation, while others considered it a deviation from educating professionals. Even with these differences, the collective of Dutch applied universities signed a treaty to fund the implementation of research in their organisations with the Ministry of Education, Science and Culture (2001). For the administrators of Amsterdam UAS in 2001, research activities were a relative welcome change. In that year, Amsterdam UAS also signed a university partnership with the research-intensive University of Amsterdam, merging their central administrative bodies and expecting increased collaboration in both research and education (ScienceGuide, 2013). Implementing applied research activities would make both universities more equal to collaborate in externally funded research. However, the Amsterdam administrators also actively strived against mission drift (Griffioen & De Jong, 2013; Kyvik, 2007; Neave, 1979), presuming that applied universities would continue to focus on innovating professional knowledge with educational programmes and professional fields as beneficiaries. Research-intensive universities focused on furthering disciplinary knowledge. Their complementarity would be the strength of this collaboration – so was the idea.

Over time, it showed that others in UASs experienced the implementation of research in the teaching-only university context as a forced-upon change. It was mostly perceived as an intervention of externally driven change and discontinuity, which the national government forced and was followed through by their own administrators. A study in six Dutch applied universities (Griffioen & De Jong, 2010), for instance, showed that administrators were significantly more positive than lecturers about the presence and quality of research in applied universities at the time. The lecturers' opinions mattered due to the intended types of changes. On the one hand, employing research professors separately from the educational programmes aimed to provide new professional knowledge to professional fields. These activities relatively were separate from the educational teams. However, the second aim was to implement research as part of the educational bachelor's and master's tracks, which fully needed the lecturers. Additionally, the national and international expectations were that lecturers would raise their level of expertise, mainly by raising their own level of education to at least the master's level. This opened up debates on what comprised high quality lecturing in higher education and influenced the notions of self-efficacy as a lecturer in applied universities (Griffioen, De Jong, & Jak, 2014). The administrative merger with the University of Amsterdam ended after a decade due to lack of administrative commitment.

Innovations Require Line-Management Responsibility

In 2015, the Amsterdam strategic programme began. An analysis of changes until 2015 shows a dual picture: the initial implementation was relatively successful in the stand-alone research activities. The funding the national government provided for the first generation of research professors, who created their own research groups. Generally, these research professors brought a network in one or more professional fields that was connected to the new research activities. Research was mainly related to developments in professional fields and in the external focus of research was developed. Their educational aim was hardly developed; most professors had not been able to influence educational programs, several did not make the effort either. Further, lecturers generally were not so positive about research or its professors. Interestingly, a 2013 study (Griffioen & De Jong, 2017) showed that when asked in six applied universities, lecturers found the effects of the implemented research activities on educational programmes more important than their contribution to theory or innovation of professional fields, as had become the main focus.

The conclusion in 2015 was that research professors had been given the task to influence education, but they were not provided with the instruments to do so. In some cases, where the effort was made and – luckily – the research professor and educational managers enjoyed working together, some successes occurred. However, changes that were considered important enough to be part of a university five-year core plan should not be left over to that slim chance. There was no clear mechanism put in place for these connections other than the central administration presuming that the new research professors would actively create these connections. The conclusion was that successes were lacking because research professors were not provided with line-management responsibility over educational programmes. In Amsterdam UAS's applied university structure, the educational managers 'owned' the bachelor's and master's programmes and research was run in other departments the research professors led as manager-researchers. The large mutual differences with, on the one hand, lecturers having thick professional experience in the local or regional setting, bachelor's degrees and didactical expertise, and on the other, research professors with PhDs and national or international networks increased the problem. The general lack of the lecturers' rich perception of research and the often more academic perspective of professional work among the research professors, made conversations about implementing research in educational programmes often very difficult and only few efforts for systematic connections were successful. Therefore, in the mechanism of the new strategic program, after the implementation process was underway for fifteen years, some responsibilities needed to shift. Understanding the origin of the proposed change meant knowing in what direction.

Differently Perceived Origin

It is important for change agents to understand a change programme's setting – the organisational structure and culture, which an upcoming section of this chapter focuses on – and to know and understand its history. By understanding its history, it becomes clear what the potential angles for change are, and what paths would be more difficult to take than others. The origin of implementing research in Amsterdam UAS still influences the actions of many involved today, even if they do not realise it. The former choices made still influence the current university's fixed structures and fluent practices, and therefore what its stakeholders find 'normal' in that context. This is passed on to new employees and new students and only slightly shifts over time.

This Amsterdam history also shows that the origin of implementing research in this teaching-only setting differs between stakeholders. At the start, for some, research was a welcome change, one that was seen as the possibility to raise the quality and better the content of the work in the applied university, also by intending to raise educational levels by changing the type of lecturers involved. For others, it was a career opportunity along with becoming educational managers. For these combined groups, the proposed change was more than Buller's (2015) 'changes that are needed because of internal rather than external'; they saw this implementation as a welcome opportunity for the university and themselves. Others did not understand why research was needed at all; they valued the focus on training professionals, and in their perception, research did not add anything to the quality of their alumni's future professional work. Therefore, they also did not understand why higher salaries were paid to the new research professors than to experienced lecturers-professionals and why colleagues were willing to work in research. In many people's perception, implementing research stole money and time from the higher-education budget. Clearly they perceived this change as being forced upon them and only recently the most firm group of stakeholders seems aware that research is here to stay.

Thus, depending on the perspective of a change agent and the particular point in history of a change topic, the viewpoint differs as should the micro-approach in the change mechanism. There should be sufficient space to manoeuvre with micro-flexibility in the context of an overall strategy. This implies the mechanism for change needs to be flexible over time as Buller (2015) and Kezar (2018) argued, but for it to be a success, it additionally needs to be flexible between the different stakeholders at the same moment as well. This is especially the case for changes where the stakeholders need to co-invent the intended changes, as is the case in research–education connections. All relevant stakeholders need to not only be 'on board', but also actively contribute to the change. They need to help invent the changes ahead by re-inventing their own practices, work and output. Therefore, the one-size-fits-all concept does not exist in changing research–education connections. Understanding origins of the change process at hand aids this intention to flexibility.

What to Change: The Particular Content of Change

The particularities of origins matter, as mentioned above, but particularities of the proposed content also need precision. In our experience, this precision is often overlooked. When asked, many change agents working on research–education connections aim to increase the connection between research and education. Follow-up questions often illustrate the multiple possible perceptions behind this statement. Obviously, ambitions for research–education connections can differ between universities or change programmes, but they can also differ between colleagues that shoulder the work to achieve the same change ambition in the same university department, or what they assumed was the same ambition. Numerous conversations have shown that every stakeholder has their own perception of what is aimed for, ranging from learning students' research competences to merging departments, and these ambitions are hardly verbalised between stakeholders.

Often this lack of verbal precision is underpinned by a lack of active awareness that research–education connections can imply many different things, ranging from including students in research activities, to systematically updating curricula with research results, to formally combining the allocation of research funds and education funds into a single management role. Somehow, stakeholders often think as far as their own proposal for research–education connections, disregarding that others have different ideas. Further, these examples already show that the field of the research–teaching nexus comprises multiple contexts in which research–education connections, with researchers in that field often narrowing down their focus to national (Griffioen, Ashwin, & Scholkmann, 2021), institutional (Daas, Day, & Griffioen, 2019; Jenkins & Healey, 2005) or HR policy (Griffioen, 2018; Xu, 2017); to organisational structures (Jenkins, Healey, & Zetter, 2007; Jenkins & Zetter, 2003); to activities of educational managers (Neumann, 1993) or academics (Åkerlind, 2008, 2011); to the intended curriculum (Verburgh, Schouteden, & Elen, 2012); or to the ways in which students experience their learning environment (Griffioen, 2019a, 2019c, 2020; Pitcher, 2011; Pitcher & Åkerlind, 2009). In this study, we call this situation the multiple layers of research–education connections. Depending on a particular university structure in a country, others more or less are present.

Another way to consider the multiplicity of research–education connections is by focusing on the connections aimed for in a university's strategy. A detailed study about intended synergy between research and education in Dutch applied universities showed that university policy can include contrasting ambitions for synergy – the added value of the research–education connection – as well as a different argumentation for this synergy's relevance (Daas et al., 2019). Collectively, seven university policy strategies again showed the multi-layeredness with intended synergies between research and education formulated as effects in students, the professional field, the academic, the educational team and the institution as a whole. Each of these ambitions was underlined with different argumentations, but also sometimes the same argumentation led to another ambition for synergy. Each of these ambitions for synergy requires different changes in the organisations' architecture as well as changes in the way stakeholders act in that context. Furthermore, each also needs another change mechanism to achieve the intended synergy (see Chapter 2) and evaluate its results (see Chapters 4 to 7).

To push this argument of multi-layeredness still a bit further, our multiple projects over the years (Griffioen, 2021a, 2021b) showed that 'research' and 'education' as wholes almost never were connected. We saw that most often an ambition started with a positive normative perspective on the research–education connection as Trowler and Wareham (2008) described. In that phase, statements would be very generic and hardly precise. The sooner change agents, administrators and other stakeholders would be able to start discussing more precise changes; therefore actual changes also would be realised sooner. Sometimes whole projects would be abandoned because the ideas between stakeholders differed too much when made explicit. However, where scholars in the field of the research–teaching nexus have shown to be able to narrow down the topic to lessons, curricula or organisational units. In our experience, change agents or administrators seem less able to do so, in particular at the start of a change process. This seems to have something to do with the 'romantic notion' of research–education connections as explained in the introduction: any increase in connection should be beneficial. However, as explained in Chapter 1, from an organisational perspective, a hybrid organisation should be very clear about where the synergy between process should be expected, as justification for sustaining the complexity of a hybrid organisation in the first place. Therefore, change agents, but even more so administrators, should be willing to formulate a very precise answer to the question: What connection between research and education should be changed when the alterations are made, and with what effect?

Multiple Layers

To be able to be precise, and based on literature and practice, potential layers and perspectives are here combined in a workable model (see also Figure 1.1).

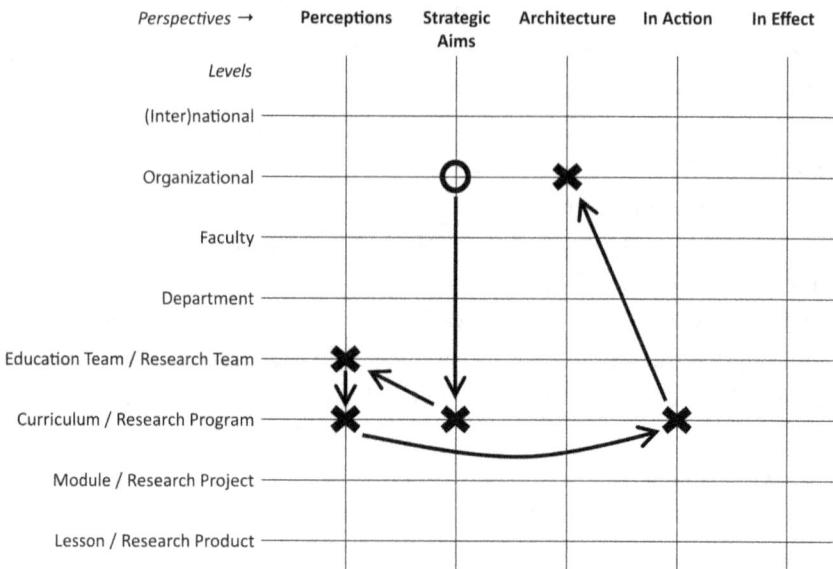

Figure 1.1 Overview of the combined layers and perspectives of research–education connections. These crosses and arrows represent the change mechanism of the Amsterdam Strategic Programme.

The proposed research–education connection can (at least) be formulated for these organisational levels of the university, therefore also different between these levels:

- in (inter)national policy,
- at the full organisation,
- in a single or multiple faculties,
- in a department or service organisation,
- in educational or research teams,
- in curricula or research programmes,
- in modules or research projects and
- in lessons or research products.

However, this list of the organisation's levels depends on the particular university's structure. For instance, Dutch universities do not have pro-vice chancellors' offices, but they do have service departments. In other university systems, organisational structures are constructed differently. Thus, depending on the university's architecture and its workings, different organisational units for change can be defined and related aims for the increase of synergy between research and education can be formulated. Also, the decision needs to be made on whether it is about one, a few, or all units of that type.

Additionally the decision needs to be made in terms of what type of synergy needs to be strived for. The aforementioned body of knowledge shows that the overall concept of changes can consider changes in the architecture of organisational levels, such as merging departments, shifts in delegated responsibilities or bachelor's learning criteria; all formal agreed upon changes. Changes can also focus on shifts in how stakeholders act; for instance, aiming for new research professors and educational programmes to work together. Another perspective is to change how stakeholders perceive research, education or its connection, as is aiming to change strategy or aiming to tune current research and education connections to have different effects as a result.

In addition to positioning the intended connection between research at an organisational unit, the type of change intended needs to be defined:

- in the stakeholders' perceptions,
- in strategic aims,
- in the universities' architecture,
- in human action and
- in the effects of the integration between research and education.

The intended connection between research and education can then be defined at the crossroads between organisational units and types of integration and build the base for the stages of a change mechanism, as is further explicated in Chapter 2. Also, the Amsterdam strategic programme was built on similar crossroads.

The Content of the Amsterdam UAS Strategic Programme over Time

The ambition of the Amsterdam strategic programme followed a new full university-level strategy focus. The combined 2015 strategic policy documents stated (authors' translation):

> Amsterdam UAS educates professionals at the bachelor's level and master's level, who are aware of the constantly changing world around them, who are able to keep their professional knowledge at the expected level and to adapt their actions

to new knowledge and changing insights. This implies they make professional decisions for action based on current (international) scientific knowledge and insights.

This requires Amsterdam UAS educational programmes to infuse their students as future professionals with knowledge, insight, skills and attitudes related to their professional fields, which lead to the appropriate professional behaviour. Knowledge, insight and skills related to research with a professional focus are herewith essential as well as a functional organisational culture and structure focussed on integrating research and education.

The Amsterdam programme's main ambition was to alter the university by changing the connections between research and education at the curriculum level, in particular in bachelor's programmes (for an overview see Figure 1.1). Thus, one organisational level of action were the about seventy bachelor's curricula of Amsterdam UAS. A second level of action was the related educational team, more precisely to their perceptions of research and professionalism (Griffioen, 2019b). The choice to include the educational teams followed from the aforementioned conclusion that while research groups had become relatively successful in serving external partners, the position of research in bachelor's programmes still was not optimal. The analysis showed that one of the causes was a lack of formal line-management responsibility for these educational programmes among the research professors. Research remained the responsibility of the researchers, lecturers and educational teams, who had been very able to omit the notion of research in their daily work.

The presumption was that if a mechanism to change the position of research in bachelor's programmes was put in place, this would create pressure on the educational teams, which could unleash the still shimmering debates about research's role in professional education. While this debate had nation-wide rounds before (Haijing de Haan-Cao & De Koning, 2016; Heest, 2018; Van Lieshout & Borgdorff, 2005), these did not always include the lecturers in the different educational teams. The expectation was that a sensible mechanism for change could bring that debate into the teams, which would then be combined with a support system to deepen the debates and reach curriculum re-design. This could open up new possibilities for research's role in professional practice and therefore its role in professional higher education, now reasoned from the educational perspective and not initiated by highly experienced researchers. A presumed shift in perceptions in educational teams was needed to alter the curriculum content, which also was the strategic programme's final aim.

Hence, the two main crossroads in the strategic programme were the perceptions of the lecturers in educational teams, and the outlines of whole curricula of bachelor's programmes, as these teams designed. To make changes in the day-to-day education, changes also were needed in modules, lessons and student–teacher interactions. However, for this change program, these were seen as an effect of the changes made, not as the initial proposed changes. It was presumed that it would not be too difficult to alter lessons or even modules, but that this would only lead to a durable change if the full curriculum outline was altered as well. Thus, the strategic programme would likely lead to altered modules and lessons, but the size of these changes was beyond the change team's activities. Furthermore, an expected serious change in multiple curricula would also yield a change in organisational structures, for instance in allocating and administering finances due to a less clear division between research and education, as was expected in HR structures due to a more frequent mixing of roles between lecturers and researchers. However, these changes were beyond the change team's responsibilities, and were also expected later in time.

Based on this description of the Amsterdam programme, it has become clear how change agents and administrators can discuss potential crossroads in a change programme, and further to then decide which ones to focus on, which to exclude and which to expect as potential by-effect of the changes made.

Chapter 2 shows how these crossroads of *what to change* needs to be, combined with a mechanism for *how to change*. In the current chapter, the relevance of the context of the change is now addressed.

What to Take into Account: The Context of Change

The literature on change management focuses on the level of groups of stakeholders in universities; it generally focuses on a systems-level change. The previously explained labels of origin of change already showed that: the labels 'from the outside' or 'from within' suggest that the organisation or its departments are seen as wholes, partly to be able to make an argument about change (as this book does), partly because that is the span of attention in change management. To consider the differences between stakeholders within groups, their notions of origin, their perceptions and ambitions, can increase the success of change programmes (or finish them quickly). Stakeholders' perceptions are the context of the change at hand, but this is not the only aspect to consider. Particular change topics increase the relevance of different organisational characteristics, as do research–education connections. Additionally, incidents in an organisation's outside world can highly influence a change programme for a long time. These contexts are elaborated on in this section.

Two types of relevant context are here considered. Firstly, the direct organisational context is considered from the perspective of the actual change at hand. Where organisations often have made the general descriptions of their set-up available, including the fixed and fluent characteristics, different elements rise when they are considered from the change topic and origin. Secondly, relevant incidents belong to the change context as potential influencers of the pace and success of the changes at hand. These incidents can be recent of from a long time ago, they can be from within the organisation or they could have happened elsewhere. Incidents are important if they are expected to still influence the change mechanism at hand.

Changing (into) a Hybrid University of Research and Education

Chapter 1 explained how the combination of research and education has resulted in university organisations of a hybrid nature. Generally, changing practices in a larger organisational context is a challenge. However, systematically changing aspects of the university that connects both research and education implies changing the core balance in this hybridity of universities. In a way, this implies changing the actual hybrid that is a university.

The knowledge about changing practices in hybrid organisations is limited, as is the body of knowledge about creating hybrid organisations (Vermeulen, Zietsma, Greenwood, & Langley, 2016). Both perspectives imply changing stakeholders' practices, where there already are two types of practices, logics or cultures, or in the case of creating hybrids, where previously there was only one. The difficulty of changing individuals' actions in such a dual situation is the presence of the duality as such. Presumably, actions of employees in organisations generally depend on the stimuli and sanctions of the organisation as a whole (Toubiana & Zietsma, 2017). While stimuli can come from intrinsic motivation as from the external organisation, sanctions follow from formalised organisational incentives. Individuals' changing practices often implies changing what they are accustomed to doing, or even what they enjoy doing, into something different. In the Amsterdam setting, lecturers who were very proud of their educational programmes were in many ways given the message that their work would improve if they also started working in research. Most lecturers would not understand how that could be the case because they considered professional work from a practice-oriented perspective, education from a didactical perspective and research from a white-coat perspective. How would white-coat research contribute to what they knew as a professional or as an experienced lecturer? Most did not strive to include research as part of their tasks and the organisation's structures and cultures allowed them to do so. Even more difficult: Lecturers who were willing or eager to include research had a hard time achieving that in their work.

This is a clear example of what is known from systematic research. Studies have shown that having two logics in a single organisation provides opportunities for employees to choose between them, which leaves space to refuse or ignore the intended change (Quirke, 2013). In the Amsterdam case, lecturers were very able to choose teaching and ignore the mere existence of research for a longer time. The organisation's structure and incentives provided much space for this choice. The existence of two practices implied two discourses and 'the tensions between these discourses produce a discursive space in which the agent can play one discourse against another' (Hardy & Phillips, 2004, in: Maguire & Hardy, 2019, p. 158). Active resistance towards the proposed changes especially rises when an existing primary process is seen as more legitimate than the newly suggested integration of both processes (Durand & Jourdan, 2012). Employees' intention to integrate or circumvent the two logics or simply intent to reduce their reality to a single logic also depends on their individual and collective values and perceptions (Toubiana & Zietsma, 2017). Additionally, stakeholders' self-efficacy related to the presumed needed skills is of influence (Griffioen & De Jong, 2015; Griffioen et al., 2014), in which stakeholders can feel the proposed changes are sensible but they do not feel able, or they feel able but do not consider them sensible.

These very individual aspects matter even more for changes, such as research–education connections. To alter these connections, individual lecturers and researchers need to actually change their own practices. Managers, policy officers and/or other support staff need to alter the organisation's fixed elements for lecturers and researchers to make these changes possible and durable. It is therefore insufficient to limit resistance, as is more or less suggested in change management literature. To alter research–education connections, academics need to co-invent the new reality. Changing the groups of stakeholders' practices is one thing. Individuals' actions often are very difficult to change within a single generation of employees, but culture also implicitly transfers between generations into newly appointed personnel's ways of working (Bystydzienski, Thomas, Howe, & Desai, 2016). Implicitly and explicitly, people hand down the practices they consider 'normal' (Foucault, 1991). Therefore, to change the research–education connections, one needs to find a mechanism that can change the universities' practices on a larger scale and across generations (freely based on Trowler, 2020, p. 138). In this mechanism, the hybrid context of the university needs to be considered.

Incidents Can Define the Tone for a Long Time

Where the hybrid context of a university can provide increased difficulties in changing stakeholders' practices, well-known incidents can make it increasingly problematic for generations. This can best be illustrated by the 'affaire' that happened in 2010 in the Dutch applied higher education sector. In that affaire, students were given a degree without providing a self-produced thesis of sufficient quality (Bakker, 2011). There had been intentional fraud on a small scale in a sector where it was relatively new to have research as part of the final thesis, but the fallout across the sector was much larger (Jäger, De Ploeg, & De Vos, 2015). The sector as a whole took responsibility, concerned that similar practices would also be present in other organisations. Many were willing to state that applied universities would never be able to conduct quality research, or that research would not contribute to educating professionals. Implementing research in curricula became much more difficult, examining in general became a bureaucratic activity to gain 'governing control'.

Looking back to the time between 2010 and 2015, the affaire publicly confirmed the point of view that bachelor's theses would not be granted without a clear research focus. This was strictly speaking in line with the European Dublin Descriptors (Nuffic, 2010), but it was also still very unclear what research competences for future professionals should look like (see also: Griffioen, 2019b); these competences were not invented yet. The general intention was to provide professionals with research competences that would aid them in their professional work, but there was no clarity about what that would look like in educational practice or in students' future professional practice. As an effect, many educational programmes implemented research as a separate competency to increase its visibility across the curriculum. The lack of definitions of 'research for professionals' often resulted in multiple solutions that highly resonated with the more academically oriented research competences of research-intensive bachelor's programmes. The lack of integrating learning to conduct research in students' professional training made quality agencies in turn often conclude that the 'level of research was too low' with again an increased academisation of the educational programs as the effect.

Thus, the message that applied universities took from this 'affaire' was that their level of research in students was too low and they needed to 'up their game', both in level and in control instruments. This resulted in a fearful implementation of tight research-related curriculum lines, copying the research-intensive university programmes and lacking collaboration with the applied research groups. For a long time, this 'affaire' took away the public space to discuss what research should be for future professionals and to formulated educational programmes accordingly. The 2015 strategic programme 'Research into Education' intended to alter this context.

To Conclude

The origin, content and context of change are different in every change programme. However, when changing research-education practices in universities, every change agent needs to take the university organisation's typical hybrid context into account, although its characteristics differ between universities as well as between change programmes within the same university. Awareness of these particularities, the specific content of change and a clear image of the organisational layers where the change needs to take place, as well as insight into the distinct contextual factors that are relevant for the changes proposed are important to distinguish. It is possible to say that by having a clear image of the origin, content and context for change, the change agents have insight in the proposed change's playing field. The next chapter introduces the approach and phases as part of the same mechanism. By adding these, change agents will have the strategy put in place.

References

Åkerlind, G. S. (2008). An academic perspective on research and being a researcher: An integration of the literature. *Studies in Higher Education, 33*(1), 17–33.

Åkerlind, G. S. (2011). Separating the 'teaching' from the 'academic': Possible unintended consequences. *Teaching in Higher Education, 16*(2), 183–95.

Bakker, M. (2011, 27 April). Bijna kwart van alle studenten Inholland kreeg onterecht diploma. *De Volkskrant*.

Bess, J. L., & Dee, J. R. (2008). *Understanding college and university organisation* (Vol. II Dynamics of the System). Sterling: Stylus Publishing.

Buller, J. L. (2015). *Change leadership in higher education.* San Francisco: Jossey-Bass.

Bystydzienski, J., Thomas, N., Howe, S., & Desai, A. (2016). The leadership role of college deans and department chairs in academic culture change. *Studies in Higher Education, 42*(12), 2301–15.

Daas, S. R., Day, I. N. Z., & Griffioen, D. M. E. (2019). *The intended Synergy between research and teaching of universities of applied sciences in the Netherlands.* Paper presented at The Higher Education Conference 2019, Amsterdam.

De Weert, E., & Leijnse, F. (2010). Practice-oriented research: The extended function of Dutch universities of applied science. In S. Kyvik & B. Lepori (Eds.), *The research mission of higher education institutions outside the university sector. Striving for differentiation* (pp. 199–218). London: Springer.

Durand, R., & Jourdan, J. (2012). Jules and Jim: Alternative conformity to minority logics. *Academy of Management Journal, 55*(6), 1295–315.

Dutch Ministry of Education Culture and Science, & Netherlands Association of Universities of Applied Sciences. (2001). *Convenant Lectoren en Kenniskringen in het hoger beroepsonderwijs.* The Hague: OCW.

Foucault, M. (1991). *Discipline and punish. The birth of the Prison.* London: Penguin.

Griffioen, D. M. E. (2013). Research in traditional universities and higher professional education: Not in its genes. In D. M. E. Griffioen (Ed.), *Research in higher professional education: A staff perspective* (Vol. PhD) (pp. 23–41). Amsterdam: University of Amsterdam.

Griffioen, D. M. E. (2018). Building research capacity in new universities during times of academic drift: Lecturers professional profiles. *Higher Education Policy, 33*, 347–66. doi:https://doi.org/10.1057/s41307-018-0091-y

Griffioen, D. M. E. (2019a). Differences in students' experienced research involvement: Study years and disciplines compared. *Journal of Further & Higher Education, 44*(4), 454–66. doi:https://doi.org/10.1080/0309877X.2019.1579894

Griffioen, D. M. E. (2019b). *Higher education's responsibility for balanced professionalism. Methodology beyond Research.* (Inaugural lecture). Amsterdam University of Applied Sciences, Amsterdam. Retrieved from https://www.hva.nl/content/evenementen/oraties/2019/10/didi-griffioen.html

Griffioen, D. M. E. (2019c). The influence of undergraduate students' research attitudes on their intention for research usage in their future professional practice. *Innovation in Education and Teaching International, 56*(2), 162–72. doi:10.1080/14703297.2018.1425152

Griffioen, D. M. E. (2020). A questionnaire to compare lecturers' and students' higher education research integration experiences. *Teaching in Higher Education, 27*(2), 185–200.

Griffioen, D. M. E. (2021a). Kijken voorbij de clusters. Een nieuwe blik op de kennisinstelling. *THEMA Hoger Onderwijs* (1), 56–62.

Griffioen, D. M. E. (2021b). Veranderingen vragen inzicht in het mechanisme. In A. UAS (Ed.). The Hague: Nationaal Regieorgaan Onderzoek.

Griffioen, D. M. E., Ashwin, P., & Scholkmann, A. (2021). Who ensures that Society has the professionals it needs? Differences in the policy directions of three European countries. *Policy Reviews in Higher Education, 5*(2), 158–73. doi:https://doi.org/10.1080/23322969.2021.1880290

Griffioen, D. M. E., & De Jong, U. (2010). Opvattingen van docenten en niet-docenten over onderzoek in het HBO. *Tijdschrift voor Hoger Onderwijs 28*(2), 83–95.

Griffioen, D. M. E., & De Jong, U. (2013). Academic drift in Dutch Non-university higher education evaluated: A staff perspective. *Higher Education Policy, 26*, 173–91.

Griffioen, D. M. E., De Jong, U., & Jak, S. (2014). Research Self-efficacy of Lecturers in Non-University Higher Education. *Innovation in Education and Teaching International, 50*(1), 25–37.

Griffioen, D. M. E., & De Jong, U. (2015). Implementing research in professional higher education: Factors that influence lecturers' perceptions. *Educational Management Administration & Leadership, 43*(4), 626–45.

Griffioen, D. M. E., & De Jong, U. (2017). The influence of direct executive managers on lecturers' perceptions on new organizational aims in times of academic drift. *International Journal of Leadership in Education*, (4), 451–67.

Haijing de Haan-cao, H., & De Koning, P. (2016). Niemand wil universiteitje spelen. *TH&MA Hoger Onderwijs* (1), 32–7.

Hardy, C., & Philips, N. (2004). Discourse and power. In D. Grant, C. Hardy, C. Oswick, & L. Putnam (Eds.), *Sage handbook of organizational discourse* (pp. 299–316). New York: Sage.

Heest, F. v. (2018, 23 May). Hbo hecht weinig waarde aan onderzoeksvaardigheden van docenten. *ScienceGuide*. Retrieved from https://www.scienceguide.nl/2018/05/hbo-onderzoeksvaardigheden-docenten/

Hogeschool Van Amsterdam. (2015a). *Nieuwsgierige Professionals. Instellingsplan 2015–2020*. Amsterdam: HvA.

Hogeschool Van Amsterdam. (2015b). *Strategisch Onderzoeksbeleid 2015–2020*. Retrieved from Amsterdam: file: //homedir.ad.hva.nl/gridm/Documents/Downloads/strategisch-onderzoeksbeleid-2015-2020.pdf

Jäger, A., De Ploeg, C., & De Vos, E. (2015). Hogescholen ervaren extreme werkdruk. Hoe komen we af van het InHolland-syndroom? *De Groene*(35). Retrieved from https://www.groene.nl/artikel/hoe-komen-we-af-van-het-inholland-syndroom

Jenkins, A., & Healey, M. (2005). *Institutional strategies to link teaching and research*. Retrieved from York: http://www.heacademy.ac.uk/assets/York/documents/resources/resourcedatabase/id585_institutional_strategies_to_link_teaching_and_research.pdf

Jenkins, A., & Zetter, R. (2003). *Linking teaching and research in departments*. Retrieved from York: http://www.livjm.ac.uk/partnership/Collab_Partner_Docs/PF_Jan_07_Martyn_Stewart_RIT.pdf

Jenkins, A., Healey, M., & Zetter, R. (2007). *Linking teaching and research in disciplines and departments*. Retrieved from York: http://www.heacademy.ac.uk/assets/York/documents/LinkingTeachingAndResearch_April07.pdf

Kezar, A. (2018). *How colleges change. Understanding, leading and enacting change*. London: Routledge.

Kickert, W. J. M. (1986). Onderzoek in het HBO. Waarom, wat en hoe? *Tijdschrift voor Hoger Onderwijs, 3*(3), 79–92.

Kyvik, S. (2007). Academic drift - A reinterpretation. In The Officers and Crew of HMS Network (Ed.), *Towards a cartography of higher education policy change. A festschrift in honour of guy neave* (pp. 333–8). Enschede: Center for Higher Education Policy Studies (CHEPS).

Kyvik, S., & Lepori, B. (2010). *The research mission of higher education institutions outside the university sector. Striving for differentiation*. (Vol. 31). Dordrecht: Springer.

Kyvik, S., & Skodvin, O.-J. (2003). Research in non-university higher education sector - tensions and dilemmas. *Higher Education, 45*(2), 203–22.

Maguire, S., & Hardy, C. A. (2019). The discourse of risk and processes of institutional change. In T. Reay, T. B. Zilber, A. Langley, & H. Tsoukas (Eds.), *Institutions and organisations. A process review* (pp. 154–73). Oxford: Oxford University Press.

Neave, G. (1979). Academic drift: Some views from Europe. *Studies in Higher Education, 4*(2), 143–59.

Neumann, R. (1993). Research and scholarship: Perceptions of senior academic administrators. *Higher Education, 25*(2), 97–110.

Nuffic. (2010). De Dublindescriptoren. Retrieved from http://www.nuffic.nl/nederlandse-organisaties/informatie/internationaliseringsbeleid/bolognaproces/achtergrondinformatie/drie-cycli/dublindescriptoren

Pitcher, R. (2011). Doctoral students' conceptions of research. *The Qualitative Report, 16*(4), 971–83.

Pitcher, R., & Åkerlind, G. S. (2009). Post-doctoral researchers' conceptions of research: A metaphor analysis. *International Journal for Researcher Development, 1*(2), 160–72.

Quirke, L. (2013). Roque resistance: Sidestepping isomorphic pressures in a patchy institutional field. *Organizational Studies, 34*(11), 1675–99.

Saarinen, T., & Valimaa, J. (2013). Change as an intellectual device and as an object of research. In B. Stensaker, J. Valimaa, & C. S. Sarrico (Eds.), *Managing reform in universities. The dynamics of culture, identity and organisational change* (pp. 41–60). New York: Palgrave Macmillan.

ScienceGuide. (2013). Werkt personele unie UvA-HvA? *ScienceGuide*. Retrieved from https://www.scienceguide.nl/2013/10/werkt-personele-unie-uva-hva/

Toubiana, M., & Zietsma, C. (2017). The message is on the Wall? Emotions, social media and the dynamics of organisational complexity. *Academy of Management Journal, 60*(3), 922–53.

Trowler, P. (2020). *Accomplishing change in teaching and learning regimes. Higher education and the practice sensibility*. Oxford: Oxford University Press.

Trowler, P., & Wareham, T. (2008). *Tribes, territories, research and teaching: Enhancing the teaching research nexus*. Retrieved from York: https://www.heacademy.ac.uk/resource/tribes-territories-research-and-teaching-enhancing-teaching-research-nexus-literature#sthash.5NK7FyDy.dpuf

Van Lieshout, H., & Borgdorff, H. (2005). *Onderzoek onmisbaar in HBO*. Retrieved from http://www.scienceguide.nl/article.asp?articleid=100270

Verburgh, A. L., Schouteden, W., & Elen, J. (2012). Patterns in the prevalence of research-related goals in higher education programmes. *Teaching in Higher Education*, 1–12. doi:10.1080/13562517.2012.719153

Vermeulen, P. A. M., Zietsma, C., Greenwood, R., & Langley, A. (2016). Strategic responses to institutional complexity. *Strategic Organisation*, 14(4), 277–86.

Xu, L. (2017). Teacher–researcher role conflict and burnout among Chinese university teachers: A job demand resources model perspective. *Studies in Higher Education*, 44(6), 903–1919. doi:https://doi.org/10.1080/03075079.2017.1399261

2

Mechanisms for Change

Didi M. E. Griffioen

Introduction

Changing the connections between research and education is a special type of higher-education change. Connections between research and education shape the core of a university's hybridity, as the logic of science (resulting in research) and the logic of pedagogy (resulting in education) shape the university's foundation (see further Introduction). Changes that touch an organisation's core increase the multiplicity of the change and the need for a smartly chosen approach as well as a fitting mechanism for change. Approach and mechanism are needed to bring action into the change process. Defining the content of the change in research–education connections is of the utmost importance to actively yield change, but a mechanism for change additionally needs an approach for changes and phases the change is expected to go through. As Kezar (2018, p. 65) states: 'Most change agents are focused on the content of the change initiative […]. However they spend little time focused on understanding the change process'. Bess and Dee (2008, p. 799) add: 'The mere perception of the need for change does not guarantee that change will occur'. For any incentive to result in organisational change, action needs to be undertaken. Further, action needs a mechanism to get stakeholders moving. Obviously, the label 'mechanism' therefore includes more firm organisational elements such as funding and structures, as well as softer elements such as perceptions and desires. Mechanism is about the possibility of putting different elements interact in motion and not about being 'mechanical'.

The approach for change provides the lens through which the change is seen; the change's origin, content and context provide information based on which the actors can weigh what perspective on the change at hand likely is most successful. Therefore, the mechanism for change consists of a combination of tools that, when combined, is expected to make the organisation move in the requested direction. The multi-layered perspective of the content as presented in Chapter 1 provides the playing field of this action. Both the approaches and mechanisms for change are founded in the existing body of literature as well as in the hands-on experience in the Amsterdam change programme.

Approaches for Change

Change processes request insight into their origins, content and context as described in Chapter 1. However, to start the change, both an approach for change and mechanism for change need to be constructed. The approach for change considers from where the content of change came – internal processes, external push, excitement among colleagues – and decides upon a general strategy for change based on this origin. The approaches are additionally based on different perspectives on what organisations are and how they can best change. The most common two approaches for organisational change are the Planned Change Strategy and the Emergent Change Strategy (Bess & Dee, 2008). The Planned Change Strategy presumes the organisation is a balance of stability and change, following the systems theory. This balance can be influenced by 'an intentional act that is driven by specific goals and plans' (Bess & Dee, 2008, p. 791). A Planned Change Strategy implies that leaders and decision makers take action to change the balance between stability and change, and to enlarge the energy towards change as a top-down approach. In this approach, the change starts with the organisation's top leaders. The Emergent Change Model follows a bottom-up approach based on social constructionists assumptions. This approach recognises 'the power for creativity and innovation possessed by people at all levels of the organisation' (Bess & Dee, 2008, p. 809). The origin of the change lies in multiple grassroots initiatives combined and results in larger changes across the organisation through the organisational leaders' activities, which Trowler (2020, p. 155) calls 'orchestration'. This implies organisational leaders recognise patterns of change across the organisation and articulate visions that 'reflect common strengths across multiple adaptations' (Bess & Dee, 2008, p. 809). We apply this difference between planned and emergent because of its clarity, but are also aware of the critique that actual emergent planning often is no planning at all due to a lack of direction (Bess & Dee,

2008; Buller, 2015), while the planned strategy can be presented as emergent for internal marketing purposes. This is in line with Bess and Dee's (2008) proposal to create a contingency framework for each change plan: a balanced combination between both approaches.

In turn, Kezar (2018) presents a more precise view through six different approaches for change, following from as many theories for change. A theory for change provides a specific view on a situation out of which a more particular approach for change follows. The first approach follows from scientific management theories, which include multiple theories that all assume strong agency among change agents. This theory resonates highly with the Planned Change Model, in which strategic planning, providing incentives and awards, restructuring organisational structures and creating a collective vision are among the basic tactics in the approach. Although the benefit of this approach is the central role of leadership, its limitation is that it tends to overestimate the role of the same leadership as those in power own, ignoring and downplaying the external context, politics and the less rational side of human involvement. In turn, evolutionary theories highly resonate to the Emergent Change Model and result in an opposite approach: 'Change happens because the environment demands that systems change in order to survive' (Kezar, 2018, p. 50). In this approach, change results depending on circumstances, changed situations and the environment. These theories' main benefit is the focus on context and human involvement. However, these theories downplay the role of change leaders and often lack explicit strategies or tactics to create change.

The third group of political theories also focuses on human agency and situational change, but starts from the notion that dominant coalitions in organisations aim to utilise their power to preserve the status quo. The outcome of a change process is a modified organisational ideology. Similarly to the Emergent Change Model, political theories focus on grassroots movements of change and have a larger focus on bottom-up leadership. This approach's main benefit is its non-linearity in a change process, considering that power shifts imply different tactics for change. However, by defining all conflicts as political and consisting of power and willingness, notions of misunderstanding or the relevant stakeholders' inability to follow-up on the proposed change can be overlooked. This omission is filled by social cognition theories, which provide a central stage for the thought processes and individuals' abilities in a changing context. Kezar (2018, p. 54) explains: 'Studies of resistance to change [as part of social cognition theories] illustrated that people were often not resisting a change because they disagreed with it, but because they did not truly understand its nature or how they might integrate it into their work and role'. Additionally, the social cognition perspective suggests that individuals hold multiple views of organisational reality, requesting for leaders who can better understand different interpretations to aid in translating and enacting the needed change. This theory adds to the perspective that not only humans and systems make the organisation; however, it has little attention for the external influences to change or the importance of organisations' structure and culture in change processes.

Cultural theories makes this connection between these mindsets and the environment or organisation. They focus on underlying values and assumptions as influencers of the change process. Their basic presumption is that there is not a single organisational reality and that activity and experience create meaning. Similar to social cognition theories, the meaning in organisations is seen as complex. However, where social cognition theories focus on individuals understanding a new way of working, cultural theories additionally focus on the values associated with that practice, which need to be learned or unlearned. This perspective resonates highly with the argument made in Section 1.2 – that it is important for change agents to know the history and context when changing a content in a university. Cultural theories additionally advise to understand the underlying values that can be addressed through examining various artefacts and symbols. Finally, institutional theory considers organisational change as an effect of changes in the influence of 'institutions', such as the government or the market. The university's hybridity in this book is argued as being based on the combined influences of the *institution of science* (Greenwood, Raynard, Kodeih, Micelotta, & Lounsbury, 2011) and the *institution of education* (Meyer, 1977); however, the change approach is less grounded in this institutional approach. Possibly, that is for the better, considering that institutional theory additionally argues that institutions influence organisational change, in which organisations with long-standing societal missions change slower and less often.

It is important to know and use these multiple approaches because experienced change agents learned that each change situation can request a different response. Most university change settings are far too complex for any single approach to work. Kezar (2018) seems to present this argument to create different multi-faceted approaches between different change programmes. However, the Amsterdam programme has shown that different approaches are needed within a single change programme.

The Amsterdam Programme's Approach

Every change programme requests its own approach. However, the Amsterdam programme illustrates that a change project requests an overall change approach – one could say a culture of the change – and additionally includes all kinds of smaller approaches that resonate to all variants as previously described in this section. The overall approach in the Amsterdam project was a thinly Planned Change Strategy in which the strategy as depict in Section 2.3 was rephrased into six additional concrete aims:

1. Each bachelor's programme has formulated a grounded rationale (or vision) for research in its related profession and therefore in the curriculum (ideally halfway through the programme).
2. In line with their new rationale, the position of research in the curriculum of bachelor's programmes is (re)considered (ideally halfway through the programme).
3. The number of lecturers and different educational programmes in the strategic programme's activities increases over time.
4. The activity of lecturers and educational programmes on the topic of research integration in the curriculum increases over time (other than activities of the strategic programme).
5. Building on aims 1–4, Amsterdam UAS has developed a combined vision for research in the professions and educational programmes, taking into account disciplinary differences.
6. Building on aims 1–4, Amsterdam UAS might define the characteristics of exciting bachelor's programmes that include research.

While the initiative of the strategic programme was taken at the central administrative level, which made the overall strategic programme based on a Planned Change Strategy, the actual strategy had the culture of an Emergent Change Strategy. Before explaining that, it is important to remember the origin of this change programme's unsuccessful history of trying to create research–education connections by bringing the new research professors in the lead, while disregarding their lack of line-management responsibility, as was more elaborately explained in Chapter 1. Following that knowledge, the strategic programme was based on the main strategy to follow line-management responsibilities and therefore position the educational teams and their managers as leading agents to create research–education connections. The idea was that aims 1 and 2 in the bachelor's curricula could be created through process aims

3 and 4 of creating activity in educational teams. The more strategic aims 5 and 6 of generating collective Amsterdam UAS frameworks on research and education would be possible derived effects.

This choice seen through the political theory lens implies an active shift in topic ownership. Generally, educational teams were not considered research specialists (also due to their educational level) and some considered placing them in the lead would result in 'other' perceptions of research than the more 'high quality' ones in the different disciplines. This argument gained weight as the effect of the still remembered national incident about the quality of bachelor's theses at another applied university (see Chapter 1). However, this implied that the strategic programme team often needed to step in when dominant voices from research or administration would try to reduce the space for the integrative task the educational teams now had. The educational teams needed time and support to develop their own perceptions of the functionality of research in their related professional fields, and therefore in their bachelor's curricula. Additionally, there was the presumption that increased developed perceptions among educators would provide a better foundation for partnering with research professors in the effort to increase research–education connections.

The approach to create activity was fully emergent in character and organised through five projects. The projects and figure 2.1 have afore been published in Griffioen and Van Ooijen (2021).

In project 1, an online tool was developed to showcase the diverse perspectives of research integration and the possibility for Q&A across the colleagues in different bachelor's programmes. This provided the possibility for educational

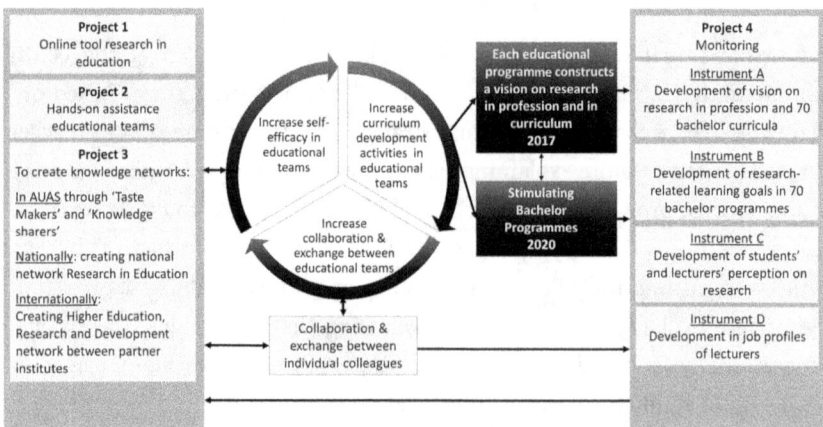

Figure 2.1 Overview of change approach based on projects.

teams to gain knowledge and assistance beyond their personal networks and independent from the strategic programme team.

Project 2 aimed to provide hands-on support to educational teams by the strategic programme team. This support reached from a low-threshold talk over coffee to working together on full curriculum development, and to a provision of custom-made workshops. The topics could range from insights at the level of lessons and modules to curriculum structures, and to handling visiting quality agencies. This project's culture was: 'How can we help?' In Chapter 3, many of the tools developed for or through the activities in this project are described for future use elsewhere.

The main aim of project 3 was to create knowledge networks across Amsterdam UAS, beyond the separate educational teams and faculties. Networks of colleagues often did not reach beyond their hallway, programme year or educational team. Every year, five university-wide symposia were organised. The topics chosen were influenced by the topics requested in project 2 as well as national and institutional policy developments or findings from the data. The topics changed over time and their importance clearly differed between educational teams who developed them at their own pace as well as between target audiences. At the start of the strategic programme, the target audience was mainly lecturers, lecturers specialised in research methods, educational managers and related curriculum developers. With the development across the university, quality agents, policy officers, research managers and researchers became target audiences.

Three of the annual symposia were called 'Knowledge Sharers' (Dutch: *Kennisdelers*), which provided the opportunity to share and celebrate local research integration activities and results; two were called 'Taste Makers' (Dutch: *Smaakmakers*) in which high-level national and international expertise presented themselves on stage. Additionally, a national network of policy officers with a focus on research integration was initiated and an international network between Amsterdam UAS's partner universities was brought to life. This project generated the excitement and interest needed to get new colleagues curious enough about a particular topic to attend a symposium. A coffee reception often followed, which led again to more extensive activities as part of project 2. In turn, the active colleagues in project 2 were the ones who were given the stage to present their challenges and solutions in a university-wide symposium. Nationally, a network of Amsterdam UAS's policy officers was initiated and those individuals would meet three times a year to share developments and generated knowledge across university developments (see also: Griffioen,

Tankink, & Van den Auweraert, 2017). Internationally, the Higher Education Research & Development (HERD) network was initiated for the same purpose, but now across Amsterdam UAS's European partners. Additionally, two Higher Education Conferences were organised in Amsterdam in 2016 and 2019, to provide the local stakeholders with access to empirical higher education knowledge. Finally, the strategic programme team initiated the first Amsterdam UAS Research Day in 2018, to add to the existing Amsterdam UAS Education Day to bring research and education to the same position of prominence. All these network activities aimed to incite creative activity and knowledge sharing between partners at the local, national and international levels as well as between the different layers.

In project 4, we created and applied a monitoring and evaluation scheme based on scientifically founded indicators with several strings of longitudinal research to provide the same academic rigor to the change programme as we would to teaching and research (Buller, 2015), and as rigorously as we intended to teach our students through the proposed change educational programmes. Underpinning this project was a strategic programme aimed to help bachelor's programmes educate research-informed professionals in a similar approach. We intended to 'walk-the-talk'. The findings of this monitoring project are presented in Chapters 4 through 7, focused on changing perceptions of research (Chapter 4), changing curriculum rationales (Chapter 5), changing curriculum learning goals (Chapter 6) and nationally changing job profiles (Chapter 7).

Finally, through project 5, a university-wide research group was developed with a focus on connections between research, education and professional action, as well as innovation processes. The university board already adopted this project, thus it made sense to include it in the change programme strategy. This project mainly focused on a provision of a body of knowledge after the change programme ended and is therefore not depicted in Figure 2.1. This research team pulled together to write this book as a collective effort to share our experiences and lessons learned (see also www.amsterdamuas/heri).

The Amsterdam Programme Followed a Combination of Approach Theories

Research–education connections started with a shift that institutional theory can indicate. The former teaching-only sector of applied higher education was dominated by the institution of pedagogy, which was confronted with mostly top-down changes in which the institution of science gained influence.

However, the strategic programme as such was not shaped through institutional theory, although the approach was aware of the differences in culture between science and pedagogy. Creating the five projects as such was in line with the Planned Change Approach of scientific management theory. Upper management delegated this responsibility to the programme team and they went ahead with formulating a change approach. However, the change approach within the five projects consisted of a combination of the social cognition theory and cultural theory approaches. The notion that lecturers and full educational teams needed to create their own understanding of what 'research' could mean for their students as future professionals followed social cognition theory. Without creating this potential of research, of providing their students with research ability, of helping them use knowledge from research and/or of employing research as pedagogy, lecturers would not be willing or able to bring research into their curricula.

Therefore, the notion of 'understanding' in this strategic programme was not based on a single, unified notion of what methodology research should include, what it's characteristics should be or even whether students needed to learn how to conduct research. The debates about potential notions of research were characterised by openness. We actively infused the possibility of multiple perspectives of research, professionalism and even education as derived from the values and multiple perspectives that cultural theory presumes. Many debates started from discussing professionalism in a particular field and followed through to potential functions of knowledge and truth as based on different types of knowledge and truth. In that context, research became a potential carrier to that knowledge and truth for their own future alumni along with gaining experience through professional practice and systematically reflecting on that practice.

Taking the time and space for these debates in educational teams, without anyone claiming any truth or telling what research should be like, activated many lecturers as potential small-level change agents. By developing their own lines of thought, lecturers and educational teams became the partners of research professors they were not before. Additionally, this approach provided the space for professionals to add the perspective of research to their notion of research as part of science (see also Griffioen, 2019).

The Amsterdam case illustrates how all theories and their lenses are needed during a change programme regarding research–education connections. However, their functionality and mutual prominence differs between change programmes, and between settings within those programmes. It is important for change agents to be aware of these lenses and shift between them when the setting requires it.

Phases of Change

Thus far an origin, a content, a context and an approach of change have been defined as part of a mechanism for change. Additionally, change projects often go through different phases in alterations that take place. Generally, change literature suggests that people and organisational structures, or the fixed and fluent aspects of an organisation, are altered in a change programme. This results in the most simple model of phases for change: To first change the structure and allow changes in organisational stakeholders' attitudes to follow; or to focus on changing the people first, and then turn to organisational-wide change (Bess & Dee, 2008). Later on, this chapter returns to the five different content layers that were introduced in Chapter 1, through discussing the mechanism of the Amsterdam case. First, the different phases for change are addressed that follow from multiple conceptual models for change. As we show, each model includes different phases, which often follow from albeit generic, perspective on what should be changed in an organisation (structures or people) and how this can be best approached. Although most change processes evolve more iteratively (Buller, 2015), it is useful for change agents to be aware of potential stages of change.

The foundational model for a stage-based perspective is people oriented and was developed as the unfreezing → changing → (re)freezing model Kurt Lewin introduced in the 1940s (Bess & Dee, 2008; Burnes, 2004; Cummings, Bridgeman, & Brown, 2016). The unfreezing step implied destabilising the equilibrium Lewin believed human behaviour was in as an effect of a context of complex forces. The second step of changing implies going to a more acceptable set of behaviours, for which action research is positioned as a change instrument in which reinforcement is needed to make the changes sustainable. Finally, the (re)freezing stage 'seeks to stabilise the group at a new quasi-stationary equilibrium in order to ensure that the new behaviours are relatively safe from regression' (Burnes, 2004, p. 986). Refreezing often requires changes to organisational culture, norms, politics and practices at the group level, which is more sustainable than individual changed behaviour.

Many models of different stages have been developed since Lewin's model. Rogers's 1962 model for adapting innovation describes five stages that include the individual stakeholder as an actor and focuses on the success factors for organisational change: awareness, persuasion, evaluation, trial and implementation (Bess & Dee, 2008).

The Kübler-Ross 1969 model compares organisational change to the process of people going through the five stages of grief: denial, anger, bargaining, depression and acceptance. This model adds the notion that in organisational change, stakeholders are likely to resist change, especially if change is presented as A is changed into B and not as A will become A+. People do not enjoy loosing A, or as Buller (2015, p. 30) states: 'people do not really fear change, they fear loss'.

The 1996 Krüger Model of Change Management distinguishes between the visible aspects in the change process, such as time and costs, and the invisible aspects, such as politics, beliefs, biases and perceptions, which can be called the human elements. Change agents are supposed to be more successful if they also focus on the invisible aspects of change (Buller, 2015).

The human element is even more present in the 2006 Kotter Model, which provides a clear longitudinal perspective in a combination of human change and structure change. This model leans more into social cognition theories and cultural theories, but still is based substantially on strategic management theories and planned change models due to its relative dominance in top-down initiatives and a leading role for all levels of management. The Kotter model includes eight phases of organisational change, which is again very people focused (Buller, 2015):

1. Establish a sense of urgency by helping members of an organisation to comprehend the need for change, as to make them do something because the pain of doing nothing is greater;
2. create the guiding coalition, which includes the leadership team, but can be expanded to early adopters;
3. develop a change vision, a clear and easily remembered image of the end of the change plan;
4. communicate the vision for buy-in through increasingly larger circles of management explaining why the new vision is beneficial to them;
5. empower broad-based action by putting new groups of colleagues in place for staff training, providing funding and working through barriers;
6. generate short-term wins, in which victories are celebrated as they occur to keep up the momentum;
7. never let up, stick to the rhetoric about the end vision, also when small victories are made; and

8. incorporate changes into the culture, to start considering the new situation as normal.

The ADKAR model for change was applied in the Amsterdam change programme (Hiatt, 2018). This model includes five phases and has a relatively large focus on altering individual people, which in the Amsterdam setting is applied in the collective context of a large university. The final phase is more structure focused. The phases of the ADKAR model are:

1. Awareness, in which individuals become aware of the proposed changes;
2. Desire, where individuals gain the willingness to contribute to the change process;
3. Knowledge, where individuals know what the requested change looks like;
4. Ability, where individuals are able to act as part of the changes; and
5. Reinforcement, to confirm the change through governance instruments.

The first two phases of the ADKAR model are rather similar to Rogers's model in that both aim for the individuals in the organisation to become aware of the proposed changes. However, the second stage in the ADKAR model, desire, is more focused on creating intrinsic motivation and an internalisation of the proposed changes; whereas Rogers's model aims for individuals to be persuaded, which resonates more to extrinsic motivation and stimuli. Where Rogers's model then mainly focuses on the content of the implementation with the evaluation, trial and implementation stages, the ADKAR model keeps its attention on the human aspect of the change in the knowledge and ability stages. In the final stage, the ADKAR model focuses more on enforcing expected changed behaviour by creating governance and other structural changes in the organisation during the reinforcement stage.

Where the phases-oriented models presents a stepwise process to organisational change, they provide limited insight into what tools can be used to achieve the change. As previously stated: To result in organisational change, action needs to be undertaken. Where the approaches for change suggest the direction for action based on a set of assumptions, and the phases-model suggests through which phases the change can be expected to go through, every change agent needs additional instruments that can actually initiate and influence the change process at hand. Chapter 3 will provide new tools for change. First, the aforementioned arguments are illustrated by the mechanism for change in the Amsterdam case.

A Mechanism for Change: The Interrelated Content, Approach and Phases of Change in the Amsterdam Case

The choice for the ADKAR model was founded in the presumed need for human attention in the Amsterdam change programme. Similar to other universities, the lecturers in Amsterdam tend to be highly autonomous, both in practice due to the high level of complexity of their work based on many different professions as well as part of their identity (Stensaker, Henkel, Välimaa, & Sarrico, 2013) as expert-professionals now teaching in their specialty. The aim of changing the research–education connections in the bachelor's curricula, implied changing Amsterdam UAS's practices at the lowest level in the organisation. Therefore, curriculum practices needed to be considered at the micro-level, across the seventy bachelor's curricula. Changing curricula entails creating different solutions for each micro-practice, ideally mutually aligned within each educational programme, then across every faculty and in the full university. These different solutions are needed for the changes to work. Trowler (2020, p. 69; 116) states in this perspective: 'Where practices which work in one context and time period are transposed to another for which they are in fact very inappropriate [...] [is shown that] maladaptive practices have disastrous results' and 'what works in change is contextually contingent'. Changing lecturers' practices yielded a human-focused approach.

This was even more needed due to this change programme's content: research–education connections. Where academics internationally thank Mick Healey (2021) for actively gathering an extensive amount of examples of research–education connections in all study years of mostly all disciplines around the world, still these examples by definition can be merely inspirational. Every single inspirational example of research–education connections needs to be redesigned to become fitting for a module, lesson or research activity elsewhere. Their general practice, professional practice and knowledge from research needs to be 'transformed' to fit a micro-setting and micro-purpose (Ashwin, 2014; Bernstein, 2000). Therefore, changing research–education connections can never just be 'rolled out'; individual lecturers and researchers need to be actively involved as co-inventing actors of the proposed changes. Thus, further than on other more instrumental change contents, the Amsterdam change programme was about changing individuals' mindsets and the values, which is more difficult when those to be changed are accustomed to having a critical stance, such as lecturers in universities who do (Stensaker et al., 2013).

Therefore, the combined projects in the strategic programme aimed to initiate change by having stakeholders interact on the topics related to research–education connections (see also the moving circle in Figure 2.1). The ground rule was that any activity on this topic would be better than no activity to achieve an increase in topic ownership. The insight and quality presumably would need to follow activity, and starting with notions of any high quality or insights from a particular perspective would kill all activity (see for the multiple perspectives on research for instance: Brew, 2001; Griffioen & De Jong, 2015). Therefore, the Amsterdam programme focused its five years on the first two phases of the ADKAR model: to create awareness of the ambition to further implement research into bachelor's curricula (added with the notion that research was there to stay), and to develop the desire to contribute to that ambition among increasingly larger groups of lecturers. With an increase in activity on the topic, hands-on experience would increase as well, which was then systematically shared among all those who were active. After the five years and through project 5, the newly created research group would be able to address the next stage of foundational-generating knowledge.

Sensemaking in Amsterdam

For the proposed changes to start occurring, Amsterdam UAS needed not only to be seen as a 'structured system [...] with procedures for assigning power, authority and responsibility for the sake of making decisions' (Buller, 2015, p. 11), but more as an organisation that is a collective of individuals with shared assumptions and valid ways of working. These ways and assumptions reach beyond the organisational structures and can differ between organisational subgroups or departments (see also: Trowler, 2020). Changing large groups of individuals (Amsterdam UAS employed 3,700 lecturers at the time) is a diffuse and often contradictory process when seen from a central focal point in the organisation (Stensaker et al., 2013). It was important to consider changes in actions as well as in sensemaking in individuals and smaller groups of lecturers to achieve real change and not just imposed, unrelated actions at the grassroots level, which would burn up stakeholders' energy for change. Sensemaking and identity are closely related in individuals. Meaning arises from the attention of processes directed towards the experience and the stakeholders' values and their priorities, and help them to decide what matters (Frolich & Stensaker, 2013). The process of sensemaking can happen in two ways: individuals attach new meanings to familiar concepts and ideas, or individuals develop new language and concepts that describe changed practices (Kezar, 2018).

In the Amsterdam setting, sensemaking was approached via the first way: to systematically attach new meanings to familiar concepts and ideas. Many educational programmes changed the formal set-up of their curricula in the years before the strategic programme started. However, many of these changes had not altered the actual modules and lessons the students received because the lecturers did not 'live' them. When they did, they mainly consisted of research ability courses that were positioned as disconnected from the professional ability courses in the curricula. Therefore, the mechanism for change in the Amsterdam project evolved around expanding the values and priorities of lecturers across the university, mainly by helping them decide how research could be useful for their students (if any) as future professionals. The values of many lecturers and educational teams traditionally were based on educating professionals in the diverse professional fields. With many lecturers being nurses, economists, teachers or social workers, it was important that they created a renewed sense of research as something that mattered to the future colleagues they educated. Mostly at the start, research was of no importance to them or even perceived as a hindrance for a proper professional education. These values were passed on to students, and new colleagues were selected based on having the similar values and educational background, again illustrating the difficulty of connecting a second primary process in a new hybrid organisation (Bystydzienski, Thomas, Howe, & Desai, 2016; see also chapter 2). In many people's perception, research in general was not part of what should matter to their students as future professionals. Lecturers perceived that professional education should be 'hands on', while they perceived research as being 'too theoretical', 'too much work for its benefits', 'not useful' and done by people wearing white coats and working in labs (see Chapter 4 for a systematic overview of changed perceptions).

Practically, the previously described projects 2 and 3 formed the core of helping colleagues address their perceptions and to test them against other's perceptions of direct colleagues and colleagues of other faculties. The support educational teams received through project 2 was the starting point for the educational programmes that were the frontrunners in this change strategy. They jumped on the possibility to get assistance, which resulted in many workshops, masterclasses and collaborations at the team or sub-team levels. Generally, lecturers in these teams already agreed that changes needed to be made and they collectively addressed the process of sensemaking. In these situations, a social cognition approach, as well as basing deliberations in cultural theory's values related to educating professionals, worked wonderfully: Colleagues simply wanted to discuss and decide upon matters of research–education integration at the intellectual level. They were clearly the frontrunners of change among the educational teams. Through the strategic programme, they became the public advocates of the intended changes. These teams were most often showcased as part of the network building in project 3. They played their role wonderfully by being willing to show not only the potential of research integration by bringing new ideas for education on stage, but also their struggles and doubts along the way. By doing so, they fully revealed the complexity of rebalancing research–education connections in their educational programmes. This worked like a charm; over time they inspired many others through large group seminars. Many new contacts among the seventy-plus bachelor's programmes followed their multiple presentations, asking for assistance for their own change. New contact, which again always started with an informal coffee reception, led to an increase in contact. The presentation of the frontrunners led many others to our programme's open door.

After initial coffee, we built in one important threshold. As change agents, it was important to enter an educational team with the formal approval of educational management. Underlying struggles in an educational team about ownership of the curriculum or of 'the definition of research' could lead to a need for taking steps away from the research–integration topic and towards creating the needed social balance in the team afore addressing this complex topic again. The local educational management's formal approval could avoid the notion that the change team was hijacking the curriculum design. For similar reasons, we always mentioned our work to policy advisors in education at the faculty level, ideally to have them active in a collaborative change effort.

Next to the frontrunning teams, several educational teams were increasingly aware of the importance of research in the sense that they knew research would not go away again. They were aware of the support project and many representatives attended the symposia as part of project 3, but often they kept their distance from the programme team. Generally, the lecturers in these teams were not convinced that research would benefit their students or that it was important to make an effort, or they felt too much resistance among colleagues. By presenting them with ongoing sessions of different topics and changes that other educational teams made through an online newsletter, over time we could persuade many into a coffee and a workshop. Many lecturers in these teams saw research as redundant for their students as future professionals: too precise, too time consuming, not practical. For this group, the aim became to attach new meaning to their current concepts such as research, professionalism and education. We achieved this through multiple discussions in educational teams as well as through presenting new concepts in written pieces for Dutch professional audiences (e.g. Griffioen, 2016, 2017a, 2017b), also following the effort with colleagues in the field to make the international knowledge of the research–teaching nexus accessible in Dutch (Griffioen, Visser-Wijnveen, & Willems, 2013) to take away barriers. Interestingly, our own Amsterdam UAS educational teams used many of our written models and concepts after disciplinary colleagues from elsewhere in the country advised them to do so. The suggestion of concepts being invented or at least used successfully elsewhere was a large incentive to Amsterdam colleagues, bringing a whole new perspective to the not-invented-here Syndrome. Visibly scaling up from the local to the national and international settings became a purposeful strategy in this regard.

A new sense of concepts was collectively created in educational teams by having a strategy to affirm familiarity and reduce strangeness in the connection between research and professionalism by applying the tools that are presented in Chapter 3. Assisting lecturers to think about possibilities for their students as future professionals provided the proper foundation to stretch their existing perceptions and attach new meanings. This assisted lecturers to come to insights such as: 'we already use theory based on research, but it is hidden in handbooks'; 'research is a way to systematically gather information, that is not so different from what we already do that in professional practice' and 'we want our students to be innovative, research methods when designed in a certain way could help them to do so systematically'. By systematically creating networks between individuals and teams across the university, these insights became dominant in institutional sensemaking as second-order change of collective understanding (Kezar, 2018), thus resulting in a changed mission for Amsterdam UAS based on a more integrated perspective of research and education (Amsterdam UAS, 2018).

Many educational teams made smaller or larger changes in their educational programmes as an effect of interacting with the change team. The teams found their way to the change team in their different developmental stages. Some were very ready for change at the start of the change programme while many others became more ready at some point during the five years of the change programmes' duration, and some still hoped research would go away. Some made impressive changes without interacting with the change team, or only when they were making their second or third round of curriculum changes towards the end of the change programme. Further, some did not initiate any change. With a focus on awareness and desire, the foundational approach was that for the duration of the change programme, all these changes were fine as long as the individuals in the organisation started to interact with the topic. The responsibility for the governance of the university as a whole did not include the programme team. The responsibility of the programme team was to generate the desire to change. With eight lecturers in the very first seminar and over 600 receiving the quarterly newsletters at the end, that is what happened across Amsterdam UAS.

References

Amsterdam UAS. (2018). Visie. Retrieved from https://www.hva.nl/over-de-hva/wie-wij-zijn/visie/visie.html

Ashwin, P. (2014). Knowledge, curriculum and student understanding. *Higher Education, 67*(2).

Bernstein, B. B. (2000). *Pedagogy, symbolic control, and identity. Theory, research, critique.* New York: Rowman & Littlefield Pub.

Bess, J. L., & Dee, J. R. (2008). *Understanding college and university organisation* (Vol. II Dynamics of the System). Sterling: Stylus Publishing.

Brew, A. (2001). Conceptions of research: A phenomenographic study. *Studies in Higher Education, 26*(3), 271–85.

Buller, J. L. (2015). *Change leadership in higher education.* San Francisco: Jossey-Bass.

Burnes, B. (2004). Kurt Lewin and the planned approach for change. *Journal of Management Studies, 41*(6), 977–1002.

Bystydzienski, J., Thomas, N., Howe, S., & Desai, A. (2016). The Leadership role of college deans and department chairs in academic culture change. *Studies in Higher Education, 42*(12), 2301–15.

Cummings, S., Bridgeman, T., & Brown, K. G. (2016). Unfreezing change as three steps: Rethinking Kurt Lewin's legacy for change management. *Human Relations, 69*(1), 33–60.

Frolich, N., & Stensaker, B. (2013). University strategizing: The role of evaluation as a sensemaking tool. In B. Stensaker, J. Valimaa, & C. S. Sarrico (Eds.), *Managing reform in universities. The dynamics of culture, identity and organisational change* (pp. 63–80). New York: Palgrave Macmillan.

Greenwood, R., Raynard, M., Kodeih, F., Micelotta, E. R., & Lounsbury, M. (2011). Institutional complexity and organizational responses. *The Academy of Management Annals, 5*(1), 317–71.

Griffioen, D. M. E., Visser-Wijnveen, G. J., & Willems, J. (Eds.). (2013). *Integratie van onderzoek in het onderwijs. Effectieve inbedding van onderzoek in curricula.* Groningen: Noordhoff Uitgevers.

Griffioen, D. M. E. (2016). Nieuwsgierige Professionals Opleiden. *TH&MA Hoger Onderwijs* (1), 54–31.

Griffioen, D. M. E. (2017a). Onderzoek en onderwijs: docenten als essentiële schakel in een complexe transformatie. Inleiding op het themanummer. *Tijdschrift voor Hoger Onderwijs, 35*(2), 2–8.

Griffioen, D. M. E. (2017b). Onderzoek is onderdeel van Professioneel Handelen. Op zoek naar nieuwe handvatten. *TH&MA Hoger Onderwijs*(5), 90–7.

Griffioen, D. M. E. (2019). *Higher education's responsibility for balanced professionalism. Methodology beyond research.* (Inaugural lecture). Amsterdam University of Applied Sciences, Amsterdam. Retrieved from https://www.hva.nl/content/evenementen/oraties/2019/10/didi-griffioen.html

Griffioen, D. M. E., & De Jong, U. (2015). Mapping Dutch higher education lecturers' discourse on research at times of academic drift. *Scottish Journal for Arts, Social Sciences, and Scientific Studies, 26*(1), 81–94.

Griffioen, D. M. E., Tankink, T., & Van den Auweraert, A. (2017). Bundel de krachten. Nederlandse hogescholen en de integratie van onderzoek in het onderwijs. *TH&MA Hoger Onderwijs* (3), 73.

Griffioen, D. M. E., & Van Ooijen, L. (2021). Awareness and desire as strategy for change. The integration of research and education at Amsterdam University of applied sciences In I. Huet, T. Pessoa, & F. Sol Murta (Eds.), *Excellence in teaching and learning in higher education: Institutional policies and practices in Europe* (pp. 217–44). Coimbra: Coimbra University Press.

Healey, M. (2021). *Resources.* Retrieved from https://mickhealey.co.uk/resources

Hiatt, J. (2018). ADKAR change management overview.

Kezar, A. (2018). *How colleges change. Understanding, leading and enacting change.* London: Routledge.

Meyer, J. W. (1977). The effects of education as an institution. *The American Journal of Sociology, 83*(1).

Stensaker, B., Henkel, M., Välimaa, J., & Sarrico, C. S. (2013). Introduction: How is change in higher education managed. In B. Stensaker, J. Välimaa, & C. S. Sarrico (Eds.), *Managing reform in universities. The dynamics of culture, identity and organizational change* (pp. 1–18). New York: Palgrave Macmillan.

Trowler, P. (2020). *Accomplishing change in teaching and learning regimes. Higher education and the practice sensibility.* Oxford: Oxford University Press.

3

Instruments to Debate Change

Didi M. E. Griffioen

Introduction

Colleagues in universities aiming for better integration of research and education often do not have a clear perspective as to what they aim to achieve, or so is our experience. This mostly is not surprising as it resonates with Trowler and Wareham's (2008) findings that notions of the research–teaching nexus are multiple and normative. The normativity finds its results in higher-education practice in a positive stance to increasing research–education connections. This positivity often does not yield the strive to precisely define what connection stakeholders are intending. For change agents, such clarity is essential to help provide direction to achieve the intended aims. Additionally, clarity is important to the stakeholders involved in the change process to avoid frustration in discovering that others intend different research–education connections. Early on, more precise insight into others' intentions can also increase the awareness of potential connections, beyond one's own ideas. Therefore, increased clarity about aims and perceptions can help to keep positivity the dominant tone in the change process.

As explained in Chapter 1, the notion of research integration potentially includes many different organisational layers and perspectives; all are relevant, depending on the particular research integration aim. Those working towards a certain increased connection often empirically work in the dark. The body of knowledge about research–education connections mostly comprises case studies about (potential) choices for research–education connections made in certain settings. These studies are hardly added with empirical testing about the workings of the choices made, let alone about their effects (e.g. Griffioen, Groen, & Nak, 2019 for an overview at the curriculum level). This is not accidental. The multiple layers of research integration and the recent tradition in this discipline make certain there is not yet a fully developed common language or conceptual model to capture the different types and layers of research integration. This standing implies that even a large insight in the body of knowledge might not lead to answers to questions such as: What best to do? How to get there? What are its effects?

The efforts in this book, particularly in Chapters 1 and 2, are to at least propose a language by advising to ask the stakeholders involved to define the origin, content in one or more layers and context of the proposed research–education connections, to result in a mechanism to achieve this change that also includes an approach for changes and expected phases that the change may likely go through. However, change agents would need additional tools to reach a collective interpretation among stakeholders of these frames, or even to gather different insights on these frames among stakeholders involved. This chapter provides several of these tools.

We have learned through the Amsterdam UAS change programme and its predecessors that most of the time, asking to explain what is meant with 'research', 'education', or their connection often is the start of a long and complex conversation in which different perspectives usually are intertwined. Stakeholders often meant different things while using the same words (see also Griffioen & De Jong, 2015; Schouteden, Verburgh, & Elen, 2011, 2014). Further, all of their perceptions could be valid, depending on the context and the perspective chosen. During sit-down debates, we often found a lack of clarity between those involved that crossed multiple levels, even when polite policy officers afore explained their interpretation of these topics or when they were written down in session agendas, project plans or even formalised definitions. The confusion also appeared among those who agreed on the topics afore, and worked at the same level of the organisation. Somehow, when working on changing research–education connections, it is rather hard to get all involved to reach the same level of mutual understanding. Change agents need to accept and even embrace that this is the case, and as we did, learn to hide their surprise and be topic-flexible. Potential aspects that can come up, often simultaneously, are: the core topic that was scheduled (what will we talk about today?); the level of research–education connections one wants to aim for; how the different stakeholders perceive this aim and all of its elements; what the means and what the end goals are; the order of means needed to achieve that aim and the role and related responsibility the stakeholders are willing to take on during that process and after. Most stakeholders reach out at the most obvious point of departure for their situation and might have never considered the context of other perspectives.

At the same time, stakeholders were often very eager to learn about these other perspectives, but this would not generally imply that their perspective would still be widened in the next session. It is up to change agents to be aware of these differences because they can occur between stakeholders in the same change project, and help stakeholders make them explicit to further the collective change process. Additionally, it is important that the change agents guide stakeholders to be aware that they also have the responsibility to know that colleagues can have rather different perceptions, which are just as valid as their own. Keeping an open mind is the most functional stance in this regard, for all involved.

Finally, it is important for change agents to be clear about who has the formal responsibility for these changes and to understand the organisational outline. In our experience, colleagues who are excited about changing research–education connections tend to overestimate their formal influence on a curriculum or department. We have seen several colleagues excitedly draw detailed plans to make changes beyond their span of influence, for instance, a faculty-wide curriculum without having any formal responsibility to do so. Obviously, they were very disappointed when finding out that the responsible line manager would not execute that plan accordingly. Thus, we learned to ask whether stakeholders had the formal say in changing, for instance, a full educational programme, a module, or even a set of lessons, to avoid future frustrations. Creating options for change should therefore always go together with a realistic view on what would be needed – formally, financially, practically – to achieve this change. When stakeholders overplayed their hand in this regard, it was up to us change agents to show them ways in which they would be able to contribute within the boundaries of their formal responsibilities.

Instruments for Conversation

The fluidity of conversations about research–education connections requires instruments. This chapter presents instruments beneficial for discussing research integration with different audiences during change processes. Several authors have afore developed similar – sometimes very famous – models and tools for similar purposes, such as the model by Brew (2001) about research conceptions, the quadrant model by Healey (2005) that provides didactical perspectives by crossing student role with research foci, and the work on how perceptions of research can influence constructions of teaching (and vice versa) by for instance Prosser and colleagues (2008), or Visser-Wijnveen and colleagues (2009). This chapter aims to contribute to this field by adding the tools, models, and instruments that have been developed over the years of the Amsterdam UAS's strategic programme. The instruments presented in Section 3.2 will assist in overseeing the field of research integration by introducing some comprehensive instruments to debate the different aspects of changing research–education connections with strategic partners, or to use as a means to discover what aspect stakeholders intend to change or discuss. Section 3.3 presents models to discuss perceptions of research from the perspectives of different stakeholders, useful when research is relatively new, such as in applied universities; and/or for disciplines where the conceptions of research are not yet uniform (Biglan, 1973; Kuhn, 1962). Additionally, they can be applied in the context of more uniform disciplinary paradigms to become more aware of detailed differences and to create new possibilities by combining stakeholders' perceptions. Section 3.4 focuses on debating changes in research–education connections at the curriculum level, as a way to balance between the many elements and multiple years of which a curriculum consists. Finally, Section 3.6 presents models to discuss research in the context of professional-oriented settings in higher education. All instruments in this chapter will be introduced, explained and suggestions for their usage will be given. The list of tools presented in this chapter invites readers to roam through it instead of reading it from beginning to end. Readers are furthermore happily invited to remodel all instruments presented to make them fit for their own settings and change programmes.

Comprehensive Instruments to Discuss 'Change Aims'

This paragraph discusses instruments that can help to provide an overview over the change in research–education-connection at hand and therefore assist in debates or reflections on change aims, the focus of change activities, or change results.

The Strategy Mapping Instrument

The Strategy Mapping Instrument's purpose is to obtain a quick overview of the strategy of a university, faculty, or department related to research–education connections. Often university strategy related to research–education connections consists of snippets of ambition written down as dense as possible (e.g. Daas, Day, & Griffioen, 2019). Most of the time, there is a lot of talk added that has not been captured in documents. As an effect, the different managers have varied perceptions of what the intentions are and for what purpose; politics also can result in different perceptions. The Strategy Mapping Instrument can assist in capturing the relevant aspects of university strategy related to research–education connections. This tool can be best applied among groups of middle- and higher-level management in universities.

As previously explained, it is important that the multiple layers of research–education connections are considered in relation to the phases of change. Another aspect to bear in mind is that the plans for change and action need to be considered in terms of the action's intentions in order for the aims to be achieved and the expected effects to occur if these changes are indeed achieved. When changing the research–education connection, the focus is often on the aims (see the middle column in Figure 3.1). For instance, students need to do research, or the collaboration between educational programmes and the professional field

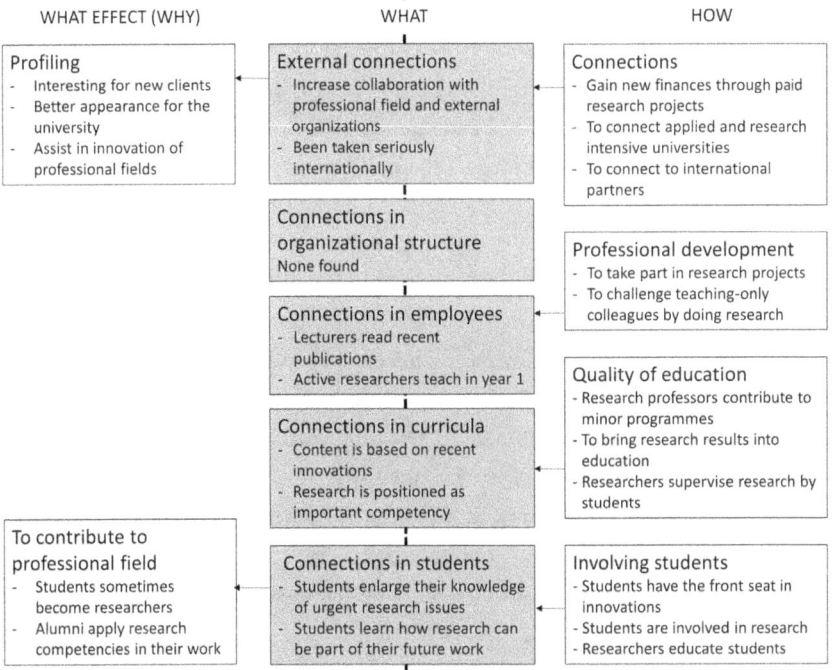

Figure 3.1 The Strategy Mapping Instrument to be used at the university-, faculty- or department-level debates on research–education connections.

needs to be increased. When asked what might be put in place to achieve that aim (the right-hand column in Figure 3.1), often the answers are diffuse. When we ask why these aims need to be achieved (left-hand column in Figure 3.1), often the answers are lacking.

This instrument can be used to map the current strategy of a university, faculty or department with a light touch, and to discuss the content and balance of all three columns with middle- or higher-level management. When needed, the same can be done over time during a change process. The power of gaining this overview is the importance of simple models. The managers can do the mapping as an exercise, or the change agent can use a filled-out model based on the most recent, relevant strategy document, as input for a workshop. With a quick stroke its content can be summarised into the different columns. The headings can be changed or add/remove boxes whenever relevant. This can easily spark a debate about university strategy to change the connection between research and education.

The String Instrument

This instrument combines the curriculum and organisational perspectives in a single model (see Figure 3.2). The model's different beads represent aspects that need to be considered, aligned, or designed during stages of change. The left model depicts beads in a sorted order: grouped in aspects of organisational set-up, curriculum set-up, content set-up, and requirements. This is the order in which change plans are most often written down. Often, the history and different beliefs that underpin the practices in an educational programme, department, faculty, or university are forgotten, but these are included here.

The right picture depicts the same beads, but now put on a string, one by one. This is the way plans normally come into action: Aspects that are easier to achieve or have more stakeholders as backup are achieved quicker, or aspects that are part of the earlier phases are put earlier on the thread. While mixing the beads, it is important to keep in mind the consistency between them, during planning as well as during implementation.

Change agents can apply this instrument to achieve an overview between the different elements (organisational, curriculum, etc.) of the change process and to discuss the similarities and differences between the theoretical and actual implementation, using the string metaphor to keep striving for consistency across all beads.

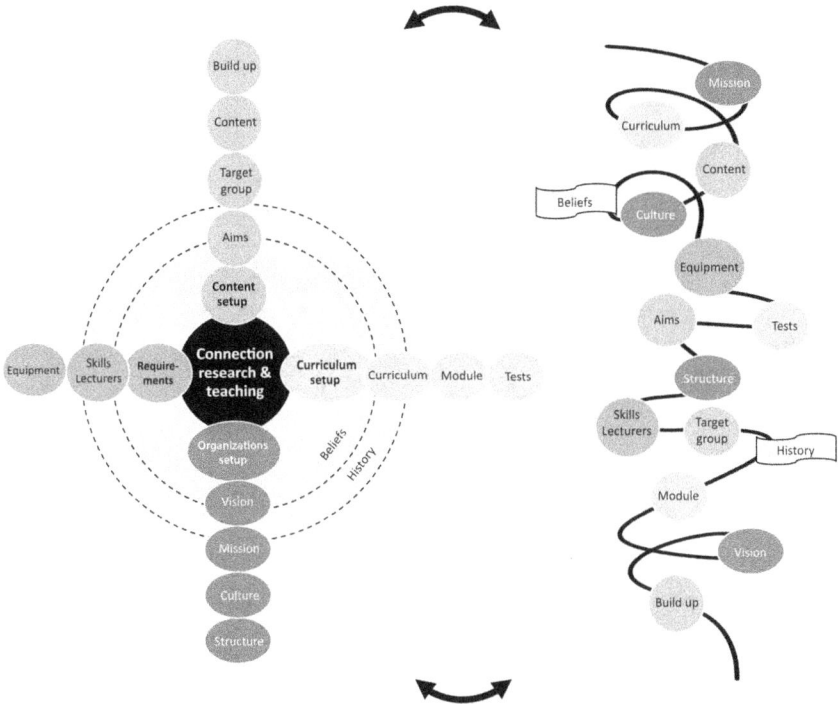

Figure 3.2 The String Instrument with sorted beads on the type of planning in the left-hand model and functionally stringed beads for implementation in the right-hand model. This instrument was previously published in Dutch in Griffioen, Visser-Wijnveen, and Willems (2013).

The Landscape Overview Instrument

Colleagues working in educational programmes often want to further connect research and education at the curriculum level. Often, their intentions follow from one or more external incentives, as can be found in the four corners of the Landscape Overview Instrument: changes in the professional or disciplinary field, changes (in the set-up of) related research programmes, changes in university expectations and/or changes in the effort to fit within legal or quality frameworks (see also Figure 3.3).

This Landscape Overview Instrument was designed because curriculum's stakeholders mostly considered their own starting point for change and did not often consider the other relevant variables in their curriculum change trajectory. Often, their basic aim was to fix the problem at hand, disregarding the problems that could be caused by addressing the other variables too late.

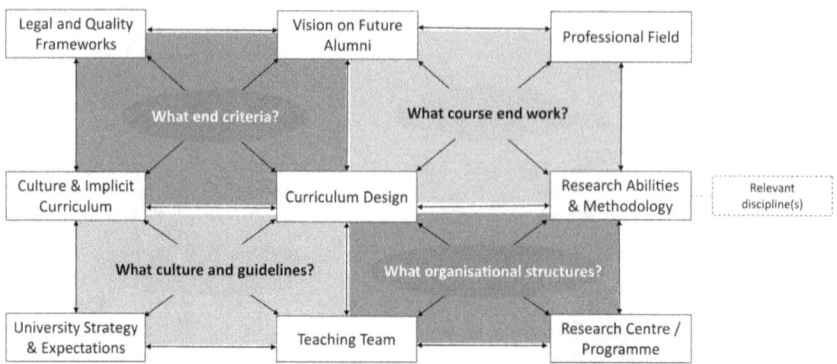

Figure 3.3 Landscape Overview Instrument.

For instance, when a quality agency requested an improved level of research in students' final projects, just changing the assignment of test criteria can result in being unbalanced with the vision of who alumni need to be when that is mostly based on the requests of professional or disciplinary fields. Another example is that changes were made due to shifted university expectations – a rewritten curriculum – but the professionalisation needed for the teaching team was ignored. Conversely, the changes made contradicted the standards for research methodology as is common in the related research, which becomes more likely if teaching and research tasks are separated. Further, when the final assignment of the final year changes, as we have seen in many educational programmes, it has implications for many other elements in the whole educational programme.

Therefore, the instrument consists of the different variables in the boxes and of the arrows between the boxes. Every one of these arrows implies a balance to be found or a question to be answered during the design, of which the details and importance differ per context, and per phase during the change project. This balance or question needs to receive attention during the curriculum change process, starting from the planning phase. Interestingly, in using the model, it does not matter where one starts. Just beginning at the most urgent, interesting, or easy arrow – and therefore following the educational team's request – will automatically lead to the need to consider the other arrows and variables. Including more perspectives can make the discussion more complex, which it needs to become, but change agents also need to have an eye out for how much an educational team can handle. Sometimes it is important to simplify in order to avoid a full stand-still.

The instrument can be applied as a talking piece to be used in meetings or workshops in the different phases of a change project. Some educational teams have used it as a foundation for a quality analysis, others have applied it in an IST–SOLL analysis.

Instruments to Discuss 'Research'

Generally, the research perceptions of experienced researchers stay implicit and only rise to the surface when they are challenged. A change process is such a situation. The notion of 'research' can be considered from many different angles, as was already empirically shown by several scholars (e.g. Brew, 2001; Griffioen & De Jong, 2015; Visser-Wijnveen, Van Driel, Van der Rijst, Verloop, & Visser, 2010). Situations of organisational change focused on the research–education connection often required to make the stakeholders' perceptions explicit. Therefore, these perceived 'truths' about what research is or should be, what it can bring, and whether that is the same for every situation normally needs to be addressed in every change process focused on research–education connections. This often implies that stakeholders with limited research experience need assistance in reaching beyond the archetype notions of research, such as the researcher as a male in a white coat working in a laboratory, or research as a science that provides generalisable truths. A dominance of archetype notions of research can limit the types of research–education connections stakeholders can imagine, design, or even accept during the change processes.

Stakeholders with substantial research experience can often reach beyond the aforementioned archetype notions of research because of their own hands-on experience. Although they are generally more able to see the nuances and more detailed possibilities in research activities, they often have difficulty debating cross-disciplinary notions of research with stakeholders of other disciplines. Notably, researchers with deep experience in a mono-discipline can feel pressured to reconsider their perceptions in debates about research–education connections with experienced researchers from other disciplines. Their vast experience can result in seeing the value of research from a specific angle.

How research can be conceived is fundamentally different between disciplines. The most foundational illustration of these differences is in Brew's (2003) work, which found four conceptions of research through interviewing senior researchers resulting in four quadrants based on two axes: the present versus absent researcher, and research as about external products versus research about internal processes. Whenever Brew's model is applied in workshops, both disciplinary differences and differences based on personal expertise and experience emerge among participants.

Another relevant focus for how stakeholders conceive research is in the context of education. Where Brew (2003) focused on researchers' conceptions of research, Griffioen and De Jong (2015) aimed their interview study to find the demarcations between research and education among lecturers. These demarcations are relevant for the design of both research and education activities. When demarcations are perceived differently, the request for combinations can result differently as well. On a more operational level, different demarcations between research and education can lead to different allocations of time and funding (see also: Bloch, Mitterle, & Würmann, 2014).

The types of findings of these two studies illustrate that change agents need to be aware of different conceptions of research that can differ largely between stakeholders of different disciplines. Moreover, stakeholders can be surprised about their own conceptions and even more about others' conceptions because the mutual differences only appear when discussed across departments or programmes. This section presents the instruments to discuss conceptions of research that were developed as part of the Amsterdam UAS change programme.

The Quality of Research Instrument

This instrument follows from empirical research among lecturers in higher applied education who were asked what they considered to be 'good research' (see Griffioen, Roosenboom, & De Jong, 2017 for details) and were applied in the Amsterdam UAS programme. This study resulted in a list of six perspectives on 'good research' that can be used in debates about what constitutes research and/or good research, including:

1. **The quality of the research design** – theory, research question, methodology
2. **The quality of the end product** (report or design) – style, content, argumentation, transparency
3. **The quality of the research's execution** – correctness, thoroughness, working with uncertainties

4. **The research's value** (after the act) – for application, for science
5. **The quality of the researcher** – the person and positioning
6. **The origin and relevance of the research topic** (before the start) – the professional/practical field, the discipline, the researcher

These six perspectives listed are not surprising. These are perspectives on the quality of research with which many are familiar. Still, when 'research' as part of the content of a change process is discussed, quality often is an issue that is discussed (fought about) while the particularities of this quality often stay implicit. Having this list on a slide in front of the room can help the debaters make their arguments more precise and therefore help increase the mutual understanding in the room.

We have seen this to be useful not only during large-scale change processes, but also during strategic debates about what to aim for in research as well as what to reward in research teams and in student work.

The Perspectives of Research Instrument

Where Anglo-Saxon colleagues are very accustomed to having several synonyms for research-related work, many other languages do not have words to make these distinctions. For instance, in the Dutch language, we only have *onderzoek*, which is close enough to 'research', but does not capture 'scholarship' or 'inquiry', and is again rather different from the connotation of 'science'. Having more words to explain what one means by 'research' can be very helpful. Therefore, we would like to introduce the Anglo-Saxon distinction between scholarship, inquiry and research.

'Research'
A systematic focus on new information

'Inquiry'
Systematically gathering existing examples

'Scholarship'
Systematically gathering existing secondary sources

Figure 3.4 The perspectives of research instrument.

While there are very many different interpretations, we will discuss here how they were applied in the setting of the Amsterdam change project, therefore an applied research setting. The importance of this instrument is not the strict demarcation between the three, but the notion that very different activities can be implied when using 'research' in a language that has just one word. For instance, in Dutch, there are no proper translations for inquiry or scholarship, which reduces the grasp of these potential differences.

In the model as was applied, *scholarship* implies that a question asked can be answered through handling secondary sources, such as articles and books, but also videos and audio recordings. Scholarship can be extended to keeping up with a field, thus reading journals and going to conferences. This can be in an academic setting – in the Anglo-Saxon world, this is most often implied as such – but it can also mean systematically keeping up with one's profession. When used as research activity, scholarship needs to be followed by an integration of the information found.

Inquiry means the systematic gathering of examples, which can be practical examples and theoretical ones. The selection of the examples requires some kind of framework that makes the examples comparable. Also for inquiry, further steps are needed to be called research. Inquiry is chosen when one expects relevant examples to exist and their comparison to be sufficient for the question asked.

Research is the systematic gathering of data along a prescribed research design that includes a question and a systematic method of working. Research also implies systematic procedures for data analysis and reporting. Further, research is chosen when a new combination of information is needed because the current information is not similar enough. This can be because there is no similar information, or because the high stakes require a high level of precision. For instance, when a new medicine is designed, it is important that this substance is tested and is not another medicine that looks somewhat like it. One can expect that in general fewer situations would request the thorough approach of research and inquiry or scholarship can often be sufficient.

In some disciplines, it is rather common to have this diversity when 'research' is discussed, even if the language does not provide the words. In other disciplines, 'research' is generally seen as only one of the three concepts explained above. For these settings, it can be important to understand these types of distinctions, especially when discussing students' research work, or that of colleagues just becoming researchers. The three distinctions can be applied in every discipline, also in the design disciplines.

The Certainty and Risk of Research Instrument

When discussing the (further) integration of research into education in the sense of students doing research, one topic to consider is what the students' research is for. This is above all the case in settings where the discipline or profession the students are educated in provides possibilities for or even demands that students' research outcomes are applicable for a specific practice. These examples can be found in both research-intensive programmes (e.g. public administration, educational sciences, medicine) and applied programmes (e.g. sales, teaching, social work). In these settings an (often implicit) dispute can be seen between those who state that student research is not valuable in the sense of not generating new scientific knowledge, and those stating that student research cannot aid practice partners in solving their proposed questions (see also the work by Elsen, Visser-Wijnveen, Van der Rijst, and Van Driel (2008) in this regard). Interestingly, both sides generally agree in their unwillingness to further integrate research into educational programmes, although for very different reasons. It is important for change agents to get clarity about these different positions to understand potential directions of development. Additionally, it is important for the stakeholders to understand their opinions' underpinnings to test whether these are the relevant limitations or whether other options are possible.

Part of the previously described dispute can be fed back to disciplinary differences for which Brew's aforementioned four-quadrant model can be informative. Another aspect of this dispute is the quality of the research's findings based on the methodological choices during the research process. Up to a certain point, this resonates to disciplinary differences as well. Those who consider research as part of science intend research to reach a certain level of truth, or even a more generalisable truth. A more elaborate and critical explanation of this line of reasoning can be found in Helga Nowotny's (2008) work. Empirical research (as distinguished from synthetic research, such as in mathematics or philosophy) that intends to achieve generic knowledge is designed through large samples and relies on systematic procedures. Providing truth is a highly important promise to society. However, as Griffioen (2017, 2019b, 2020) also argues, generic truth is a more difficult notion when intended to apply that knowledge to a particular setting and/or intended for a specific outcome. Generalisable truths, especially in the more social disciplines, results at best in a probability of a certain outcome, which is not always the outcome societal partners, clients, or even the students intend.

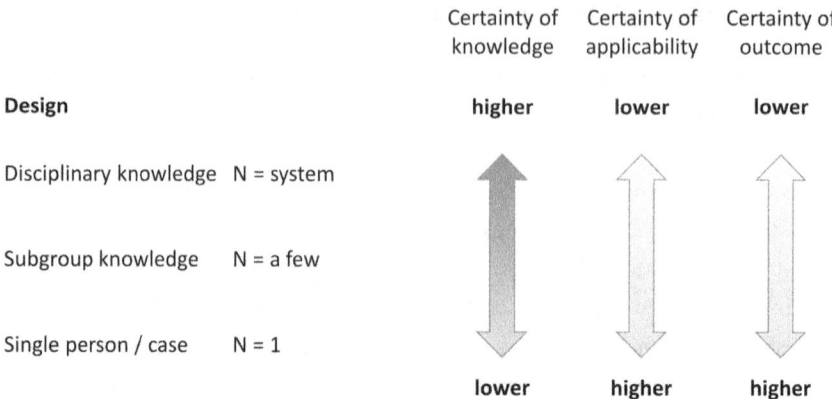

Figure 3.5 Levels of certainty and risk model: What is research in the educational programme for?

In most settings, it is important to discuss these notions to have clarity about the function of the research that students and others perform. Figure 3.5 can assist in that debate, often not to solve the dispute, but to provide clarity about the underpinnings of the statements stakeholders make, and to increase the mutual understanding. Knowing that these underpinnings do not change easily, it still is important to collectively make clear choices. The choices made about certainty (and therefore risk) related to students' research influences the range of designs presented to them. Creating clarity about intentions and design helps students and lecturers to establish a better educational setting and better research outcomes, considered at least from the chosen perspective.

The Phases of Research Instrument

The widely known model to explain different phases of research is the Empirical Research Cycle. This model distinguishes different research phases, such as formulating hypotheses, testing and reporting. This model has been considered as very valuable for the more fundamental types of research, but has been experienced as lacking for research that aims to implement change during the research process, such as in design research (e.g. Oskam, Souren, Berg, Cowran, & Hoiting, 2017) and in action-based research (e.g. Bradbury, 2015). For these situations, the Regulative Research Cycle (Van Strien, 1986) was developed, which contains phases such as problem formulation, diagnosis, planning, implementation and evaluation. Already these two partly contradictory models can be of great use in debates about what is meant when the notion of 'research' is discussed among stakeholders.

During workshops we came across three problems that we addressed with this new instrument, which also considers research phases. The first problem was realising that many stakeholders addressed 'research' in an incomplete way; leaving out or reducing the importance of activities in their discussion about research, such as deducing a solution or reporting, therefore not including it in their educational provision, while students were assessed on these activities. Similar omissions were seen in the expected research work of colleagues. We have seen this incompleteness in two types. The first type was seen among stakeholders who addressed research from the perspective of the Empirical Research Cycle, so focused on the formulation of a question or hypothesis, the systematic gathering of data and the writing of a report. While these stakeholders gave the most attention to the activities that were part of the Empirical Research Cycle, often additionally an advice or design to implement in the research setting, was expected.

A similar incompleteness was found among a second group of stakeholders who addressed 'research' as solving a design problem, which is more in line with the Regulative Research Cycle in which the main focus was on the activities in the design process, the characteristics of the design and (sometimes) on its actual usage in the research practice. While the attention was on these design elements, the design was created based on a list of characteristics that followed from multiple interviews, sometimes focus groups, and several talks to clients, while the importance and quality of these activities were hardly discussed or approached in a systematic manner.

These perceptions of incompleteness and their complementarity can result in a few issues. In many cross-disciplinary debates about research–education connections, the willingness to understand other stakeholders would be reduced by the notion that the first group of stakeholders were mostly from health, economics and the social sciences related disciplines and the second group were mostly from creative and technical disciplines. Stakeholders across these groups simply concluded they were different than the others and hence sharing examples or even working together would not lead to anything.

An even more important issue is that the implicitness of important research activities in the process can result in student grading for elements of the model that were not part of the explicit curricula. It is however important that all elements that are assessed were also part of learning opportunities for the students. The new model makes this issue crystal clear to educational design teams, as we have seen many times. The silence of the curriculum designers was often deafening when the message hit home in workshops.

The Phases of Research Instrument can assist in debates about what activities and assignments comprise research. The instrument consists of two sides (derived from Andriessen, 2014) that represent the two perspectives of the previously explained groups of stakeholders. For clarity, in Figure 3.6, the simple model is depicted, while Figure 3.7 depicts the fully detailed model.

The right-hand side is called 'practice-based evidence' and combines activities that can be part of the Empirical Research Cycle and therefore systematically brings together evidence from practice, just to know or to use later on as input for a design task. The model does not address anything about the quality or precision expected in the different activities implied by a specific research task, currently it only distinguishes the activities as such. The right side results ends new knowledge through an integration of research findings.

The left-hand side is called 'evidence-based practice'. This side includes activities that use integrated knowledge as a start to design a process or product that can be implemented or used in an empirical setting. The integrated knowledge can be of the researcher or student or a body of knowledge that was given, used to finally result in the implementation of a new design.

Researchers or students can conduct the full cycle or choose/be assigned one of either cycles, if only one is relevant. Still, as soon as the other side's output is expected of the researcher or the student, the quality criteria of that output need

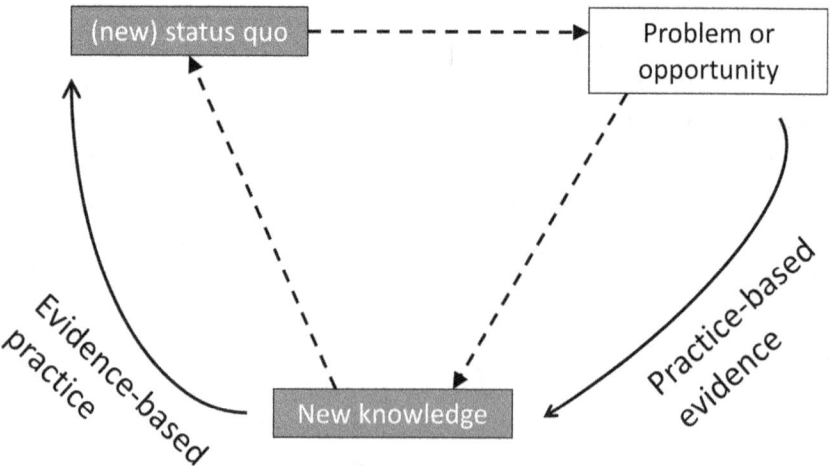

Figure 3.6 The research phases model: short version.

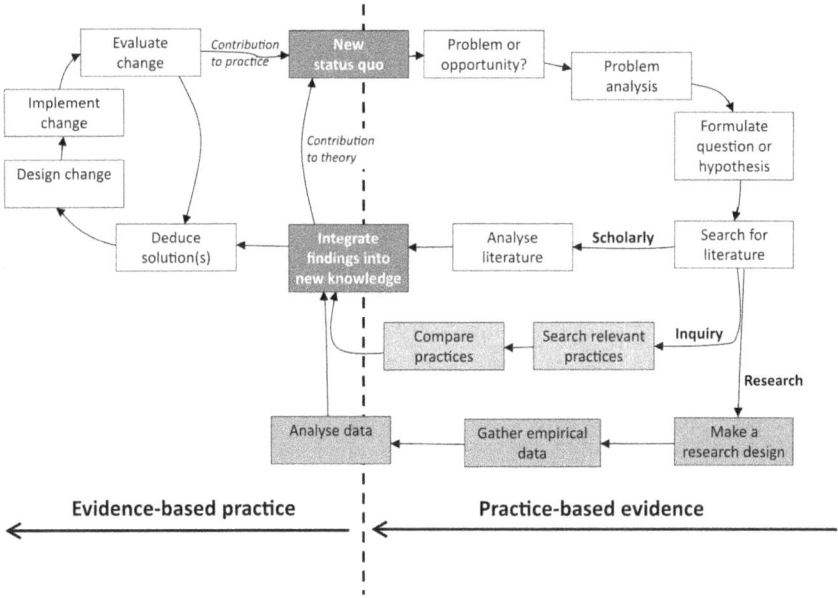

Figure 3.7 The phases of research instrument.

to be formulated and the activity needs to be educated as part of the regular curriculum.

Finally, the Perspectives to Research Instrument also is integrated in this model. As illustrated in Figure 3.7, different routes of practice-based evidence are depicted, assisting stakeholders to distinguish between scholarship, inquiry and research in the project, or curriculum end terms, even if their native language does not provide a discourse to do so. Often, not all researchers or students need to do 'research', sometimes doing 'inquiry' or being a 'scholar' is sufficient.

Bringing these three elements into this model enlarges the variance about research in educational programmes. More generally, all included activities in the instrument can be replaced for others when relevant for that distinct context or masterclass. However, the aim is always to present a fair curriculum to students, which implies that whatever is assigned for grading needs to be sufficiently educated and learned as well.

Level of Autonomy and Complexity in Research

Curriculum parts that aim for educating students in research competences imply a debate about the level at which students need to become adequate.

Where the previous section provided the Phases of Research Instrument as a tool to discuss the content, notably the content of research steps students need to go through as part of their education, in this section the Research Level and Content Instrument (RLC-I) is provided to discuss the level and content at which students need to become adequate. This instrument consists of two elements: first, the Research Autonomy and Complexity Tool (RAC-T), which provides a collective language to debate levels of research. This tool is then combined with the New Aspects of Research Tool (NAR-T), which is also the starting point for the empirical analysis of changed learning goals in Chapter 6. The combined RLC-I can be used for debates about the level and content of research in the curriculum as well as to conceptually cross-compare study years or full educational programmes as part of a change trajectory. Both elements and their combination will be discussed.

The Research Autonomy and Complexity Tool (RAC-T)

This tool aims to provide a language to debate the level of research expected of students (and other stakeholders) in a certain context. The tool is disciplinary generic in nature, meaning it can be adapted to any discipline or context. Here, the depicted tool is a research-oriented adaptation of a tool that Bulthuis (2011) first developed for all competencies. The RAC-T consists of two axes: One axis indicates the amount of autonomy the student receives while fulfilling a research assignment; the other axis indicates the complexity of the research assignment, based on the assignment's complexity as well as the assignment's context. Autonomy and complexity are positioned as complementary-level indicators, which combined results in five distinguishable levels for research. These five levels can be adapted or made more precise when needed for a particular context (see Table 3.1 for an overview).

New Aspects of Research Tool (NAR-T)

The RAC-T is combined with the NAR-T. This tool is an empirical adaptation of the six aspects of research that Verburgh, Schouteden, and Elen (2012) originally developed. The adaptation was done through the empirical study on changing higher education learning goals. The NAR-T provides six aspects of research that have shown to be part of higher education curricula: critical attitude, curiosity, knowledge about research results, knowledge about research

Table 3.1 Overview of the Research Autonomy and Complexity Tool (RAC-T)

	Level C	Level D	Level E
<- AUTONOMY ->	**Complexity: low** - Single element assignment, one context - Limited number of themes of a single order/scale level - Application of the student-known procedures - Mono-disciplinary - Location: within the context of the educational programme or for the student-familiar context **Autonomy: high** - A lot of self-steering, supervision upon request or at low frequency - A high amount of freedom to make process choices - Large responsibility for the end result - Supervises others in a team - Strategic role	**Complexity: middle** - Multiple (part) assignments in a single situation, or a single element assignment in multiple situations - Limited number of themes of different order/scales, or multiple themes of a single order/scale - Assignment requests adaptation of known procedures - Limited interdisciplinary - Unfamiliar context but can be overseen in size and system complexity **Autonomy: high** - A lot of self-steering, supervision upon request or at low frequency - A high amount of freedom to make process choices - Large responsibility for the end result - Supervises others in a team - Strategic role	**Complexity: high** - Diversity in (part) assignments in different contexts - Multiple themes of different order/scale - Unknown procedure - New knowledge and skills need to be developed - Multidisciplinary - Location: context is unknown, large and complex **Autonomy: high** - A lot of self-steering, supervision upon request or at low frequency - A high amount of freedom to make process choices - Large responsibility for the end result - Supervises others in a team - Strategic role

Level B	Level C	Level D
Complexity: low - Single element assignment, one context - Limited number of themes of a single order/scale level - Application of the student-known procedures - Mono-disciplinary - Location: within the context of the educational programme, or for the student-familiar context **Autonomy: middle** - Reasonable amount of autonomy and average amount of guidance, added with supervision upon request - Freedom in making choices within a fixed framework - Final responsibility of a part of the final assignment - Tactical role	**Complexity: middle** - Multiple (part) assignments in a single situation, or a single element assignment in multiple situations - Limited number of themes of different order/scales, or multiple themes of a single order/scale - Assignment requests adaptation of known procedures - Limited interdisciplinary - Unfamiliar context but can be overseen in size and system complexity **Autonomy: middle** - Reasonable amount of autonomy and average amount of guidance, added with supervision upon request - Freedom in making choices within a fixed framework - Final responsibility of a part of the final assignment - Tactical role	**Complexity: high** - Diversity in (part) assignments in different contexts - Multiple themes of different order/scale - Unknown procedure - New knowledge and skills need to be developed - Multidisciplinary - Location: context is unknown, large and complex **Autonomy: middle** - Reasonable amount of autonomy and average amount of guidance, added with supervision upon request - Freedom in making choices within a fixed framework - Final responsibility of a part of the final assignment - Tactical role

Level A	Level B	Level C
Complexity: low - Single element assignment, one context - Limited number of themes of a single order/scale level - Application of the student-known procedures - Mono-disciplinary - Location: within the context of the educational programme, or for the student-familiar context **Autonomy: low** - Limited autonomy and intensive guidance - Asks for assistance for unexpected circumstances - Does not make independent decisions - Responsibility for own actions - Final responsibility for part of the assignment - Assisting, operational role	**Complexity: middle** - Multiple (part) assignments in a single situation, or a single element assignment in multiple situations - Limited number of themes of different order/scales, or multiple themes of a single order/scale - Assignment requests adaptation of known procedures - Limited interdisciplinary - Unfamiliar context but can be overseen in size and system complexity **Autonomy: low** - Limited autonomy and intensive guidance - Asks for assistance for unexpected circumstances - Does not make independent decisions - Responsibility for own actions - Final responsibility for part of the assignment - Assisting, operational role	**Complexity: high** - Diversity in (part) assignments in different contexts - Multiple themes of different order/scale - Unknown procedure - New knowledge and skills need to be developed - Multi-disciplinary - Location: context is unknown, large and complex **Autonomy: low** - Limited autonomy and intensive guidance - Asks for assistance for unexpected circumstances - Does not make independent decisions - Responsibility for own actions - Final responsibility for part of the assignment - Assisting, operational role

<- COMPLEXITY ->

methods, research skills and competency to be a researcher. For a more elaborate explanation about these six research aspects and its empirical underpinning, see Chapter 6.

Research Level and Content Instrument (RLC-I)

Combining the RAC-T and the NAR-T can be integrated to the RLC-I (see Figure 3.8). By integrating both the aspects of research and the proposed levels for each of these aspects, stakeholders can have a more precise debate about research in the curriculum, but also in professionalisation or requested levels of work in a research appointment. It also becomes possible to compare choices across study years or across different educational programmes. However, note that in the current state of the instrument this is more a conceptual comparison than an empirical comparison, for which the demarcations in the current instrument need to be argued per setting. However, it has been shown to be a valuable instrument to provide language to university settings focused on changing research–education connections.

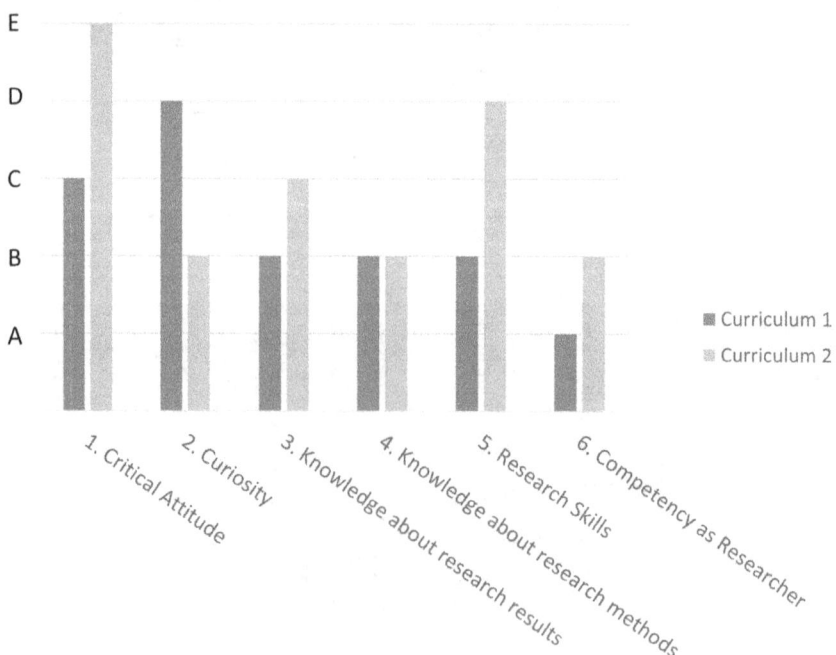

Figure 3.8 Research level and content instrument, example comparison.

Instruments to Discuss 'Research' in Relation to 'Professionalism'

The Amsterdam change programme took place in an applied university. Applied universities distinctly focus on educating high-level professionals. Research and professional practice do not automatically resonate, as is much easier for research and disciplines, which were developed mutually. Still, many problem-solving capabilities nowadays are related to research ability (Brew, 2007; Verburgh, 2013). Therefore, one of the arguments to implement research in professional higher education is to educate future professionals to interact with the complexities of a knowledge society (Baggen, 2005; Barnett, 2000; Griffioen, 2013). Professional practice is increasingly based on complex knowledge and professionals increasingly are expected to be accountable for their choices and actions (American Nursing Association, 2010; Payne, 2014). However, changing research–education connections yields debates about the definitions of research for professionals and whether these are different between professions. Therefore, in this chapter, two models are presented that can assist these debates in applied universities, and in the more vocationally oriented programmes of research-intensive universities.

Routine versus Innovation in Professional Action

In debates with professionals and educators of professionals, it is often asked what the benefit of research for daily professional action would be. As previously explained, research in the tradition of science aims to provide generalisable truths, which paradoxically often implies reducing the certainty for and applicability in certain cases or contexts. Still, national and international governments state that research is important for high-quality professional action (Griffioen, Ashwin, & Scholkmann, 2021); a notion educators of professionals and curriculum developers in higher education need to wrap their heads around.

One way to make this presumed contradiction less dominant is by distinguishing between professional routine and professional innovation. Professional action is based on professional knowledge. According to Young and Muller (2014), two types of professional knowledge can be distinguished: know that (something exists) and know-how (to use). These two knowledge types are closely related in professional practice, considering that knowing that for a professional almost always needs to result in knowing how. According to Young and Muller (2014), knowing how exists of three parts:

1. knowing about relationships between pieces of knowledge;
2. knowing how pieces of knowledge can be useful for professional action (see also Winch, 2014) and
3. knowledge about the procedures for judging, testing, and acquiring this knowledge.

However, as a professional, it is insufficient to know about something; a professional needs to be able to act upon their knowledge. Therefore, a professional requires 'embodied knowledge' (Polanyi, 2009), or 'do' knowledge. As one does not only need to know how to ride a bike, but more importantly one needs to practice riding. Something similar is the case for physical therapeutic action, teaching or designing a sensor as an engineer. Finally, we expect professionals are able to trace back their tracks systematically (see also Griffioen & Wortman, 2013), thus they need 'evaluation' knowledge. Combined, this results in the four types of professional knowledge as depicted on the second line in Table 3.2.

Table 3.2 Elements of professional routine and professional innovation

	KNOW	KNOW	DO	EVALUATE
Professional Routine	**Know That** The existence of particular professional knowledge **Know How** Relations between sections of professional knowledge	**Know That** The existence of particular professional procedures **Know How** Know how professional knowledge and procedures can be useful for certain contexts	**Embodied Skill** To have the ability for context-specific effective and efficient professional action	**Reflect** To validate, reflect upon and justify professional choices made
Professional Innovation	**Know How** Procedures for judging, testing and acquiring (new) knowledge	**Know How** Knowing what procedures for acquiring knowledge are useful in specific contexts	**Embodied Skill** To be technically able to develop new knowledge in different contexts	**Reflect** To validate, reflect upon and justify the provision of new knowledge

Research competences fulfil a limited or latent role in professionals' routine activities (see white circle around the upper globe in Figure 3.9). In everyday work, the professional applies routines and protocols in changing contexts. This does not imply professionals' routine work is easy. Their work intrinsically is complex also due to tuning actions and knowledge to different contexts. However, professionals do not have to innovate their work every day. They do need to be critical of their own actions and others' actions and register when there is a possibility for systematic improvement (see also the upper box of Figure 3.9).

In addition to routine actions, professionals find themselves in situations where innovation is needed, due to raised problems or to follow new opportunities. Then, research-related activities can be useful. Research activities have their own basic knowledge and ways of working (know that), their own contexts of application (know how), practice needed for action (do) and ways to look back on process and results (evaluate). Table 3.2 provides an overview of this duality.

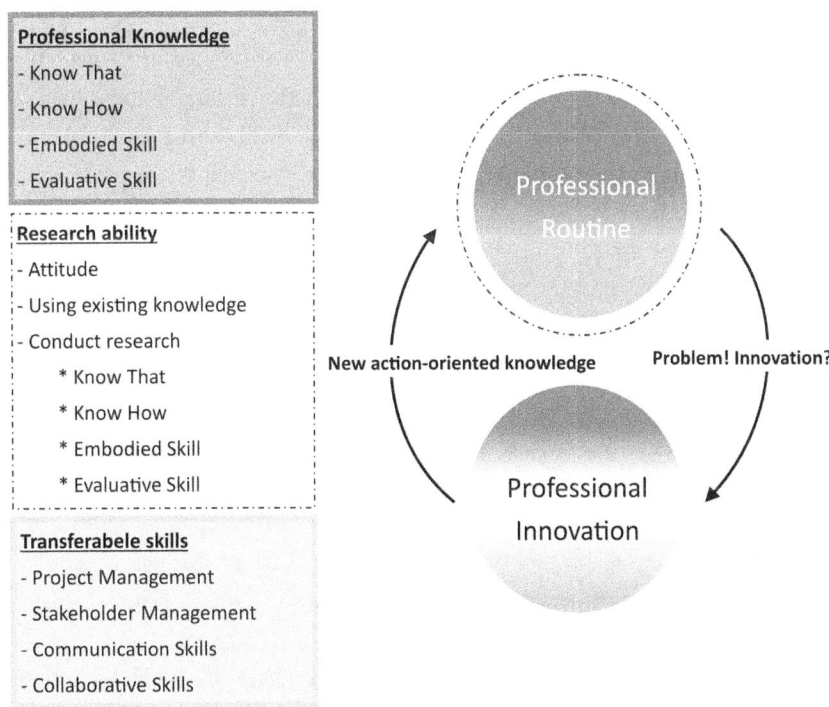

Figure 3.9 Routine versus innovative professional action.

It is important to be aware of this duality when implementing research in professional curricula. When stakeholders aim to make this duality more precise and applicable for their field, endless debates about what role research is supposed to play in professionalism can be made more functional. Using research principles to innovate professional action implies a separate strand of learned competences, although closely related to the core profession as such. Change agents can assist in showing the multi-layeredness of conversations in this regard.

Perspectives of Professional Differences: Framework

As we know from empirical research (Brew, 2006; Visser-Wijnveen, 2013), research–education connections can be different between disciplines, also due to differences in the perceptions of research (Brew, 2001). What is less considered is that professions can also be different between professions. Initially, interviews with educational managers of programmes in professional higher education resulted in distinguishing four types of professions in how they position research in the profession (see also Griffioen & Wortman, 2013, for the methodological underpinnings).

The first group of professions is the *research-dependent professions*, such as dietary and applied law. It is essential for professionals working in these fields to keep up to date with the swift information renewal. Not keeping up could make the professionals outdated, and quicker than in other segments, the professional might lose their licence.

The second group is the *researcher professions*, in which conducting research is considered part of the core activities. Examples are marketing-related professions, applied chemistry and applied forensics.

Thirdly, a group of *reflective professions* can be distinguished, for instance social work. These professionals perceive research as something that lies very close to their day-to-day professional actions and is more reflective than systematic empirical in nature. The aim mostly is focused on a short cycle way to improve the professionals' actions, as well as those of the clients. Additionally, they intend to improve protocol-based professional actions through research.

The final group is the *design-oriented professions*, such as product design, architecture and fashion and design. Professionals in this group design technical or creative products, such as buildings, clothing or usability tools. Essentially, research is part of this design process, at least through inventories that result in design requirements. Additionally, usability research of concept products is part of the design process. Interestingly, the professionals in this field we talked to do not seem to consider the first 'research', while they apply research methods from social sciences, they do not seem to know or apply the ground rules for scrutinising the research. However, they do consider the second part 'research'. In between is an iterative design process that is largely based on well-considered leaps of insight (Oskam et al., 2017).

These four groups of professions resonate with Biglan's (1973) well-known categorisation of disciplines. The first group of professions can be seen as hard and life, the second as soft and non-life. The reflective professions can be clustered as soft and life, while design professions are non-life. Interestingly, Biglan originally found a creative/non-creative distinction, which did not make it into his final scheme. Empirical studies have shown that differences between disciplines and professions matter for how research is implemented into curricula (Visser-Wijnveen et al., 2009) as well as for how students perceive the presence of research in the curriculum (Griffioen, 2019a).

Many talks with lecturers and even more with educational managers have shown the importance of the self-positioning the profession in relation to research. Who are we, and what is research to our students' future work? One very explicit example of this importance came from an educational manager from another applied university who read about these four types of professions and realised her programme was allowed to be different from the other programmes in the same social faculty. Up until that moment, the manager and his team had tried to create a collective research curriculum for their students, but that had resulted in very difficult conversations and a sub-optimal concept curriculum. This division into four types made her realise that her programme and the related profession could be characterised as 'research-dependent', while the other programmes in their department were 'reflective' in nature. She realised that at the most foundational level of what constitutes research as part of the profession, these different programme types could not be integrated in a single collective curriculum. Since then, they have changed course and created separate curricula.

Instruments such as these are created to help stakeholders increase their insight and perspective in such a way that it generates options and solutions for research–education connections. Change agents can apply these four types of educational programmes as an instrument to assist stakeholders in considering their core profession in relation to research. Such consideration influences how research is further implemented into the curriculum as well as the department. Sometimes the only thing needed is for a change agent to say 'well that makes sense if you conclude that you are different'.

Final Remark

As shown, this chapter is rather practical in nature when compared to the other, more academic chapters. The numerous models assisted the team of Amsterdam UAS to help bring clarity to the debates that are part of every change process, aiming to further integrate research and education. All instruments are meant to add new perspectives to the existing models and to those involved in changing the research and education connection. The models presented become tools when change agents add their own ways of working, adapting and applying. Change agents can use and adapt the models to use for their own change purposes. They would need to (re)design their own pedagogies for certain purposes; however, some suggestions are given. These models were designed and adapted based on usability in practice and were – while often research-informed in nature – not yet systematically tested through an empirical process. However, that was not the intention.

References

American Nursing Association. (2010). *Nursing social policy statement. The essence of the profession.* ANA: Silver Spring.
Andriessen, D. (2014). *Praktisch relevant én methodisch grondig.* Retrieved from Utrecht: https://www.bibliotheek.nl/catalogus/titel.375166009.html/praktisch-relevant-%C3%A9n-methodisch-grondig—dimensies-van-onderzoek/
Baggen, P. (2005). De wereld veranderen: universiteit en overheidsbeleid in Nederland, 1960–2000. In L. J. Dorsman & P. Knegtmans (Eds.), *Universitaire vormingsidealen. De Nederlandse universiteiten sedert 1876* (pp. 93–108). Hilversum: Verloren.
Barnett, R. (2000). Supercomplexity and the curriculum. *Studies in Higher Education, 25*(3), 255–65.
Biglan, A. (1973). The characteristics of subject matter in different academic areas. *Journal of Applied Psychology, 57*(3), 195–203.
Bloch, R., Mitterle, A., & Würmann, C. (2014). *Time to teach: Contextualizing teaching time in German higher education.* Paper presented at the Society for Research into Higher Education, Newport, UK.
Bradbury, H. (Ed.) (2015). *The Sage handbook of action research.* New York: Sage.
Brew, A. (2001). Conceptions of research: A phenomenographic study. *Studies in Higher Education, 26*(3), 271–85.
Brew, A. (2003). Teaching and research: New relationships and their implications for inquiry-based teaching and learning in higher education. *Higher Education Research & Development, 22*(1), 3–18.

Brew, A. (2006). *Research and teaching. Beyond the divide.* New York: Palgrave Macmillan.
Brew, A. (2007). *Research and teaching from the students' perspective.* Retrieved from http://w3.unisa.edu.au/easdeanteaching/colloquium/2008/Angela%20Brew%20and%20Kerri-Lee%20Krause/angela_brew%203.pdf
Bulthuis, P. H. (2011). *Handleiding voor HBO-niveau. Handleiding voor het onderzoeken, realiseren en verantwoorden van het HBO-niveau.* Retrieved from Deventer.
Daas, S. R., Day, I. N. Z., & Griffioen, D. M. E. (2019). *The intended synergy between research and teaching of universities of applied sciences in the Netherlands.* Paper presented at the Higher Education Conference 2019, Amsterdam.
Elsen, M., Visser-Wijnveen, G. J., Van der Rijst, R. M., & Van Driel, J. H. (2008). How to strengthen the connection between research and teaching in undergraduate university education. *Higher Education Quarterly, 63*(1), 64–85.
Griffioen, D. M. E. (2013). Onderzoek in Universiteit en Hoger Beroepsonderwijs: niet in de wortels. In D. M. E. Griffioen, G. J. Visser-Wijnveen, & J. Willems (Eds.), *Integratie van onderzoek in het onderwijs. Effectieve inbedding van onderzoek in curricula* (pp. 11–30). Groningen: Noordhoff Uitgevers.
Griffioen, D. M. E. (2017). Onderzoek is onderdeel van Professioneel Handelen. Op zoek naar nieuwe handvatten. *TH&MA Hoger Onderwijs,* (5), 90-7.
Griffioen, D. M. E. (2019a). Differences in students' experienced research involvement: Study years and disciplines compared. *Journal of Further & Higher Education, 44*(4), 454–66. doi:https://doi.org/10.1080/0309877X.2019.1579894
Griffioen, D. M. E. (2019b). *Higher education's responsibility for balanced professionalism. Methodology beyond Research.* (Inaugural lecture). Amsterdam University of Applied Sciences, Amsterdam. Retrieved from https://www.hva.nl/content/evenementen/oraties/2019/10/didi-griffioen.html
Griffioen, D. M. E. (2020). *Open science and the responsibilities of higher education (Keynote).* Paper presented at the National Finnish 'Open Science in Autumn 2020' Conference, Helsinki, Finland. https://www.researchgate.net/publication/348049778_Keynote_Open_Science_and_the_Responsibilities_of_Higher_Education
Griffioen, D. M. E., & Wortman, O. (2013). Onderzoek in het onderwijs van de Hogeschool van Amsterdam. *Tijdschrift voor Hoger Onderwijs, 31*(1&2), 16–31.
Griffioen, D. M. E., Visser-Wijnveen, G. J., & Willems, J. (Eds.). (2013). *Integratie van onderzoek in het onderwijs. Effectieve inbedding van onderzoek in curricula.* Groningen: Noordhoff Uitgevers.
Griffioen, D. M. E., & De Jong, U. (2015). Mapping Dutch higher education lecturers' discourse on research at times of academic drift. *Scottish Journal for Arts, Social Sciences, and Scientific Studies, 26*(1), 81–94.
Griffioen, D. M. E., Roosenboom, B. H. W., & De Jong, U. (2017). Opvattingen over 'Goed Onderzoek' van Docenten in het Hoger Onderwijs. *Tijdschrift voor Hoger Onderwijs, 34*(2).
Griffioen, D. M. E., Groen, A., & Nak, J. (2019). The integration of research in the higher education curriculum: A systematic review. *The Higher Education Journal of Learning and Teaching, 10*(1).

Griffioen, D. M. E., Ashwin, P., & Scholkmann, A. (2021). Who ensures that Society has the professionals it needs? Differences in the policy directions of three European countries. *Policy Reviews in Higher Education.* doi:https://doi.org/10.1080/23322969.2021.1880290

Healey, M. (2005). Linking research and teaching to benefit student learning. *Journal of Geography in Higher Education, 29*(2), 183–201.

Kuhn, T. S. (1962). *The structure of scientific revolutions.* Chicago: University of Chicago Press.

Nowotny, H. (2008). *Insatiable curiosity. Innovation in a fragile future.* Cambridge: MIT Press.

Oskam, I., Souren, P., Berg, I., Cowran, K., & Hoiting, L. (2017). *Ontwerpen van Technische Innovaties.* Groningen: Noordhoff BV.

Payne, M. (2014). *Modern social work theory* (4 ed.). New York: Palgrave Macmillan.

Polanyi, M. (2009). *The tacit dimension.* Chicago: The University of Chicago Press.

Prosser, M., Martin, E., Trigwell, K., Ramsden, P., & Middleton, H. (2008). University academics' experience of research and its relationship to their experience of teaching. *Instructional Science, 36,* 3–16.

Schouteden, W., Verburgh, A. L., & Elen, J. (2011). *The use of drawings to assess lecturers' conceptions of research.* Paper presented at the American Educational Research Association, New Orleans.

Schouteden, W., Verburgh, A. L., & Elen, J. (2014). Teachers' General and contextualised research conceptions. *Studies in Higher Education, 41*(1), 79–94. doi:10.1080/03075079.2014.914915

Trowler, P., & Wareham, T. (2008). *Tribes, territories, research and teaching: Enhancing the teaching research nexus.* Retrieved from York: https://www.heacademy.ac.uk/resource/tribes-territories-research-and-teaching-enhancing-teaching-research-nexus-literature#sthash.5NK7FyDy.dpuf

Van Strien, P. J. (1986). *Praktijk als wetenschap. Methodologie van het sociaal-wetenschappelijk handelen.* Assen: Van Gorcum.

Verburgh, A. L. (2013). *Research integration in higher education. Prevalence and relationship with critical thinking.* (PhD). KULeuven, Leuven.

Verburgh, A. L., Schouteden, W., & Elen, J. (2012). Patterns in the prevalence of research-related goals in higher education programmes. *Teaching in Higher Education,* 1–12. doi:10.1080/13562517.2012.719153

Visser-Wijnveen, G. J. (2013). Vormen van de integratie van onderzoek en onderwijs. In D. M. E. Griffioen, G. J. Visser-Wijnveen, & J. Willems (Eds.), *De integratie van onderzoek in het onderwijs. Effectieve inbedding van onderzoek in curricula*(pp. 60–73). Groningen: Noordhoff B.V.

Visser-Wijnveen, G. J., Van Driel, J. H., Van der Rijst, R. M., Verloop, N., & Visser, A. (2009). The relationship between academics' conceptions of knowledge, research and teaching – a metaphor study. *Teaching in Higher Education, 14*(6), 673–86.

Visser-Wijnveen, G. J., Van Driel, J. H., Van der Rijst, R. M., Verloop, N., & Visser, A. (2010). The ideal research-teaching nexus in the eyes of academics: Building profiles. *Higher Education Research & Development, 29*(2), 195–210.

Winch, C. (2014). Know-how and knowledge in the professional curriculum. In M. Young & J. Muller (Eds.), *Knowledge, expertise and the professions* (pp. 47–60). London: Routledge.

Young, M., & Muller, J. (2014). *Knowledge, expertise, and the professions*. London: Routledge.

4

Changes in Perceptions of Research Integration

Mette Bruinsma and Didi M. E. Griffioen

Introduction

Institutional change in higher education affects – and is affected by – a number of groups of stakeholders, such as students, lecturers, future employers of students, supporting staff and managers. Moreover, and following Jenkins and Healey's (2005) work on research integration in universities, this change should take place on different levels: from policymakers' and managers' decisions on the pace of implementing change (Griffioen, Doppenberg, & Oostdam, 2017) to developing practical guidelines for collaborative curriculum designs (Griffioen, 2020). More than other stakeholders, lecturers and students are the embodiment of the integration of research and teaching in higher-education institutions. It is particularly in their teaching and learning interactions within the lecture hall, the classroom or the labs that students' research skills, as well as their attitudes towards research are developed, and that lecturers potentially translate and reshape their own research into curricular content. Students and lecturers share educational experiences, but their perceptions of such experiences might be very dissimilar (Griffioen, 2020). The interaction between lecturers and students is 'two-way traffic': Higher education institutions form a dynamic and hybrid context in which different conceptions of what research entails, why research is important and what the expectations are of the relationship between research, education and future employment mingle. The students' and lecturers' perceptions implicitly and explicitly shape attitudes to organisational change, and are thus interesting starting points to consider such change.

 This chapter will connect the thinking of the perceived 'ideal' relationship between research and teaching within the context of higher education. Studying conceptions of research addresses how research is understood from different perspectives. Brew (2001), for instance, identified four ways of understanding research after interviewing senior academics, mainly indicating differences between disciplinary fields. In her research-as-domino concept, academics aim to add objective blocks of knowledge, while in the research-as-trading approach, new knowledge is seen as being exchanged. In turn, the research-as-layer concept perceives research as internally adding layers of understanding, while a research-as-journey approach perceives research as an individual pathway of the academic. Griffioen, Roosenboom, and De Jong's (2017) study shows that lecturers in research-intensive universities share the same five elements that make them perceive what 'good research' is in terms of lecturers in professional universities: the design of the research, the quality of the final product, the way the research is conducted, the qualities of the researcher and the relevance and origin of the topic. They differ somewhat in their interpretation of the sixth element, where research-intensive lecturers focus on the scientific value of research, and lecturers of professional higher education value its utility. In turn, Åkerlind's (2008) study has shown that academics' perceptions of research are distinguishable on five different elements: who is affected by the research (intentions), the anticipated impact of the research (outcomes), the nature of the object of study (questions), how the research is undertaken (process) and the researchers' feelings about the research (affection).

Additional models have been designed that depict perceptions about connections between research and education, of which Healey's (2005) model is the most prominent. This model of four types of research integration is constructed based on two axes that focus on students as participants versus students as audience and on the research's content in its methods. In turn, Schouteden, Verburgh, and Elen (2014) studied academics' research conceptions in the context of educational settings by letting them draw, resulting in the research-as-steps concept, as qualities of research processes and as qualities of researchers. The particular context of education tuned the research conceptions to the academic or professional focus as well as to the specific level of mastery that the academics expected of the students.

Interestingly, all these mentioned models as such do not call for change; they merely present options for how to perceive research from a certain perspective or how to perceive research as part of educational settings. As Chapter 2 suggested, for actual change to take place, a focus for change is needed to indicate the direction in which to change. Although the mentioned models were merely developed to distinguish important differences, with the insight they provide in potential focus for change, they are now widely used in masterclasses and workshops worldwide. Correctly used, they can present potential change agents with new options for how to perceive research and research integration. However, for this effect to take place, this perspective needs to be added to each of the models. The discrepancy between what is – respectively according to lecturers and students – versus what should be, formulates potential directions for future organisational change. For change to appear in curricula, modules and lessons, lecturers' and students' ideals for research integration need to change to provide them with a new focus on which to concentrate.

Change is needed. Generally, the support for research integration is increasing, also in applied universities (Griffioen, 2018). This is happening in interactions with changing national and institutional policies (Teichler, 2014). Largely, there seems to be a stronger emphasis on research integration at the institutional and departmental levels (e.g. Durning & Jenkins, 2005; Lucas, 2007), or at the microscale of lessons or modules (e.g. Healey & Jenkins, 2015; Visser-Wijnveen, 2009), but when examining the directions of change close-up, the picture becomes diffuse. Different stakeholders seem to have varying ideas on how research and education should be further integrated, or why. Therefore, it is beneficial to study lecturers' and students' perceptions on how and why research is, or should be, integrated. The collection of views can operate as a large-scale inquiry of the practical operation's current status of integrating research and teaching in higher professional education, as well as its future perspectives of the 'how' and 'why' of research integration.

Lecturers' and students' perceptions can be functional for the organisational change perspective if not only the current but also their ideal notions of research–education connections are considered. As explained in the Introduction, the mechanism for changing research–education connections requires an intended synergy between the two, which one could also call an ideal. Some of the few scholars who considered lecturers' proposed research–education connections are Visser-Wijnveen, Van Driel, Van der Rijst, Verloop, and Visser (2010), who researched lecturers' 'ideal' research–teaching nexus. In that study, participants were asked to describe in detail what they believed the linkage was between research and education. Based on these 'imaginations', the researchers distinguished five profiles of the research–teaching nexus academics held. The preferred profiles were respectively 'teach research results', 'make research known', 'show what it means to be a researcher', 'help to conduct research' and 'provide research experience' (Visser-Wijnveen et al., 2010, p. 208). These findings focused on what the 'ideal' nexus should look like in the eyes of lecturers, and therefore offers direction for changed research–education connections, other than the aforementioned models, which do not intend to present a 'best way' of connecting research and teaching (see also Elsen, Visser-Wijnveen, Van der Rijst, & Van Driel, 2008). The research Visser-Wijnveen and colleagues undertook is an example of researching ideal conceptions and perceptions, yet it exemplifies the disciplinary focus on research-intensive higher-education institutions.

Few scholars have addressed ideals for research integration. The 'ideal' combined with the perceptions of the current connections between research and education provides direction for change. A more general insight into lecturers' and students' perceptions of research and research–education connections can contextualise their ideal and current perceptions. The analysis of such rich data provides a valuable starting point for exploring institutional change.

Therefore, this chapter presents the findings of lecturers' and students' perceptions of research at both the start and end of the Amsterdam strategic programme. By asking both groups about the importance of research, its function as well as their current and ideal practices, this study yields the particular organisational layers to which lecturers and students connect research. The duality of two groups in a longitudinal perspective provides the opportunity to consider perception differences as well as changes over time. Therefore, next to presenting the Amsterdam project's findings, this chapter also is an example of a light touch, a scientifically sound instrument to monitor change across a higher education organisation.

Perceptions of Research and Teaching versus Perceptions of Research Integration

When addressing perceptions of research integration – the integration of research in educational curricula – it may be an obvious starting point to start with collecting and analysing perceptions of research and perceptions of education. However, the perceptions of research integration are not necessarily the sum of the two other perceptions. As Brew (2012) addresses, discussing research integration has a very specific context:

> The suggestion that teaching and research should be more firmly drawn together should not be seen as an argument for educating all students to become academics, nor is it merely an academic exercise to prop up arguments that

all academics should engage in research. Rather, it is a response to a number of changes in higher education which have challenged the relationship. These include: the move to a mass higher education system (Elton, 1992; Westergaard, 1991), the amount of time available both for teaching and for research (Hattie & Marsh, 1996), as well as changes in the nature of research and in the nature of teaching in higher education (Rowland, 1996) and changes in the nature of knowledge (Brew, 1999). Also of relevance is a changed policy context.

(Brew, 2012: 101)

Research, teaching and their integration are conceptualised in different ways, but are also likely to be defined differently by various stakeholders, such as lecturers and students. Brew subsequently argues for the need to 'reconceptualise the role of higher education and to renegotiate relationships between teachers and students' (Brew, 2012). These potential differences yield the exercise to think respectively about research, teaching, or research integration while taking the aims, roles and values of higher education in general into consideration. This is in line with Griffioen's call (2020, p. 3): 'When we aim to have students as our partners in how we integrate research into education, a comparison between the perspectives of both groups can provide critical information'. It is especially the value of this comparative exercise that upholds the contribution to the broader scholarly discussion on research integration.

This exercise follows the conception of students as partners, a relevant conception within higher-education studies because of its transformative power (Healey, Flint, & Harrington, 2016). Additional arguments emphasise inclusion and ethics of care as important values of the students-as-partners approach in higher education (e.g. Matthews, Dwyer, Hine, & Turner, 2018). The discussion relates to a gap in knowledge on how lecturers and students share certain perceptions of research within the organisation and within the hybrid space of the higher-education organisation or how these perceptions potentially contradict each other. Ashwin (2014) argues that research into students' experiences of studying in higher education has 'been dominated by studies that focus on teaching and learning, the majority of which tend to separate teaching from learning' (p. 123).

Earlier publications on research integration have not often resulted in measurement instruments comparing lecturer and student perspectives and experiences. Griffioen's (2020) study shows that students and lecturers shared perceptions about the role of research in their related vocational field and about research integration. However, important cognitive and affective differences were found between students and lecturers regarding students' research practice. The study also suggested that lecturers believe students have more positive views of research's function as a provider of new knowledge for professional action than students in fact have. This led to suggesting 'the importance of lecturers explicitly discussing these differences with students and enhancing attitudes through curriculum design and classroom practice' (p. 10). The data set for this chapter is the related qualitative data in the same study, added with the second qualitative measurement of this longitudinal study. These participants' observations, examples and remarks in the open questions provide an additional perspective on the hiatus between the current status of research in higher vocational education and their 'ideal' scenario.

Therefore, in this chapter, we focus on lecturers' and students' perceptions as a way to include the hybrid and multidimensional nuances, ideas, ideals and attitudes one's experiences shape. The centrality of perceptions in research, rooted in cognitive science and psychology, offers a unique perspective within other social sciences, among which higher education studies. There are many examples of perception studies in this field, reaching from studies on specific educational tools and methods, such as the perceptions of students participating in so-called 'reflective learning experiences' (e.g. Fullana, Pallisera, Colomer, Fernández Peña, & Pérez-Burriel, 2016), on specific formative experiences, such as perceptions on the transition from secondary to higher education (e.g. Noyens, Van Daal, Coertjens, Van Petegem, & Donche, 2020), to studies taking a broader perspective, for instance on the perceived workload of students in higher education (e.g. Kyndt, Dochy, Struyven, & Cascallar, 2011).

Researching Perceptions: The Amsterdam Case

Exploring comments, ideas, doubts and experiences provide insights into how research integration is conceptualised and considered. This chapter particularly focuses on lecturers' and students' change of perceptions of research integration during the Amsterdam strategic programme. The perceptions of 3,459 students and 695 lecturers in two time points provided the possibility to reveal in-depth qualitative data on attitudes and experiences of different stakeholders within the higher-education institution. Such analyses based on rich data sets on perceptions are informative and could even be an impetus for organisational change.

This study reveals rich insights into lecturers' changing perceptions about the role and position of research at an applied university and about potential future directions to develop this role on what this role and its position should be. Additionally, in the second time frame, the lecturers' perceptions are compared to those of students. The chosen emphasis in this project, comparing perceptions of students to the perceptions of lecturers, adds a comparative layer to this research, which reveals different key groups' diverse lines of thought. To demonstrate the central role of the concept of perceptions in change in higher education, this and the following section will explore one case study of such an analysis of perceptions. First, the research objectives and the research design will be explored, followed by a discussion of our experiences with data collection and data analysis in this comparative perception research project.

Research Objectives

In the process of continuously building connections between research and education in an applied university, lecturers and students can have fixed or changing perceptions of research, related to one or more of the multiple organisational layers that the change process affects (see also Chapter 2). Therefore, in this study, we have monitored the changing concept of 'research' as perceived by lecturers and students in a holistic way, providing an opportunity to include definitions of research, teaching and/or research integration in any way the respondents associated with this subject matter on any of the relevant organisational levels of the university.

The in-depth engagement with the answers to open questions provided the opportunity to thoroughly analyse causes, consequences and nuanced changes in lecturers' perceptions over time. Additionally, we included students' perceptions because they are central to the 'learning side' of education. In this, we do not approach lecturers and students as two homogeneous groups: it is important to emphasise the variety within groups of lecturers and groups of students. Thus, comparing can happen between lecturers and students as well as among the groups. This research aims to answer the following research question:

To what extent are shifts in perceptions about research and research integration seen during the organisational change programme?

Following from this research question, the differences and similarities between lecturers' and students' perceptions on the current integration of research and education and the ideal integration of the two is central is an entrance point in exploring past changes as well as potential future pathways.

Research Design

This project is based on a data set consisting of the input from 3,459 students and 695 lecturers from one higher-education institution, the Amsterdam University of Applied Sciences (Amsterdam UAS). Most participants completed a research survey in 2016 or 2019, while a small number of respondents (eighty-six lecturers) completed the survey in both years. Therefore, this study's units of analysis are 'lecturers' and 'students' and it is not possible to distinguish potential changes in individuals' perceptions. All lecturers and students of Amsterdam UAS were invited as respondents to collect as many individual perceptions as possible. The research was not designed to focus on a number of specific disciplines or groups within the organisation, but to provide an overall perspective of the existing perceptions and attitudes at Amsterdam UAS. There was no significant overrepresentation or underrepresentation of specific disciplines. The qualitative data applied in this chapter is a subset of a mixed methods research project focused on the interaction between research integration in education and students' intended research behaviour in vocationally oriented higher education (see also Griffioen, 2019a; Griffioen, 2019b, 2020).

Using the survey allowed investigating the entire organisation. The open-ended questions in the survey provided participants with the opportunity to reflect elaborately on the theme of research in the curriculum in order to indicate their perceptions at the time.

The open-ended questions asked to students and lecturers were:

1. Why is research important or not important for Amsterdam UAS?
2. What role does research have in your studies/in your teaching right now?
3. What role should research ideally have in your studies/in your teaching?

In general, lecturers provided more elaborate answers to the open-ended questions, whereas many students were relatively short in answering these questions.

The qualitative data was analysed in three rounds using Atlas.ti9. First, the researcher and two research assistants immersed themselves in the data through grounded coding (Charmaz, 2006), which resulted in an initial codebook. Second, this codebook was applied to the data in which it was expanded by discussing the coding process. Third, several codes were merged to fit both the lecturers' data of both time points as well as the students' data in the second time point. Finally, this codebook was applied to all data. Five themes emerged from the data, each subsequently consisting of one or more different codes.

Comparisons of lecturers' shifting perceptions through the time of current integration of research in education and their perceptions of the 'ideal' nexus may offer certain directions for institutional change. Supplemented with the data collected from students at one moment in time (2019), the research reveals an even richer picture. Earlier quantitative analysis (see Griffioen, 2020) of this same research project revealed that students and lecturers shared perceptions about the role of research in their field and about research integration in 2015. They also described important cognitive and affective differences between the two groups of stakeholders with regard to research practice. Such findings evoke follow-up questions about the characteristics in the differences within groups of stakeholders. While staying close to specific examples participants of the survey gave, in the next section we address potential future pathways of integrating research in the undergraduate professional curriculum, exploring some small-scale as well as large-scale suggestions lecturers and students offered. To do this, we will first address different perspectives on the current situation.

The Current Status and Perceptions of 'Ideal' Research Integration as a Driver for Institutional Change

The findings showed that lecturers and students perceive research along five themes that emerged from the data and relate to research–education connections: a) research in the curriculum; b) stance to research integration; c) research competencies; d) research and professional practice; and e) roles, tasks and collaborations in research. This section is structured by means of these themes. Two other emergent themes were: f) the purpose of research and g) conditions for including research. When relevant, the content of these two themes is selectively added to the storyline of the first five. In their answers, both lecturers and students reflected on the 'current status' of the integration of education and research. These experiences are explicitly personal and subjective, but collectively, they provide some shared, as well as different, experiences.

Theme 1: Research and Its Place in the Curriculum

Both in 2016 and 2019, many lecturers described the integration of research in the curriculum as 'fragmentary'. The key reflection on research in the curriculum was that students solely did research concerning their thesis in their final year. Lecturers described their own central research 'task' in thesis supervision. There was a small perceptible shift when comparing both years: compared to 2016, in 2019 more lecturers referred to the design of a research trajectory in the curriculum, and more lecturers addressed the centrality of evidence-based practice in education. In 2019, fewer mentioned the lack of a 'continuous' research line in the curriculum. However, overall, lecturers addressed the thesis as the key research component in the curriculum, with some lecturers, in both years, mentioning the role of research in the curriculum design as a whole and the use of research examples in individual lectures and teaching sessions. Research integration in education depends on lecturers' own perspective, role and expertise with regarding research:

> 'I am both a researcher and a lecturer. The results of my research are translated to the content of the curriculum'.
>
> (Lecturer, 2016)

In both years, some lecturers reflected on their own process of doing PhD research, and explained how this affected their teaching. However, others were more cynical about their own research:

> Unfortunately, research happens in my own time.
>
> (Lecturer, 2019)

This indicates there are certain practicalities, such as time, but also hiring practices, facilities, funding, the presence or absence of supporting staff and the attitude of managers that affect how, and how much, lecturers engage with research. Subsequently, this evidently impacts students' learning experiences.

The students who filled out the survey, in 2019, presented a very diffuse image of research as a part of the curriculum: from students who explained that research was almost non-existent in the curriculum to students addressing research as a component that was intertwined in the entire curriculum. The following quotes demonstrate the scope of students' reflection on the current situation, varying from a strong agreement with the significant role of research to comments expressing no enthusiasm for research in their curriculum:

> We've had a few sessions on 'research', but these classes were not very exciting and interesting. They wouldn't even discuss examples of research. (Student, 2019)

> In every course of the curriculum, research plays a significant role. (Student, 2019)
>
> Sometimes we have to do research, but usually this is only 'desk research'. (Student, 2019)

In their answers, students mentioned 'how much' research was in the curriculum, but in many cases, they connected their answers to their own opinions about research. For instance, the first quote demonstrates that there were 'a few sessions', but noted that these were not interesting. In turn, the final quote reflected on the nature of research in the curriculum as 'only' desk research. This student's remark demonstrates they expected more or other research components in the curriculum, as many other students also illustrated.

Some lecturers reflected on their fear of research taking up too much time that could better be spent otherwise, such as the following lecturers:

> So much of our attention goes to research, causing the development of 'basic knowledge' to suffer. (Lecturer, 2019)
>
> The focus on research and research competencies in our teaching education takes up too much precious time, which is urgently needed for professional ethics or professional knowledge. (Lecturer, 2016)

However, overall, these kinds of comments decreased when comparing the data from 2016 and 2019. In the last year, less than twenty comments appear that specifically mentioned a negative result for education because of too much attention for research, whereas in 2016, there were around fifty comments. The students, surveyed solely in 2019, still provided this relatively higher number of the consequences of 'too much research' in the curriculum:

> Research costs so much time, it would be better to spend that time on practice and theory, to become a better [disciplinary professional] in professional practice. (Student, 2019)

The perspective of research negatively influencing other parts of the curriculum was to some extent shared by lecturers and students, but comparing the lecturers' data through time reveals a small shift in how present this conception is throughout the lecturers.

However, another cluster of comments on research in the curriculum was about how research was imposed on students:

> I find research important, but it needs to be taught from the first year. What the tools are, and how you conduct research. Now you are being thrown into the deep end in the final year. (Student, 2019)

Lecturers recognised how this affected students, and how lecturers had to impose research on students. On the other hand, students experienced this as 'just something we have to do'. Such comments might indicate it would be possible to make improvements in the embeddedness of research in the curriculum. Besides research having too big of a role in the curriculum and being imposed, lecturers and students expressed concerns about the lack of constructing a 'research learning trajectory': research plays a big role in the undergraduate dissertation and final assignments, but in the first two years, research is dispersed throughout the different courses, as the following quotes illustrate:

> To be honest, I do not notice that research plays a role in my current education. It only starts to play a role when you have to write your undergraduate dissertation. (Student, 2019)
>
> Applied research is not stimulated enough during courses. Students only actively work on an applied research question when writing their thesis. (Lecturer, 2016)

Students mentioned this slightly more than lecturers. The 'misfitting' of research in the curriculum was not the only aspect lecturers and students wanted to improve, as will be discussed in later sections.

Theme 2: Advocating or Resisting? The Arguments for and Against Research Integration

The second theme focuses on lecturers' and students' stance towards research, which shows differences between as well as within both groups.

Lecturers that were advocating for research integration recognise and emphasise both the importance of research for the institution as a whole, and more specifically, for students as future professionals. The first was expressed in comments about the 'status' of Amsterdam UAS, and its position in the wider network of knowledge institutions and professional organisations:

> 'Research is essential for [Amsterdam] UAS. The organisation is suited to support innovation in professional practice and to prepare students for an innovative world. By sharing research in education, students will get used to that the world around them changes by means of research and that they could be the source of positive change.
>
> (Lecturer, 2019)

This quote addresses that the matter of status and position of the institution is not necessarily only about status, it also affects the possibilities and futures of all students. A strong institutional appearance and position in a wider network benefit students, and these, for most respondents who were advocating research integration, are the prime reason for research integration. The benefits of research integration lead to better quality education and a better preparation for changes and innovations in the future.

> Reciprocal interdependence of research and education makes sure that teaching material is up-to-date, and it invigorates the quality of research. (Lecturer, 2016)
>
> By doing research, lecturers could be role models for students with regard to 'life-long learning'. (Lecturer, 2019)

As both quotes suggest, bringing research and education together in one organisation and context is perceived as beneficial for the future professionals. When comparing the lecturers' responses from 2016 and 2019, there was a slight shift to more positive comments on the importance of research for students' futures. However, the perception of the irrelevance of research specifically in professional higher education, as well as the lack of time and embeddedness in the curriculum, as conditions for its realisation, prevails throughout these years, sometimes in firm statements:

> We must be careful to avoid research that does not in some ways tie back to our goals as a higher vocational education institute. (Lecturer, 2016)
>
> The unique quality of higher professional education (learning by doing, hands-on, internships, professional attitude) could be undermined by this 'research fetishism'. (Lecturer, 2019)

However, a small number of students were perfectly happy with the amount of research in the curriculum, or would like to see more research, as the following illustrates:

> Research does not play a substantial role in the curriculum, but it is present. For me, this is fine. (Student, 2019)
>
> At the moment, I am satisfied with the role that research plays in my education. (Student, 2019)

These findings demonstrate it is erroneous to address students as a homogeneous group. They have different experiences, different backgrounds and different ambitions – both personally and professionally. However, despite this diversity, both the 'research-prone' students and the 'research-hesitant' students, address some very useful potential future pathways, which is further discussed in a later section.

Theme 3: Research Competencies: What Does Research in Education Currently Look Like?

The prior sections provided a diffuse image of research integration in the undergraduate curriculum and in the organisation as a whole, which suggests there is still a lot to gain in this matter. Before turning to potential future pathways, first lecturers' and students' perceptions of what research integration truly entails is discussed: What are they talking about when discussing research in their education?

Both in 2016 and 2019, lecturers – more than students – discussed the need for students to develop a critical attitude, skills regarding logical reasoning and evaluating knowledge and facts, and dealing with 'fake news':

> Students learn to find and evaluate scientific evidence, and they learn how to translate this evidence into their own actions. (Lecturer, 2019)

> It helps to develop critical thinking and in developing one's own opinions, and it also generates new knowledge.
> (Lecturer, 2016)

With regard to instrumental research skills, lecturers described the skill of doing desk and literature research as an important aspect: coping with and reflecting on different kinds of source material were important in the curriculum, and regarding to lecturers, also in students' future professional practice. As illustrated by:

> Through desk research, students learn to find relevant and reliable sources and they learn to process these sources in their final research projects. This contributes to the development of the student's own visions.
> (Lecturer, 2016)

In relation to instrumental skills and research attitudes, there was not a significant shift in lecturers' attitudes between 2016 and 2019: The code 'results', comprising comments on the results of research and the ability to apply knowledge gained through research, was in both years the most found code.

The students who answered the survey in 2019 mainly emphasised the methods of doing research as a specific competency they had to develop to become a professional: some described this as an evidence-based practice. One student stated:

> The capacity to find information, to read it, apply it and explain it is essential for a professional working in [professional field].
>
> (Student, 2019)

Students mentioned less the research attitude, understood as a certain disposition towards research. If mentioned, they often described the competency of solving problems, whereas lecturers often emphasised the competency of critical thinking, logical thinking, evaluating one's own conceptions and dealing with 'fake news'. One exception in a student was:

> We have to learn to base our work on facts and not on assumptions. If we base our work on assumptions, we create products that users do not need or which are not functional.
>
> (Student, 2019)

Besides research methods, students regularly mentioned the role of research in gaining a better understanding and developing new knowledge and techniques, the importance of basing professional action on facts and being able to support one's arguments for specific choices (e.g. medical treatments, lesson designs).

In their reflections on how much attention instrumental research skills need, students provided, yet again, a diffuse view: Some students addressed the time spent on developing such research skills as too much, others as too little. It is unclear from the data whether these differences were based on differences in curricula, expectations and students' ambitions, or on differences in students' prior education. A widely shared student perception was the emphasis on designing research, finding literature and reflecting on research, but generally less on executing research. Many students called or implied these research projects 'superficial', for instance:

> In my current education we mainly conduct literature research, and we learn a little bit about conducting practical research.
>
> (Student, 2019)

However, there were students who described very specific forms of research, for instance, target audience analyses or pupil observations: these are examples of 'research' assignments that were closely connected to professional practice, and students did not always consider them as research. To illustrate:

> Research should be much more important, but it should be fitting as well. Conducting scientific research is not essential for a [professional], but target audience analyses or conducting user tests are.
>
> (Student, 2019)

> Conducting research plays an important role in my development to become a [professional]. Market analyses, target audience analyses, functional analyses and user analyses are important for determining and giving direction to a project. Studies with technical data are essential for finding the best solutions.
>
> (Student, 2019)

These findings indicate a potential hiatus between the richness of what research activities can comprise and the different conceptions of what 'research' is to undergraduate students. To what extent is research recognisable for students when it is intertwined in assignments?

These findings reveal that there is a very broad variety of considerations regarding research, with students recognising or not recognising different elements as research. However, the conception of what research is, is inextricably connected to their normative attitudes regarding research; the scope of the considerations is traceable throughout the analysed data. The same can be expected among lecturers, which asks for a more detailed debate about research activities between lecturers and students to provide increased clarity.

Theme 4: Research and Professional Practice

As discussed throughout this book, research has a different role in higher professional education than in higher academic education. The distinction between both might converge and diverge through time, but is generally widely shared. Considering the context of the Amsterdam case in an applied university, professional practice unsurprisingly played a significant role in both the lecturers' and students' answers when asked about research and education. Lecturers, more than students, considered internal and external partnerships with 'the field'. Many of them specifically mentioned Amsterdam UAS research groups, especially in 2019. Comparing the 2016 and 2019 data, it seems that research groups, in general, take up a more central role in the organisation; however, a lack of contact between the educational 'context' and the research 'context' is a widely shared concern. As the following two quotes address, some lecturers were concerned about researchers' lack of interest to get involved with students:

> Research groups [lectoraten] are aloof from our undergraduate programmes. Students only come into contact with research groups when lecturers actively bring them into contact with each other. (Lecturer, 2019)

> Our research groups do research that is very interesting for our [discipline] lecturers and students. More interaction would be enriching for both. (Lecturer, 2019)

In that same year, there were a few lecturers who already described shifts towards more interaction and exchange between research groups and education within the institution:

> Stronger connections between research groups and lecturers are needed, and these will happen (this is already happening).
> (Lecturer, 2019)

Students' perceptions focused mainly on the function of research for their work as future professionals. In this applied university, they were educated to become professionals in often very specific professional contexts. The findings show that whether students were 'research-prone' or 'research-hesitant', they mainly valued research when it was directly connected to this professional practice. As the following two quotes indicate, students referred to their specific future professional context. Both students addressed very practical reasons why they should be learning certain research skills themselves:

> I use research articles on a daily basis, especially during my internship when I have to deal with difficult or rare cases. I am able to find useful information which I can use in practice afterward. I also base all my reports on current research. (Student, 2019)
>
> As a future teacher, I will need to be able to teach my students to research.
> (Student, 2019)

These findings show that the perspective of research and professional fields somewhat differed between lecturers and students. Where both perceived the need for research in education that was relevant for students' professional practice, some lecturers in 2019 added the dimension of relevance for their students' learning being connected to Amsterdam UAS's research groups. Although these last indications of change still are relatively scarce, it is interesting that these remarks about research groups were only found in the 2019 data – not in the 2016 data. This might hint towards shifts within the organisation, or at least some 'best practices'.

Theme 5: Roles, Tasks and Collaboration

The aforementioned research groups play – or would potentially play – an important role in the connection between research and teaching. However, besides these collaborations within the wider organisation, both lecturers and students also reflected on lecturers' and students' collaboration as well as the different roles and tasks both groups have. Lecturers, unsurprisingly, strongly connected their own research activities to the role research had in the curriculum within which they were teaching, just a few students mentioned the importance of lecturers' own research: In these cases, they all argued that discussing lecturers' own research did not happen enough. In 2016, many lecturers reflected on the lack of a research culture in the wider organisation:

> I notice an almost hostile-like attitude against research, and this is fatal for improving the curriculum. Knowledge is important [...] yet lecturers should have the time and enthusiasm to develop and keep up their own knowledge.
>
> (Lecturer, 2016)

> Many researchers are not interested in didactics, and 'hard core' lecturers are not interested in the research done at [Amsterdam] UAS. Barely anyone is able to build bridges between the two.
>
> (Lecturer, 2016)

Such quotations sketch an image of an organisation with two faces: educational practice and research practice as two separate activities and communities. The answers from lecturers in 2019 provide a slightly more united perception of research and education, but the changes seem to come slow and still are relatively small. For instance:

> To integrate research and education, you have to communicate it persuasively and in simple terms, otherwise you will lose the support of too many lecturers. Projects will only be successful if most of the lecturers are on board.
>
> (Lecturer, 2019).

> An important task, I think, is to persuade applied educated lecturers that scientific research is important.
>
> (Lecturer, 2019)

In reflections on colleagues and peers, a number of students reflected on the lack of interest in their peers' attitude towards research:

> Motivation is very important in doing research. I am not sure if the average student is that motivated. I am motivated, that's why I would like to do more research.
>
> (Student, 2019)

> Many fellow students do not want to be bothered with conducting research. Indeed, many of my peers often do not see the point of conducting research.
>
> (Student, 2019)

> Many students understand that they need to know how to conduct research. But I am not sure if they also think it is important to do so.
>
> (Student, 2019)

These quotes emphasise the already discussed diffuse image that appears in this research, in which the approach of students, as well as lecturers, as a heterogeneous group, should be central: different students have different ambitions, interests and talents, and these play a role in how they perceive the role of research in their education. The following section addresses such differences, similarities and shifts in more detail.

Future Pathways

In the previous section, we discussed lecturers' and students' perceptions with regard to research integration by distinguishing five themes. In this section, these same five themes will be addressed, but here the potential future pathways as the lecturers and students described them are emphasised. These 'ideal' futures are sometimes broad ideas and other times very specific small changes; however, together they provide a collection of perceptions that could provide directions for organisational change. Furthermore, this research project's broad scope of analysis means that participants were able to address their own key concerns and solutions without a strict 'framework' the researchers provided. As this section demonstrates, these future pathways are thus very diverse in nature, and consequentially, would need to be translated from a more operational level of organisational change to a tactic or strategic level of change when applied to a particular setting. However, they might be food for thought for institutional policymakers as well as researchers.

Theme 1: Research and Its Place in the Curriculum

The lecturers' and students' perception about research and its ideal place in the curriculum is a notion that was shared widely in the findings, of which differing perceptions emerged. The two most substantial topics emerging were the notions of choice and of integration.

A small number of lecturers as well as students addressed their impression that there should be freedom of choice in the curriculum with regard to research: not only the extent of research in the curriculum, but also the specific 'form' or 'type' of research.

> It should not be dictated by the organisation. I think it is important that students have the freedom to conduct research and are facilitated appropriately.
>
> (Lecturer, 2016)

> It is good to let students experiment with conducting research, but we should not force students to conduct scientific research within the [university]. It should be a choice. Students that have an affinity with conducting scientific research should have the freedom to do so, so that they can prepare themselves for a possible master's degree.
>
> (Lecturer, 2019)

Some lecturers presupposed that by giving students the choice to do research, the students who then make that decision are more motivated for research, which students also mentioned:

> Because not everyone finds conducting research interesting, it would be ideal if there would be more research-oriented elective courses for students that are interested in doing research, next to the regular research-oriented courses.
>
> (Student, 2019)

This can be seen as a logical argument; however, this means that research is only done by the few, and not the many students of every curriculum. A choice to make research more flexible and optional could be beneficial because it personalises the educational experience and gives students the option to do what they prefer to do, what they are good at, or what they think is best for their future career path. That said, this presupposes that research is not something with which all graduates from higher professional education should be acquainted. Thus, it takes a different perspective on what role the undergraduate degree should take with it. This is one example of how some relatively 'straightforward' suggestions for future change are strongly related to wider visions and strategies on a higher policy level.

Besides the matter of the curriculum's flexibility with regard to research components in the curriculum, many lecturers argued that developing research skills should not – or not only – be addressed in specific research-focused trajectories as part of the curriculum, but rather they should be integrated into the curriculum's regular courses. This means that, for instance, training in research skills is integrated into more 'knowledge-focused' courses. For instance:

> Knowledge in the course that I give is always situational. That is why I am not in favour of separate research-oriented courses. I would like to integrate research more in the curriculum.
>
> (Lecturer, 2016)

> I would like research, practical and applied, to play a role in every course and also in the first few years, so that it builds up towards the final dissertation.
>
> (Lecturer, 2019)

Theme 2: Advocating or Resisting: The Arguments for and against Research Integration

Building on the discussions and ideal images on research and its place and the curriculum, the future scenarios lecturers and students sketched were still very diverse, and both voices advocating and resisting the emphasis on research integration were found in the two groups of stakeholders. Some lecturers envisaged a smaller role:

> I don't want to educate future researchers, I want to educate researching, critical, curious professionals.
>
> (Lecturer, 2016)

Whereas others addressed the need for a larger role:

> Research should be connected to everything we [lecturers] do when teaching.
> (Lecturer, 2019)

When looking at the number of responses, far more respondents envisaged a smaller role than a larger role of research in their ideal future scenarios. This was the same for the 2016 respondents as well as the 2019 respondents, which addresses that change towards a stronger research integration, if decided through a top-down approach, can meet hesitant – or perhaps even resistant – attitudes of stakeholders within the organisation.

Additionally, many students expressed aversion to the role of research in their studies:

> Personally, I don't like doing research, and I think it doesn't add anything to know how to do research as a professional. I have made the switch from academic education to professional education because I disliked research.
> (Student, 2016)

Such findings do not offer specific grounds for change, but they do reveal the 'target audience' of higher professional education: To some, studying at an applied university was a conscious choice not to do research. There are multiple possible perspectives that can be formulated, for instance, the role of information evenings and 'open days': explaining that research is a fundamental part of being a professional. If higher professional education institutions aim to integrate research in education, this message – that research is a prominent component of professionalism – should be more explicitly shared among stakeholders.

Theme 3: Research Competencies

The future perspectives of research competences mainly focus on critical research attitudes. Lecturers in 2016 as well as in 2019 addressed the need to emphasise a critical research attitude as well as some specific instrumental research competences, such as using academic literature. However, the lecturers' perceptions on developing research competences and a critical research attitude were slightly different from the students' perceptions on these themes. Students often mentioned relatively 'small' research competences they wanted to develop.

These competences were more about specific methods of data collection and data analysis, or about a distinctive research activity:

> I want to learn about how to approach my target audience [doelgroep]. (Student, 2019)
>
> I just want to learn where to find research material and how to analyse this. (Student, 2019)
>
> I want to learn how to approach the writing of a research report. (Student, 2019)

These three quotes indicate that students did not interpret research skills and research competences as skills and competences that played a wider role in their development as a professional. Some lecturers also noted this:

> Make the presence as well as access of research clearer.
>
> (Lecturer, 2019)

Thus, to develop research competences, it is first important to establish some common ground in discussing what they comprise, before continuing to discuss what the role of research should be in higher professional education. This could also mean thoroughly discussing what the role of research should be in professional practice and then defining the particular research competences that come with that perspective. Either way, a greater clarity on research competences is requested. The very specific examples students gave about what they wanted to do more in their educational programmes demonstrate there are specific points they would want to start at, which can be added with the lecturers' broader understanding of the future of research found in this study.

Theme 4: Research and Professional Practice

As discussed earlier in this chapter, both lecturers and students placed a strong emphasis on professional practice in their thoughts on research integration in higher professional education. This comes as no surprise, but many respondents seemed to separate research components in the curriculum from professional practice components in the curriculum, such as internships. Problem-based education might be a solution to address the interconnectedness of these two domains, and the suggestion to work on 'actual cases' in the classroom was mentioned often:

> It would be ideal if teams of lecturers would research actual problems from clinical practice. This way, lecturers will learn from each other and be motivated

> to develop themselves. This would also set the tone for others as well as for students.
>
> (Lecturer, 2016)

> For me personally, a little bit less research would be great. I think discussing specific experiences in professional practice of me and others is so much more useful than filling in the umpteenth unimaginative form.
>
> (Student, 2019)

This last quote expresses a very cynical perspective of what research is and how it is something that is completely separate from professional practice. Many student respondents expressed a clear passion for their future professional practice, and some seemed to consider research as standing 'in the way' of their development towards becoming a professional instead of as an integral component of professionalism. An interesting follow-up question would be to consider how this perspective developed over time, but first of all, it is important to note that perceptions of what research truly is might be very different for some students and lecturers. This might also be a chance for advocates of research integration: by making visible that research and professional practice are definitely not mutually exclusive but strongly connected, the aversion against research might slowly change.

Theme 5: Roles, Tasks and Collaboration

The last theme that will be discussed here is the only one in which a clear difference between respondents of 2016 and 2019 can be found. In 2019, far more lecturers addressed their wish to have more time for research as an integral part of their responsibilities than in 2016. Furthermore, they also expressed a need for clearer interweaving of the role of research groups [lectoraten] in educational practice:

> In an ideal situation, researchers could be asked to identify trends and developments and find relevant literature [to curate this] by which lecturers genuinely have input in their teaching programmes.
>
> (Lecturer, 2019)

Lecturers want to 'research together with students' and are searching for ways to collaborate with internal as well as with external partners. Some lecturers described a relatively detailed image of what future roles and collaborations should look like, but connected this directly to their experienced lack of space and time to work on their own research ideas. The earlier mentioned importance of autonomy and differentiation (making research an optional activity instead of a mandatory one) goes for lecturers' job description as well. Some teams within the organisation reported in the findings that might be considered 'early adapters' of this approach in 2016:

> Within our team, lecturers are stimulated to do research: in time and space. Lecturers who are not interested in research are taken in consideration as well. In my eyes, this is a perfect balance.
> (Lecturer, 2016)

Thus, future pathways might be motivated by good practices within the organisation.

Conclusion

It is valuable to collect specific ideas, potential causes for certain perceptions and attitudes and possible 'ways forward'; these offer perspectives on what kinds of changes students and lecturers genuinely need or desire. Listening to the many voices by means of a large-scale, qualitative study, such as conducted in this research project, is not only academically insightful, but also important, systematically gathered information from an organisational change perspective, as here demonstrated. The shared idea of respondents sketching potential future pathways that emerge from the findings is the wish for togetherness. This sense of togetherness can be found in the proposed collaborations between students and lecturers, collaborations between teaching-only staff and researching staff, and collaborations between education and professional practice.

However, combined with this togetherness comes an overall cynicism of the feasibility of developing new ideas and new educational practices, due to the needed conditions:

> That they [the students] will learn that research is something they can do, that it is not out of their reach. That practical research is something different from academic research. That it is possible to practice a lot with the right feedback at the right moment. Let them discover things for themselves, an old-fashioned 'learn-to-learn' situation. But that will ask a lot of time of lecturers, and, sigh, that, will be too expensive.
> (Lecturer, 2016)

This cynicism did not change in the short timeframe studied here, although there might be a small shift in the lecturers' conceptions about the shapes research potentially might take in the undergraduate professional curriculum. Thus, this broad-scope research might conclude in a less cynical conclusion: Organisational change with regard to research integration needs time for discussion, time for clarification and time for experience. It needs time over time: It is a marathon, not a sprint.

References

Åkerlind, G. S. (2008). An academic perspective on research and being a researcher: An Integration of the Literature. *Studies in Higher Education, 33*(1), 17–33.

Ashwin, P. (2014). Knowledge, curriculum and student understanding. *Higher Education, 67*(2), (123–6).

Brew, A. (1999). Research and teaching: Changing relationships in a changing context. *Studies in Higher Education, 24*(3), 291–301.

Brew, A. (2001). Conceptions of research: A phenomenographic study. *Studies in Higher Education, 26*(3), 271–85.

Brew, A. (2012). Teaching and research: New relationships and their implications for inquiry-based teaching and learning in higher education. *Higher Education Research & Development, 31*(1), 101–14.

Charmaz, K. (2006). *Constructing grounded theory. A practical guide through qualitative analysis.* Los Angeles: Sage Publications.

Durning, B., & Jenkins, A. (2005). Teaching-research relations in departments: The perspectives of built environment academics. *Studies in Higher Education, 30*(4), 407–26.

Elsen, M., Visser-Wijnveen, G. J., Van der Rijst, R. M., & Van Driel, J. H. (2008). How to strengthen the connection between research and teaching in undergraduate university education. *Higher Education Quarterly, 63*(1), 64–85.

Elton, L. (1992). Research, teaching and scholarship in an expanding higher education system. *Higher Education Quarterly, 46*(3), 252–68.

Fullana, J., Pallisera, M., Colomer, J., Fernández Peña, R., & Pérez-Burriel, M. (2016). Reflective learning in higher education: A qualitative study on students' perceptions. *Studies in Higher Education, 41*(6), 1008–22.

Griffioen, D. M. E. (2018). Building research capacity in new universities during times of academic drift: Lecturers professional profiles. *Higher Education Policy.* doi:https://doi.org/10.1057/s41307-018-0091-y

Griffioen, D. M. E. (2019a). Differences in students' experienced research involvement: Study years and disciplines compared. *Journal of Further & Higher Education, 44*(4), 454–66. doi:https://doi.org/10.1080/0309877X.2019.1579894

Griffioen, D. M. E. (2019b). The influence of undergraduate students' research attitudes on their intention for research usage in their future professional practice. *Innovation in Education and Teaching International, 56*(2), 162–72. doi:10.1080/14703297.2018.1425152

Griffioen, D. M. E. (2020). A questionnaire to compare lecturers' and students' higher education research integration experiences. *Teaching in Higher Education, 27*(2), 185–200.

Griffioen, D. M. E., Doppenberg, J. J., & Oostdam, R. J. (2017). Organisational influence on lecturers' perceptions and behaviour towards change in education. *Studies in Higher Education, 43*(11), 1810–22.

Griffioen, D. M. E., Roosenboom, B. H. W., & De Jong, U. (2017). Opvattingen over 'Goed Onderzoek' van Docenten in het Hoger Onderwijs. *Tijdschrift voor Hoger Onderwijs*(2).

Hattie, J., & Marsh, H. W. (1996). The relationship between research and teaching: A meta-analysis. *Review of Educational Research, 66*, 507–42.

Healey, M. (2005). Linking research and teaching: Exploring disciplinary spaces and the role of inquiry-based learning. In R. Barnett (Ed.), *Reshaping the university: New relationships between research, scholarship and teaching* (pp. 67–78). McGraw Hill: Open University Press.

Healey, M., & Jenkins, A. (2015). *Linking discipline-based research with teaching to benefit student learning through engaging students in research and inquiry*. Retrieved from http://www.mickhealey.co.uk/resources

Healey, M., Flint, A., & Harrington, K. (2016). Students as partners: Reflections on a conceptual model/student response. *Teaching and Learning Inquiry, 4*(2), 1–13.

Jenkins, A., & Healey, M. (2005). *Institutional strategies to link teaching and research*. Retrieved from York: http://www.heacademy.ac.uk/assets/York/documents/resources/resourcedatabase/id585_institutional_strategies_to_link_teaching_and_research.pdf

Kyndt, E., Dochy, F., Struyven, K., & Cascallar, E. (2011). The perception of workload and task complexity and its influence on students' approaches to learning: A study in higher education. *European Journal for Psychology in Education, 26*, 393–415.

Lucas, L. (2007). Research and teaching work within university education departments: Fragmentation or integration. *Journal of Further and Higher Education, 31*(1), 17–29.

Matthews, K. E., Dwyer, A., Hine, L., & Turner, J. (2018). Conceptions of students as partners. *Higher Education, 76*(6), 957–71.

Noyens, D., Van Daal, T., Coertjens, L., Van Petegem, P., & Donche, V. (2020). Assessing students' perceptions of fit between secondary and higher education: A validation study of the SPFQ. *Higher Education Research & Development, 39*(2), 1–15. doi:doi:10.1080/07294360.2019.166237

Rowland, S. (1996). Relationships between teaching and research. *Teaching in Higher Education, 1*(1), 7–20.

Schouteden, W., Verburgh, A. L., & Elen, J. (2014). Teachers' general and contextualised research conceptions. *Studies in Higher Education, 41*(1), 79–94. doi:10.1080/03075079.2014.914915

Teichler, U. (2014). On the move towards a new convergent design of higher education systems. In J. C. Shin & U. Teichler (Eds.), *The future of the post-massified university at the crossroads* (Vol. 1) (pp. 229–48). Switzerland: Springer International Publishing.

Visser-Wijnveen, G. J. (2009). *The research-teaching nexus in the humanities: Variations among academics.* (PhD). Leiden University, Leiden.

Visser-Wijnveen, G. J., Van Driel, J. H., Van der Rijst, R. M., Verloop, N., & Visser, A. (2010). The ideal research-teaching nexus in the eyes of academics: Building profiles. *Higher Education Research & Development, 29*(2), 195–210.

Westergaard, J. (1991). Scholarship, research and teaching: A view from the social sciences. *Studies in Higher Education, 16*(1), 23–28.

5

Changes in Curriculum Rationales

Linda van Ooijen-van der Linden, Indira N. Z. Day,
Jolieke Timmermans and Didi M. E. Griffioen

Introduction

Changes in research–education connections are expected to become visible in the rationales of curricula, especially if a change programme focuses on changing this connection at the university organisational level. This chapter focuses on these potential changes during the Amsterdam change programme.

Barnett described a curriculum as 'a pedagogic vehicle for effecting changes in human beings through particular kinds of encounters with knowledge' (Barnett, 2009, p. 429). He rephrased this to the questions 'what should we teach?' and 'how should we teach?', explicitly noting the conceptual flattening of these questions compared to the original description. While a curriculum does serve to allow transmitting knowledge and learning, this description of what it is supposed to do, does not capture the rich complexity of what a curriculum is and how it relates to its aims, purposes and effects (Young, 2014). A curriculum can be further explicated as 'a set of teaching and learning prescriptions, [which is] in essence a knowledge-forming activity' (Scott, 2014, p. 14). At the same time, '[curricula] set limits on what is possible to learn in schools or other educational institutions' (Young, 2014, p. 7). According to these definitions, the curriculum provides directions and boundaries for student learning. As Scott (2014, p. 27) states, 'those relations between curriculum contents, pedagogic forms, evaluative processes and criteria are a function of how knowledge is conceived and used within a curriculum, rather than they being independently derived'.

While we often discuss the curriculum as if it were a unified object, it consists of many different elements that need to be aligned through purposeful curriculum design (Biggs, 1996; Huizinga, 2014; Van den Akker, 2003, 2013).

Different missions of higher education, such as to provide general education, educate specialists, educate researchers or educate educators, require knowledge to be organised in the curriculum differently (Short, 2002). This suggests the importance of deliberate and collaborative curriculum design in which curriculum designers explain the rationale: The underlying reasons why they include specific knowledge, information or learning activities in the curriculum (Scott, 2014; Van den Akker, 2003). How a curriculum is conceived and designed is influenced by ideas of what a curriculum is and the role learners can or should fulfil in the design and implementation process (Bovill & Woolmer, 2018; Karseth & Sivesind, 2010).

In addition, the curriculum is altered when lecturers redesign learning activities during and in between teaching; when students respond differently; when the professional field requires different knowledge, skills and attitudes; or when policies change (Bovill & Woolmer, 2018; Wiliam, 2013), as will its rationale.

In this chapter, we first outline different strands of conceptualisations of curricula. They serve as the foundation for an overview of the function and content of rationales on research in higher education bachelor's curricula across time and disciplines as well as related to actual research integration in changing curriculum rationales. Then we report the findings of a monitoring study focused on changes in the curriculum rationales of bachelor's programmes in Amsterdam UAS during the Research into Education strategic programme. Findings are discussed in terms of different stakeholders who can be served by research integration and the curricula conceptualisations to which they relate.

The Curriculum

Much has been written about what constitutes a curriculum. In this body of knowledge, (at least) three strands can be seen: a 'student-centred' strand, a 'structure and instruments' strand, and a 'knowledge and content' strand. The student-centred strand focuses on the purpose of curricula in how they allow each student to be a whole person (Roberts, 2015) and to become a professional with a professional identity in an uncertain world (Barnett, 2012). The focus on students' development contrasts with teacher-focused education in which transmitting knowledge from teacher to student is centralised from the perspective of a sending teacher. Young (2014) sees this social function of the curriculum through offering constraints and possibilities, shaped by acts, beliefs, motivation, and by all involved: as a 'social fact'. Overall, this strand mainly focuses on developing certain dispositions in students (Barnett, 2012) and developing human power (Deng, 2021). Although the simultaneous focus on effectiveness and efficiency intends to empower both lecturers and students, Tam (2014) criticises that in real life this easily amounts to an outcome-based and instrumental approach. Then, contrary to the intentions, the curriculum is easily reduced to a collection of stand-alone active learning activities in which lecturers coach their students towards passing the examinations, thus merely demonstrating the learning goals have been achieved and not focused on full-person learning.

The second strand of curriculum design mainly focuses on the curriculum's structure and its instrumental functionality for learning. This functionality is defined in systematically striving towards certain outcomes (Roberts, 2015) and is characterised by a thick focus on consistency across all elements. Constructive alignment of objectives, assessment and teaching/learning activities helps students and lecturers realise the intended curriculum (Biggs, 1996). Backward design is an often used design strategy that helps to reach constructive alignment from the desired results to acceptable evidence of these results, and then to a design of learning and instruction accordingly (Wiggins & McTighe, 1998). Part of this strand are the practical lenses for curriculum structures, such as Van den Akker's (2003) Spider Web Model, which positions the curriculum rationale at the core of the model, with other elements, such as aim and objectives, content, lecturers' roles and location circling it. All elements are interconnected through the threads of the spider web, presuming that if one element is changed, the others will need to as well. The rationale and the notion of interconnectedness, therefore, are positioned to capture the curriculum complexity as Barnett (2009) and Young (2014) described. Alternative models that consider the curriculum structure are, for instance, the Four Component Instructional Design (4CID) model, which offers detailed steps for the design of learning activities structured in a curriculum (van Merriënboer, 2019), and the ADDIE (Analysis, Design, Development, Implementation and Evaluation) model (Branch, 2009), which considers analytical phases that, when combined, lead to a thorough and well-founded curriculum design. Such focus on the structure of the design process or the curriculum entails the risk of paying less attention to the curriculum's content than it deserves.

The third strand focuses on knowledge and content of the curriculum. The afore described notions of constructive alignment, backward design and their related models focus on the curriculum structures, mainly disregarding the learning activities' content. This strand however zooms in on notions of knowledge in general and students' relations to certain forms of knowledge and their understanding of the discipline they study (Ashwin, Abbas, & McLean, 2013), as well as the transformation of that knowledge in the curriculum into student learning (Ashwin, 2014; Bernstein, 2000). Liminal space, as Land, Rattray, and Vivian (2014) described, is an interactionist view on how threshold concepts in acquiring a certain knowledge base can contribute to curriculum design and transformative learning. Threshold concepts and their teaching are very content driven in expecting the learner to transform, to make a discursive shift and to understand the concept. Luckett and Humna (2013) described another, yet conceptually adjacent, approach to working with different kinds of knowledge, in which they combined the specialised dimension of legitimation code theory (Maton, 2010, 2013) with Bernstein's concepts of classification and framing to surface what counts, what is valued or worthy of distinction and what is recognised as specialised practice. This resulted in a detailed analysis of the implicit layers of meaning and meaning making in the curriculum (see also (Paxton & Frith, 2013). Knowledge structures of four humanities courses were discerned to consist of knowledge codes and knower codes, explicating that students are required to develop different ways of relating different kinds of disciplinary knowledge, different dispositions and attributes and different ways of intellectual practicing in different courses. Uncovering and explicating these implicit knowledge structures and the to-be-developed professional actions and interactions with knowledge are expected to unlock the possibility of designing a curriculum that makes these knowledge structures accessible for students and allows them to consciously learn the rules of the game (Luckett & Hunma, 2013).

The different perspectives on curriculum content can be connected to the curriculum structures via applying the concept of 'pedagogical content knowledge' (PCK). PCK bridges the gap between content-wise 'empty' design models, the disciplinary knowledge and pedagogical approaches by taking all into account and making them mutually dependent (Shulman, 1986). How to best teach subject matter depends on the specific subject matter, what students already know and many contextual factors influencing the learning process, such as identity, college management, national policies for funding, inspection and wider social and economic contexts (James, 2013). Therefore, '[PCK] affords a space for what Cousin (2008) has termed "forms of transactional curriculum inquiry"' (Land et al., 2014, p. 215), where teaching and learning are neither student-centred nor teacher-centred.

Added to the PCK notion, and as an integration of the strands of curriculum perspectives is here argued that Van den Akker's curriculum 'rationale' is the direction-giving element of curriculum design. The curriculum rationale can balance the instrumental approach of curriculum structures including the need to include specific aims and objectives with the profession's bigger ideas and the lecturers' freedom and responsibility to teach in a transforming way. The connection is made when lecturers plan forward and reflect backward on their student interactions (Wiliam, 2013). If formulating a shared rationale is not prioritised, if the elements of the curriculum are not aligned to this shared rationale and if the communication within the teaching team and with students is not properly addressed, then it might not function up to its full potential as a curriculum in the sense of transforming knowledge and individuals. Thus, the rationale and the curriculum design strands or perspectives are interrelated, influencing one another, shaping the curriculum as Young's (2014) 'social fact'. Research integration in curricula requires a rationale on research in professional practice and on how education could or should prepare students for this (Ashwin, 2014).

Rationales of Research in Curricula

Historically, curriculum rationales have both included and excluded 'research' as a variable. Schimank and Winnes (2000) explain how pre-Humboldtian, Humboldtian and post-Humboldtian types of relationships between research and education can be discerned. For pre-Humboldtian, the relationship is categorical in nature; research and education are two entirely different things, organised in separate institutions. Universities were dedicated to teaching, research took place in 'learned societies' or 'academies'. Later on, and following the Humboldtian university ideal, universities framed their teaching responsibility as inseparable from the professors' research activities. Research was seen as the connecting factor between lecturers and students as both searched for new knowledge. In the post-Humboldtian pattern, a differentiation of roles and/or organisations and/or resources for teaching and research occurs within universities (Schimank and Winnes, 2000). National research policies and institutional governance in, for instance, England and the Netherlands led higher education to become more focused on efficiency, effectiveness and outcome-based cultures (Leisyte, Enders, & de Boer, 2009). Accountability and funding mechanisms pushed these institutions into a post-Humboldtian relationship between education and research. Currently, the balance becomes more diverse. Research-intensive universities strive to establish better opportunities for academics to build a career on teaching by advocating a more diverse perspective of recognition and rewards based on contributions other than scientific publications (te Pas, 2019). In turn, universities of applied sciences started strengthening their research capacity around the turn of this century (Witte, van der Wende, & Huisman, 2008), which still is a work in progress (Griffioen, 2020). A multiplicity can be seen moving from the ideal Humboldtian perspective to more diverse research–education connections.

A diversification of research–education connections at the curriculum level requires changes in its rationale. Formulating a curriculum rationale generally answers the question 'to what purpose?', or shorter, 'why?' a curriculum is shaped the way it is. Answers to this question can be informed by the body of knowledge on the history of education, human learning, the discipline (or multi- or trans-disciplinarity), and more or less dominant perspectives of relevant stakeholders. Decisions on curriculum rationales in higher education are influenced and made at the macro-, meso- and micro-levels that differ in their interdependencies across countries. The Bologna process set out with a curriculum focus, but it also influenced policy and funding in such a way that it influenced rationales' focus and boundaries (Berndtson, 2013). Some socio-political, economic and geopolitical forces influencing curricula are relatively stable in time and well known. Others, such as technology and decolonisation, are relatively new (Krause, 2020; Lotz-Sisitka, Wals, Kronlid, & McGarry, 2015). The academic discipline is a major influencer in curriculum decisions, as are lecturers' beliefs about educational purpose. Broader conceptions of research have been found to coincide with more diverse integration of research in education as course content, skills, inquiry learning and students doing research (Roberts, 2015). How lecturers fulfil their role as change agents is just as an interrelated process as is curriculum change, determined by factors at all levels, and resulting in progressive, oppositional, territorial, bridge building and accommodating agency (Annala, Lindén, Mäkinen, & Henriksson, 2021; Annala, Mäkinen, Lindén, & Henriksson, 2020). Changing parts of a programme's curriculum can be done in isolation by individual lecturers and, preferably, in collaboration (Anakin, Spronken-Smith, Healey, & Vajoczki, 2017). Several forces such as ownership, identity, and resources (e.g. time) influence the outcome of the change process in an intended curriculum, at the level of individual lecturers, their department or institution. The degree of influence of each force, whether it operates at the individual, department or institutional level, and whether the influence enables or inhibits curriculum change, is determined locally. This renders curriculum change highly context-specific (Anakin et al., 2017). Change teams at programme level need time, opportunities for collaboration with other redesign teams and guidance on curriculum design (Turner, Healey, & Bens, 2020).

National and institutional priorities tend to shift focus faster than teaching and learning practices can accordingly be designed, implemented, redesigned and become good practices (Hénard & Roseveare, 2012; Krause, 2020). Therefore, Brew and Cahir (2014) propose that a sustainable approach of change in higher education institutions would be to do three things: 1) hold on to the values and principles of their profession, 2) see and know the broader patterns and development and 3) reframe the current priorities and associated changes in a way that serves the profession and the professionals. For curricula with a professional focus, serving the profession and the professionals includes designing education in such a way that it allows teaching and learning as intended by the rationale, aims and objectives. That is, only if rationale, aims and objectives have been well chosen and formulated to include all that is relevant for starting professionals, and nothing else. The continuous becoming by balancing one's current professional identity, action and knowledge with new information and experiences requires the professional to ask the right questions (Griffioen, 2019). This requires knowledge and professional action in education and research to be tailored to the current state of the society, profession, lecturers and students, taking into account their history and relevant contextual elements (Krause, 2020; Robertson & Bond, 2005), as well as taking into account both expected and unknown changes in the future (Barnett, 2018).

The Changing Role of Research in a Curriculum

The complexity of curriculum design and integrated research rationales can be explained by considering the nature of knowledge on education and curriculum design. This is not just another type of academic disciplinary knowledge with a specific focus and dedicated set of agreed upon methods of research. Short (2002) would call the knowledge on education mission-oriented knowledge. The distinction between discipline-oriented knowledge and mission-oriented knowledge serves to explain that the complexity of mission-oriented subjects cannot be broken down into separate and researchable building blocks, as is common in mono-disciplinary fields; they require to be considered and researched as complex wholes. Knowledge creation in mission-oriented subjects, such as education, is achieved in multiple ways: in formal research, on-the-go in professional practice and both inside and outside research institutions. In line with the knowledge strand in curricula perspectives described above, Short (2002) argues how curricula are built, or should be built, on four types of knowledge (see also Roberts, 2015). The first is general knowledge on citizenship, how to act wisely as a person in different contexts and situations. The second is disciplinary knowledge, which is needed to function professionally in a specialised field. The third is research knowledge, as universities have the responsibility to educate researchers on how to advance their field. The fourth is educational knowledge, as lecturers teaching any type of knowledge need to be educated in how to educate and how to educate that specific type of knowledge. Short (2002) suggests students in higher education need all four types of knowledge, but their relative contributions within a specific curriculum should be tailored to the type of education: general education, education of specialists, education of researchers and education of educators. Indeed, in higher education daily life, the rationales of academic disciplines are interwoven with the rationales of research in academic curricula (Hessels, Lente, & Smits, 2009; Lepori, 2007; Neumann, 2001; Roberts, 2015). For example, the health disciplines have been advocates of evidence-based practices for a long time (Burke et al., 2005; Ruzafa-Martínez, López-Iborra, Barranco, & Ramos-Morcillo, 2016; Shorten, Wallace, & Crookes, 2001).

However, the large number of advocates does not imply a firm body of knowledge on how to bring research into the curriculum. In a systematic review on research integration in curricula, only seven of 121 papers pertained to curriculum rationales of a single curriculum or as disciplinary guidelines (Griffioen, Groen, & Nak, 2019). Six of these seven focused on disciplinary guidelines (macro-level), and five of these were on medical education, anatomy and pharmacy or nursing. The only study on the micro-level of a single curriculum focused on educational research in PhD programmes. No studies related to the curriculum at the national or institutional level (meso-level). Hence, insight and knowledge on curriculum rationales are scarcer in peer-reviewed journals than, for instance, insight and knowledge on aims and objectives or learning activities, as these subjects yielded forty-six and forty-eight papers, respectively. This thin body of knowledge on curriculum rationales might be due to a lack of knowledge or to a lack of knowledge as written down in peer-reviewed and published papers.

Still, the curriculum and its rationale are the vehicles for clear choices that lead to students' transformation from student to professional and their learning on how to use different types of knowledge in different types of professional action. However, comparisons of the planned, enacted and experienced curriculum (Cao, Postareff, Lindblom-Ylanne, & Toom, 2021) are relevant in this respect because they do not necessarily pertain to the same professional knowledge and actions (Annala et al., 2021; Ashwin, 2014). The planned curriculum as written down in policy documents, study guides and course manuals can result in multiple enacted curricula, depending on the lecturers responsible for teaching parts of the curriculum. Yet, if lecturers collaborate intensively to ensure consistency or even if the same lecturer(s) teach all students, that does not mean all students' experiences of the curriculum are alike. Therefore, changes in the planned curriculum are not automatically followed by corresponding changes in the enacted curriculum, which in turn do not automatically coincide with changes in the experienced curriculum.

The Focus of Curriculum Rationales

One of the Amsterdam strategic programme's main ambitions were the changes in the curriculum layer across the university. Further, one of the presumptions was that relevant curriculum changes would be visible in the learning goals of curricula as reported in Chapter 6 as well as in the curriculum rationales. A shift in the role research plays in the educational programmes' purpose would become visible over time in written down curriculum rationales, in answers of educational teams on 'why' research is part of the curriculum, or at least in a change in the characteristics or presence of research in these rationales. As with all monitoring studies in the Amsterdam change programme, the intention was to intervene as little as possible in the daily processes of education, which resulted in using the educational programmes' periodic self-reports as data for its analysis. These self-reports are part of a periodic system of quality enhancement for higher education. Nationally, educational programmes in the Netherlands undergo a quality assessment every six years. Most universities apply a similar system internally after three years. Therefore, educational programmes write a self-report for this assessment every three years.

The general standard for applied educational programmes, the 'HBO standard' for bachelor's programmes in the Netherlands provides the overarching framework for programme-specific national profiles (HBO-raad, 2009). National committees agree upon the discipline-specific national profiles and serve to ensure the programmes' quality across institutions. The standard consists of four parts: intended learning outcomes, curriculum and learning context, assessment and achieved learning outcomes (Beoordelingskader accreditatiestelsel hoger onderwijs Nederland, 2018). A curriculum's rationale is mostly described as part of the first part, where the educational programme's focus and purpose are explained. This section was used in detail as data for this study, while the rest of the documents were scanned for relevant, additional content.

Self-reports generally come to life through teamwork, with the dual purpose of providing information for the quality-enhancement process, which also includes one or more site visits, and passing the six-year accreditation that is a prerogative for government funding. Additionally, there are the rationales and the programme objectives tuned annually as programme objectives in legally bounding education and assessment regulations. They are obviously tuned again during curriculum design and teacher–student learning interactions based on a backward design starting from programme objectives (Cao et al.). Thus, some difference can be expected between the written-down rationales and educational practice. Still, as ready-for-use documents, the self-reports are the most official information about changed curriculum rationales.

The self-reports of all Amsterdam UAS programmes were requested from the local Amsterdam UAS quality agency. For the period 2013–2015, prior to strategic programme Research into Education, fifty-nine self-reports were available and

Table 5.1 Overview of included self-reports in both time periods

Number of self-report documents per faculty and period		
Faculty	No. of docs in 1st period	No. of docs in 2nd period
Business and Economics	10	6
Sports and Nutrition	3	2
Digital Media and Creative Industries	7	4
Health	4	3
Applied Social Sciences and Law	7	5
Education	1	1
Technology	9	4
Teacher Education	18	17
Total	**59**	**42**

for 2016–2018 we received forty-two self-reports. In these documents quotes on the integration of research in education were selected and coded in Atlas.ti to signify which stakeholder was being served by the integration: professional practice, the educational programme, the student or some 'instrumental' stakeholder, such as the obligation to follow the HBO standard. Two researchers discussed the initial codebook and wrote a coding guide to ensure consistent coding. Quotes that the first coding researcher had doubts about were discussed until agreement on inclusion (or exclusion) and its code.

Categories of Research in Curriculum Rationales

The analysis of all documents in the two time frames showed a dominance of different stakeholders in how research is positioned in the curriculum's rationale. Where the educational programmes are set up to educate students as future professionals, our research question of 'with what purpose is research included in the curriculum?' was not always answered with the student as the most important or final receiving stakeholder. The four types of argumentation are explained briefly here and further depicted in the upcoming subsections.

The first type of argumentation on rationales is related to the stakeholder' professional practice. Educational programmes state that they integrate research into the curriculum to enable students to meet the demands from professional practice, or to improve the quality of professional practice in the end. The second argumentation focuses on the educational programme as a stakeholder. Integrating research into the curriculum in these educational programmes is assumed to improve educational quality, or research is used as a pedagogical instrument to teach different skills. The third type of stakeholder argument about the rationales is the student, where educational programmes state to incorporate research into the curriculum so that students acquire research skills or a research-minded attitude, or so that students can further develop professionally. Interestingly, the first student-oriented rationale focuses on the student while studying, where the second orients more towards the alumnus as professional and/or the professional field as a whole in which alumni are assimilated. The fourth type of argumentation is not related to a specific type of stakeholders, which could presume content as part of the argumentation; the arguments are more instrumental, in that they serve an obligation by including research in the curriculum. Rationales that are related to instrumental reasons often focused on accountability structures. Programmes note, for example, that they incorporate research into the curriculum because national guidelines for programmes mandate it, or that they include research because that is in line with university policy or faculty policy.

Changes in Curriculum Rationales over Time

In this section, the changes in curriculum rationales over time are considered. The educational programmes showed a different prominence of the four types of argumentations about research, and some changes were seen over time (Figure 5.1 provides an overview of percentages across two time points). In the first time period, of the fifty-nine programmes across seven faculties, thirty wrote down rationales of research in their curriculum serving professional practice, nineteen argued with a focus on their educational programme, twelve positioned research to serve the student and eight programmes presented instrumental reasons. Three programmes did not show any argumentation about research in their curriculum. These numbers were influenced by the dominance of eighteen teacher education programmes, which had a shared and similar rational on professional practice, added with argumentations with research as a didactical tool serving their educational programme, research serving their

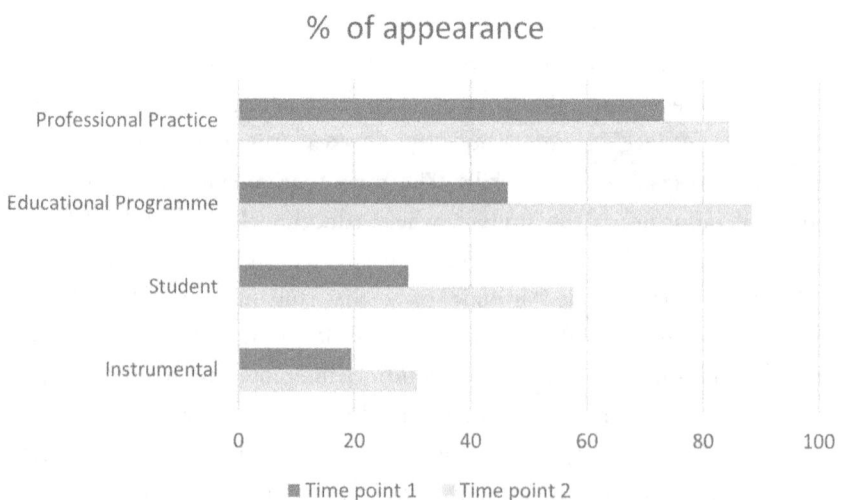

Figure 5.1 Percentage of appearance of the four types of argumentation on including research in the curricula.

students and no statements about instrumental reasons for including research into the curriculum.

In the second time point, of forty-two programmes, twenty-two had rationales on professional practice, twenty-three on the educational programme, fifteen on student and eight on instrumental. Now all forty-two programmes had rationales about research (for the difference between numbers of programmes, see Table 5.1). Because of their number, again a dominance of the teacher education programmes can be seen.

The findings showed that the strategic programme Research into Education was accompanied in time by an increase in curriculum rationales as formulated in self-report audit documents. Where the first time point showed a strong focus on professional practice, which was met in the second time point, this was then added with a thick focus on research in the curriculum to benefit the educational programme. Also an increase in the prevalence of the student as a stakeholder in the curriculum was found, and instrumental rationales showed the smallest increase.

Research in the Curriculum to Serve Professional Practice

When we consider the different rationales' content in the first period, the professional practice was the most prevalent stakeholder at Amsterdam UAS overall, and in six out of seven faculties, which emphasises the role of Amsterdam UAS in professional education. In four faculties, the number of quotes increased a few years later. Educational programmes at Amsterdam UAS mentioned different reasons for integrating research into the curriculum with regard to professional practice. Rationales in this category could be related to professional practice's demands. These demands in turn could be related to national frameworks such as professional profiles, as is apparent in the following quote: 'to ensure that future [structural business administrators] measure up to this profile, we prepare students for a career where research skills, technical craftsmanship, managerial skills, and an entrepreneurial attitude play an important role'. Additionally, the need for future professionals to use research skills is apparent in the rationale: 'our programme aims to teach sufficient knowledge and skills for new professionals to conduct fiscal research'. In several programmes, integrating research into the curriculum is related to evidence-based practices: 'starting from the first year, students are taught that professional action should be based on evidence based practice'. Rationales could also pertain to the quality of professional practice. Such rationales are related to students developing skills to improve practice, such as this example from the pedagogical programme:

> The current societal and political developments in the profession and field require an integrative competence. The pedagogical profession has become less defined and is characterised by an increase in flexibility and entrepreneurship. Creativity and authenticity are important parts of this. All those changes require an inquisitive and reflexive attitude. Additionally, the pedagogue must be able to use his knowledge and skill at different levels. He is like a spider in the web and can act, collaborate and respond to new situations from a multi-disciplinary approach (in multi-disciplinary teams).

The self-reports document the collaboration of programmes with representatives of their professional fields in higher vocational education on aligning the curriculum with professional practice.

Research in the Curriculum to Benefit the Educational Programme

The content of the rationales on education shows that in the first period, only the faculty of technology had the educational programme as the most prevalent stakeholder. In the second period, the focus on the educational programme was larger in the number of quotes than those with a focus on professional practice, overall and in four out of seven separate faculties. Rationales regarding the educational programme focused on incorporating research as a measure to increase the quality of the educational programme, such as in this example: 'The programme aims to further increase the graduate goals (in line with Centre of Expertise ambitions). In the past two years the programme has become more challenging, with an increased focus on research skills and quantitative methods'. Educational programmes could also use research as a pedagogical tool. In some instances, research was incorporated in the curriculum as a way to teach students different skills: 'They develop their research knowledge further by writing individual papers on an Asia- related subject and they learn how in various Asian societies, cultural approaches influence business negotiations and relations, and how to improve their own communications skills'; or to prepare students for their graduation assignments, 'Students work on practice-based research projects fitting their specialisation. Research-lecturers supervise students during these projects. This is a prelude to graduation, where students work independently on a practice-based research project'.

In the second time frame, across the university, the self-reports contained forty-two more quotes on research integration that benefited the educational programme, while seventeen fewer documents than in the first time frame were included. The findings also show that the rationales' content had changed; the 'why' of research integration was present more explicitly then, for example: 'Students use research to come to substantiated advice for method development' and 'The test of competence is a professional assignment, of which practical research is an important part motivated by a practical problem or a wish for improvement on the part of the external client. The research has a theoretical and practical component'. The prior focus on professional practice has become a dual focus with equal attention for the educational programme as a stakeholder in research integration.

Incorporating Research into the Curriculum for Students

The rationales' content serving students are complex, where many educational programmes argue about students in their rationales, but these argumentations are not usually related to 'research'. When educational programmes do integrate research to benefit students, they focus on research as a way for students to develop professionally, such as, 'in this context, conducting research and gaining research skills is one way to further professionalise lecturers' (teaching programme). Further, rationales for the student focus on them developing research skills or a critical research-minded attitude: 'We value the research skills of our students. [...] The first results of the research line are clearly visible. Current fourth-year students have developed research skills during every year of the educational programme and clearly benefit from this'.

In the second time frame, the student as a stakeholder to be benefited by research integration again was less prevalent than professional practice and the educational programme, but the faculty of health, the faculty of digital media and creative business, and the faculty of social sciences and law all showed an increase in student-focused rationales on research integration. The faculties of education and of sports and nutrition showed no change in the number of quotes on student rationales, but as described before, these faculties wrote down their rationales on research integration in separate documents instead of incorporating them in the audit documents. Two of the seven faculties showed a slight decrease in the number of quotes on student-focused rationales. The faculty of technology focused their self-reported research integration efforts on the stakeholders' educational programme and professional practice. Yet one of their programmes did not report on the student as a stakeholder in the first period, but in the second they wrote: 'Research and knowledge allow our alumni to suggest innovative logistic solutions'. The faculty of business and economics showed a slight decrease in student-focused rationales and only a slight increase in rationales pertaining to the other stakeholders.

Incorporating Research into the Curriculum for Instrumental Reasons

Rationales that are 'instrumental' generally lack content related to the educational programme. Instrumental rationales are focused on accountability towards external frameworks or standards. Programmes incorporate research in line with Dutch national frameworks for professional education, or because it is an Amsterdam UAS policy, but do not add any other content to their argumentation. For example, 'Research ability belongs to the [Amsterdam] UAS standard and is an important area of action for the [Amsterdam] UAS in its education and research agenda 2011–2014'. Note that in the Netherlands, the general 'HBO standard' for bachelor's programmes provides the overarching framework for programme-specific national profiles (which were coded as professional practice), and respectively, universities and educational programmes are expected to provide their own relevant content, also related to the positioning of research. Another example refers to how the programme responded to an external audit: 'With the curriculum review, research has also been given a recognisable place in the curriculum'. Overall, instrumental rationales showed the most modest increase in prevalence.

Disciplinary Differences in the Changes of Curriculum Rationales on Research

This section considers the differences in reasoning on research in the rationales in the different faculties of Amsterdam UAS. An overview of the seven faculties conveys that six of them showed increases pertaining to argumentations for research serving professional practice and instrumental argumentations. The faculty of sports and nutrition was the exception, with professional practice dropping from eleven to five quotes and instrumental from two to zero. The second time frame of the faculty of sports and nutrition was based on two documents, whereas the first was based on three documents. Similar to the faculty of education, for the faculty of sports and nutrition, the reflection documents did not address what happened at the faculty level with regard to rationales on research in education. In the second period, the reflection document of one of the two programmes that provided documents contained a description of the process of designing and implementing a dedicated research line throughout the bachelor's programme. This research line would replace some curriculum parts that were still embedded in the theoretical line at the time of writing the second document. This means that the change at the faculty level for sports and nutrition was not fully captured by the reflection documents as units of analysis.

The faculty of health stands out in the opposite direction, with an overall increase of twenty-one rationales on research in education. Their audit documents reported a strengthening of evidence-based practices in educational innovations throughout the faculty programmes, exemplified in the following quotes:

> In 2014, the educational programme concluded, after analysing the situation, that the developments in healthcare required a substantive reorientation. The potential of interweaving education, research, and patient care was insufficiently exploited and students were not optimally supported in their learning and development.
>
> The [Amsterdam] UAS and AMC worked closely together to develop 'Polyphysics', an academic workplace for the faculty and inter-professional care facilities. Here the health care professionals, lecturer-researchers, and students from the faculty of health work together on the care of rehabilitating patients (e.g. cardiac rehabilitation), linked to research and education (such as clinical lessons and clinometry).

A somewhat similar change in research rationales occurred with the faculty of technology. Just as the faculty of health, the faculty of technology already had a relatively strong emphasis on research compared to other vocational programmes. Professional practices in which research is incorporated could require educational programmes in which that research is incorporated, as exemplified by the quotes below.

> Research abilities are firmly incorporated in the curriculum: evidence based practice (EBP) is extensively discussed in the propaedeutic phase, EBP concepts

are made explicit and processing assignments are included in the learning path, in which students have to develop a professional product – such as a guideline, care path or course.

The goals of the assignment on board are: the student can demonstrate to solve nautical/technical problems systematically and methodically, the student demonstrates in the research to work responsible with the methodology and the student demonstrates that he or she is able to conduct research specifically related to that particular ship.

The most remarkable change occurred with the faculty of education; that faculty went from thirty-eight to thirteen quotes on research serving professional practice in the second period. The explanation is that in the second period, a faculty-wide vision on research in education had been written, covering the vision on and content and assessment of research in education. Sixteen self-report audit documents all referred to this document and no longer included recurring statements on research in education, as was the case in the first period. This new faculty-wide vision document is not part of the documents chosen for this study, but not mentioning it would suggest a decrease in attention for research rationales with the faculty of education while that is not an accurate description of what happened.

The faculties of digital media and creative industries, of applied social sciences and law and of business and economics show less prominent changes, although all three show an overall increase in quotes while fewer documents were available for analysis in the second period. In the faculty of digital media and creative industries, one programme first only stated to integrate research in 'the research project'. In the second period, a much more coherent statement was made on 'research in all years and types of learning activities' and now a strengthening of the relation with the faculty knowledge centre is mentioned. In the faculties of digital media and creative industries and of applied social sciences and law, it was primarily the educational programme, followed by the student as a stakeholder, on whose behalf the increases in quotes were made. In applied social sciences and law, one of the programmes extended 'Research skills help to further develop professional practice and contribute to reflective skills in daily professional action of the student' to

> Research helps students to develop an inquiring, curious, open attitude. They learn to zoom out from $N = 1$, individual client level, to think systematically, to

analyse, problematise, and to handle sources and information. This is necessary to execute the job as a whole. This allows the professional to firmly position himself and solidify his profession in a dynamic and complex society.

The faculty of business and economics already had relatively high numbers of quotes on professional practice and educational programme in the first period, and in the second period, three instrumental rationales for integrating research in education were added, but the overall distribution of quotes over the four stakeholders did not show major changes in this faculty. One of the programmes of business and economics states in the second self-report that, 'extra research classes were offered to students who had little research in their curriculum and to support them in writing their thesis'. The 'work-in-progress' aspect of research integration in this faculty is highlighted by a reflective quote: 'Students in year 1 and 2 still experience research as something that needs to be done (to be able to finish) instead of as a means to provide valid advice or process improvement'.

Returning to the curriculum perspectives, student-centred teaching can be, unsurprisingly, recognised in curriculum rationales on the student as stakeholder: 'As a result, the student develops the research capacity to develop concrete solutions for metropolitan societal issues and learns to reflect on his own actions'. Sometimes, the formulation is quite broad, such as: 'The practice-orientated education of the program is aimed at stimulating the curiosity of students from the first period'. The structure and instruments curriculum design perspective was recognisable in the rationales for the educational programme as stakeholder. For example, 'The curriculum works towards the graduation programme. Research (task competences, the regulatory cycle of our profile) is anchored in the project line from the second semester of the propaedeutic phase and students write a "thesis light" during their internship'.

The knowledge and content strand can be found across the four stakeholders. For professional practice:

> Expertise is still important. But cross-curricular competencies, such as research and reflective skills, problem-solving skills, critical thinking, (inter-disciplinary) collaboration and communication are becoming increasingly important in order to function in a future-oriented way. These competencies are also important for the productivity and innovation capacity of the construction industry. We, therefore, find it important that students gain experience with practice-oriented research and are able to critically evaluate, but also systematically examine

(developments in) professional practice. Their actions (professional attitude) must always be based on analyses. This gives depth to their craftsmanship, sharpens reflective and cognitive skills and enables students and graduates to contribute to innovations in professional practice.

For the educational programme:

That means that we are involved with our students, we are person-oriented and we are aware of our pedagogical and educational task. This involves an investigative attitude on several levels: towards one's own functioning, the development of the student and current developments in the professional field.

For the student:

The basic principle of the experiments is that a student can best develop in an environment in which education, research and the professional fieldwork together on challenges from practice. In this ideal learning environment, the student, teacher, researcher and professional work inter-disciplinary and have control over their own learning process.

Instrumental:

At Amsterdam University of Applied Sciences, more and more structural attention is being paid to knowledge development in and with practice. In the institutional plan of Amsterdam University of Applied Sciences, Amsterdam UAS formulates knowledge development in and with practice as an important spearhead. Research is stimulated through the lectorates, but also through new positions as a university researcher in training.

The growing attention for the educational programme as a stakeholder to be served by research integration matches the attention for the research–teaching nexus in the higher-education literature (see also: Hénard & Roseveare, 2012). The clearest finding is the increase in attention for the integration of research, given the higher numbers of quotes in the second time period in fewer documents. The quotes also show how the different stakeholders' interests sometimes are combined in single statements. For example, in the educational programme quote above, the students' interests are mentioned, and refers to the role of an investigative attitude in fulfilling the pedagogical and educational task. Of course, the self-reports provide a rather abstract overview of what is deemed important for the educational programme. The directions the curriculum rationales offer are explicated in learning outcomes or learning goals for the educational units at learning line, module, course and/or class levels.

Overall, the programmes do appear to see the possibilities opening up by viewing learning as active, social and contextual and more dynamic views on professionalism are being developed (Griffioen, 2019), thereby extending the dynamics of research in the curriculum.

To Conclude

The quantitative increase in numbers of quotes on research in education in programme self-reports and the development of documents dedicated solely to research in education in two faculties suggests the initiation of an institution wide shift towards assigning research a larger role in vocational education and professional practice. Several qualitative changes towards strengthening and nuancing research rationales appear visible, though relating them to other documents and shop-floor practices would be required to offer a full view on each programme rationale and the implementation in the curriculum.

What the changes in rationales on research–education connections in these self-reports offer is space for further changes at most of the multiple layers mentioned in Chapter 1: department level, in curricula or research programmes, in modules or research projects and in lessons or research products educational or research teams. As the changes in language in self-reports open up space for further discussion of the rationales for research in education, it helps change agents in educational and research teams to further develop these rationales and their follow-up in learning goals (Chapter 6) and shop floor practices. As more people discuss research–education connections and collaborate on designing and implementing them, a knowledge-base is built on what research–education connections serve agreed upon purposes, serving the students, professional practice, educational programme quality and/or national standards. The data described in this chapter indicate an awareness of and desire to work on purposeful research–education connections, as the change programme intended to do. As the number of change agents increased over the years (Chapters 1 and 2), space opened up for the next phases in the ADKAR model for change, the construction of knowledge and ability (Hiat, 2018).

Positioning research as a core aspect of professional practice as the Dutch government did requires professionals in education to reconsider their curriculum rationales and design in serving the changing professional practices

(Brew & Cahir, 2014; Van den Akker, 2003, 2010). Examples of other push towards reconsideration of rationales and of how higher education could or should serve its purpose can be read in Barnett (2009, 2012) and Young (2014). The acknowledgement of the complexity of the issues societies over the world face and of global issues could be argued to add complexity to the connection of different types of knowledge in curricula of bachelor programmes (Short, 2002). For example, beyond knowledge on citizenship, disciplinary knowledge, research knowledge and educational knowledge, professionals in education and the professionals they educate may need knowledge on transdisciplinary, complex collaboration. In line with the conceptualisation of research as a personal and possibly transformational journey (Brew, 2001), research can simultaneously be an individual and collective learning process. One step further, viewing learning through this particular research lens Brew offers, framing learning in a bachelor programme as researching one's possible purpose in life might be a useful perspective in considering research–education connections in curriculum rationales and development. Of course, this should be balanced with other relevant conceptualisations and types of research (that are part of the profession) and research–education connections. A growing number of researchers, educators and others involved is working on constructing knowledge on curriculum development and research–education connections (e.g. Anakin, Spronken-Smith, Healey, & Vajoczki, 2017; Bovill & Woolmer, 2018; Brew, 1999; Cao et al., 2021; Griffioen et al., 2019; Turner et al., 2020). As the efforts increase, we step by step gain a better understanding of creating transformational learning as envisioned in curriculum rationales.

References

Anakin, M., Spronken-Smith, R., Healey, M., & Vajoczki, S. (2017). The contextual nature of university-wide curriculum change. *International Journal for Academic Development, 23*(3), 206–18. doi:10.1080/1360144x.2017.1385464

Annala, J., Lindén, J., Mäkinen, M., & Henriksson, J. (2021). Understanding academic agency in curriculum change in higher education. *Teaching in Higher Education*, 1–18. doi:10.1080/13562517.2021.1881772

Annala, J., Mäkinen, M., Lindén, J., & Henriksson, J. (2020). Change and stability in academic agency in higher education curriculum reform. *Journal of Curriculum Studies*, 1–17. doi:10.1080/00220272.2020.1836261

Ashwin, P. (2014). Knowledge, curriculum and student understanding in higher education. *Higher Education, 67*(2), 123–6. doi:10.1007/s10734-014-9715-3

Ashwin, P., Abbas, A., & McLean, M. (2013). How do students' accounts of sociology change over the course of their undergraduate degrees? *Higher Education*, *67*(2), 219–34. doi:10.1007/s10734-013-9659-z

Barnett, R. (2009). Knowing and becoming in the higher education curriculum. *Studies in Higher Education*, *34*(4), 429–40. doi:10.1080/03075070902771978

Barnett, R. (2012). Learning for an unknown future. *Higher Education Research & Development*, *31*(1), 65–77. doi:10.1080/07294360.2012.642841

Barnett, R. (2018). *The ecological university: A feasible utopia*. New York: Routledge.

Beoordelingskader accreditatiestelsel hoger onderwijs Nederland. (2018). Retrieved from https://www.nvao.net/files/attachments/.89/Beoordelingskader_accreditatiestelsel_ hoger_onderwijs_Nederland_2018.pdf

Berndtson, E. (2013). Contradictions of the Bologna process: Academic excellence versus political obsessions. *European Political Science*, *12*(4), 440–7. doi:10.1057/ eps.2013.24

Bernstein, B. B. (2000). *Pedagogy, symbolic control, and identity: Theory, research, critique* (rev ed.). London: Rowman & Littlefield Publishers, Inc.

Biggs, J. (1996). Enhancing teaching through constructive alignment. *Higher Education*, *32*, 347–64.

Bovill, C., & Woolmer, C. (2018). How conceptualisations of curriculum in higher education influence student-staff co-creation in and of the curriculum. *Higher Education*, *78*(3), 407–22. doi:10.1007/s10734-018-0349-8

Branch, R. M. (2009). *Instructional design: The ADDIE approach*. New York: Springer-Verlag New York Inc.

Brew, A. (1999). Research and teaching: Changing relationships in a changing context. *Studies in Higher Education*, *24*(3), 291–301. doi:10.1080/03075079912331379905

Brew, A. (2001). Conceptions of research: A phenomenographic study. *Studies in Higher Education*, *26*(3), 271–85. doi:10.1080/03075070120076255

Brew, A., & Cahir, J. (2014). Achieving sustainability in learning and teaching initiatives. *International Journal for Academic Development*, *19*(4), 341–52. doi:10.1080/136014 4X.2013.848360

Burke, L. E., Schlenk, E. A., Sereika, S. M., Cohen, S. M., Happ, M. B., & Dorman, J. S. (2005). Developing research competence to support evidence-based practice. *Journal of Professional Nursing*, *21*(6), 358–63.

Cao, Y. L., Postareff, L., Lindblom-Ylanne, S., & Toom, A. (2021). A survey research on Finnish teacher educators' research-teaching integration and its relationship with their approaches to teaching. *European Journal of Teacher Education*. doi:10.1080/02 619768.2021.1900111

Cousin, G. (2008). Threshold concepts: Old wine in new bottles or new forms of transactional curriculum inquiry? In R. Land, J. H. F. Meyer, & J. Smith (Eds.), *Threshold concepts within the disciplines*. Rotterdam and Taipei: Sense Publishing.

Deng, Z. (2021). Powerful knowledge, transformations and Didaktik/curriculum thinking. *British Educational Research Journal*, *47*(6), 1652–74. doi:10.1002/berj.3748

Griffioen, D. M. E. (2019). Higher education's responsibility for balanced professionalism: Methodology beyond research. In Amsterdam University of Applied Sciences.

Griffioen, D. M. E. (2020). Differences in students' experiences of research involvement: Study years and disciplines compared. *Journal of Further and Higher Education*, 44(4), 454–66. doi:10.1080/0309877x.2019.1579894

Griffioen, D. M. E., Groen, A., & Nak, J. (2019). The integration of research in the higher education curriculum: A systematic review. *The Higher Education Journal of Learning and Teaching*, 10(1). doi:10.24384/vhs6-1j85

HBO-raad. (2009). *Kwaliteit als opdracht*. Retrieved from Den Haag: https://www.vereniginghogescholen.nl/system/knowledge_base/attachments/files/000/000/394/original/Kwaliteit_als_opdracht.pdf?1443430484

Hénard, F., & Roseveare, D. (2012). *Fostering quality teaching in higher education: Policies and practices*. Retrieved from https://learningavenue.fr/assets/pdf/QT%20policies%20and%20practices.pdf

Hessels, L. K., Lente, H. v., & Smits, R. (2009). In search of relevance, the changing contract between science and society. *Science and Public Policy*, 36(5). doi:10.3152/030234209X442034

Hiat, J. (2018). ADKAR change management overview.

Huizinga, T. (2014). *Developing curriculum design expertise through teacher design teams*. (PhD), University of Twente, Enschede.

James, D. (2013). Investigating the curriculum through assessment practice in higher education: The value of a 'learning cultures' approach. *Higher Education*, 67(2), 155–69. doi:10.1007/s10734-013-9652-6

Karseth, B., & Sivesind, K. (2010). Conceptualising curriculum knowledge within and beyond the national context. *European Journal of Education*, 45(1), 103–20.

Krause, K.-L. D. (2020). Vectors of change in higher education curricula. *Journal of Curriculum Studies*, 1–15. doi:10.1080/00220272.2020.1764627

Land, R., Rattray, J., & Vivian, P. (2014). Learning in the liminal space: A semiotic approach to threshold concepts. *Higher Education*, 67(2), 199–217. doi:10.1007/s10734-013-9705-x

Leisyte, L., Enders, J., & de Boer, H. (2009). The balance between teaching and research in Dutch and English universities in the context of university governance reforms. *Higher Education*, 58(5), 619–35. doi:10.1007/s10734-009-9213-1

Lepori, B. (2007). Research in non-university higher education institutions. The case of the Swiss Universities of Applied Sciences. *Higher Education*, 56(1), 45–58. doi:10.1007/s10734-007-9088-y

Lotz-Sisitka, H., Wals, A. E. J., Kronlid, D., & McGarry, D. (2015). Transformative, transgressive social learning: Rethinking higher education pedagogy in times of systemic global dysfunction. *Current Opinion in Environmental Sustainability*, 16, 73–80. doi:10.1016/j.cosust.2015.07.018

Luckett, K., & Hunma, A. (2013). Making gazes explicit: Facilitating epistemic access in the humanities. *Higher Education*, 67(2), 183–98. doi:10.1007/s10734-013-9651-7

Maton, K. (2010). Progress and canons in the arts and humanities: Knowers and gazes. In K. Maton & R. Moore (Eds.), *Social realism, knowledge and the sociology of education: Coalitions of the mind* (pp. 154–78). London: Continuum.

Maton, K. (2013). *Knowledge and knowers: Towards a realist sociology of education.* London: Routledge.

Neumann, R. (2001). Disciplinary differences and university teaching. *Studies in Higher Education, 26*(2), 135–46. doi:10.1080/03075070120052071

Paxton, M., & Frith, V. (2013). Implications of academic literacies research for knowledge making and curriculum design. *Higher Education, 67*(2), 171–82. doi:10.1007/s10734-013-9675-z

Roberts, P. (2015). Higher education curriculum orientations and the implications for institutional curriculum change. *Teaching in Higher Education, 20*(5), 542–55. doi:10.1080/13562517.2015.1036731

Robertson, J., & Bond, C. (2005). The research/teaching relation: A view from the edge. *Higher Education, 50*(3), 509–35. doi:10.1007/s10734-004-6365-x

Ruzafa-Martínez, M., López-Iborra, L., Barranco, D. A., & Ramos-Morcillo, A. J. (2016). Effectiveness of an evidence-based practice (EBP) course on the EBP competence of undergraduate nursing students: A quasi-experimental study. *Nurse Education Today, 38*, 82–7.

Schimank, U., & Winnes, M. (2000). Beyond Humboldt? The relationship between teaching and research in European university systems. *Science and Public Policy, 27*(6), 397–408.

Scott, D. (2014). Knowledge and the curriculum. *The Curriculum Journal, 25*(1), 14–28. doi:10.1080/09585176.2013.876367

Short, E. C. (2002). Knowledge and the educative functions of a university: Designing the curriculum of higher education. *Journal of Curriculum Studies, 34*(2), 139–48. doi:10.1080/00220270110069181

Shorten, A., Wallace, C., & Crookes, P. A. (2001). Developing information literacy: A key to evidence-based nursing. *International Nursing Review, 48*(2), 86–92.

Shulman, L. S. (1986). Those who understand: Knowledge growth in teaching. *Educational Researcher, 15*(2), 4–14. doi:10.3102/0013189x015002004

Tam, M. (2014). Outcomes-based approach to quality assessment and curriculum improvement in higher education. *Quality Assurance in Education, 22*(2), 158–68. doi:10.1108/qae-09-2011-0059

te Pas, S. (2019). Career paths in teaching Thematic Peer Group Report. In T. Zhang (Ed.), *Learning and Teaching paper #2*: European University Association. Brussels: European University Association.

Turner, N. K., Healey, M., & Bens, S. (2020). Developing the curriculum within an institution using a Change Academy approach: A process focus. *International Journal for Academic Development, 26*(2), 150–62. doi:10.1080/1360144x.2020.1840988

Van den Akker, J. (2003). Curriculum perspectives: An introduction. In J. Van den Akker, W. Kuiper, & U. Hameyer (Eds.), *Curriculum landscapes and trends* (pp. 1–10). Dordrecht: Kluwer Academic Publishers.

Van den Akker, J. (2010). Building bridges: How research may improve curriculum policies and classroom practices. In S. M. Stoney (Ed.), *CIDREE, Consortium of Institutions for Development and Research in Education in Europe*, (pp. 175–95). Amersfoort.

Van den Akker, J. (2013). Curricular development research as a specimen of educational design research - Part A: An introduction. In T. Plomp & N. Nieveen (Eds.), *Educational design research* (pp. 52–71). Enschede: SLO.

Van Merriënboer, J. J. G. (2019). *The four-component instructional design model: An overview of its main design principles*. Retrieved from Maastricht: https://www.4cid.org/publications/

Wiggins, G., & McTighe, J. (1998). *Understanding by design*. New Jersey: Merrill Prentice Hall.

Wiliam, D. (2013). *Principled curriculum design. In redesigning schooling* (Vol. 3) London: SSAT (The Schools Network) Ltd.

Witte, J., Van der Wende, M., & Huisman, J. (2008). Blurring boundaries: How the Bologna process changes the relationship between university and non-university higher education in Germany, the Netherlands and France. *Studies in Higher Education, 33*(3), 217–31. doi:10.1080/03075070802049129

Young, M. (2014). What is a curriculum and what can it do? *The Curriculum Journal, 25*(1), 7–13. doi:10.1080/09585176.2014.902526

6

Changes in Curriculum Learning Goals

Linda van Ooijen-van der Linden, Natalie Pareja Roblin,
Jason Nak, Iris Jong and Didi M. E. Griffioen

The Curriculum and Research–Teaching Nexus

Higher-education institutions are challenged to prepare 'future-proof' professionals who think critically, solve complex problems and adapt to a rapidly changing society (Griffioen, Ashwin, & Scholkmann, 2021; van Laar, van Deursen, van Dijk, & de Haan, 2017). These demands have led them to increasingly see research and inquiry as key in students' development (Brew, 2010; Brew & Mantai, 2017). As a consequence, universities worldwide are making growing efforts to strengthen the integration of research and teaching in undergraduate programs (Brew & Mantai, 2017; Healey, 2005a).

Research plays a fundamental role in student learning within higher education (Jenkins, Healey, & Zetter, 2007) because it can positively impact the quality of teaching (Taylor & Canfield, 2007) and students' opportunities to develop research competences (Ruzafa-Martínez, López-Iborra, Barranco, & Ramos-Morcillo, 2016). Currently, most educational programs attempt to enhance the connection between teaching and research in the curriculum; however, there is little empirical ground to guide such efforts (cf. Griffioen, Groen, & Nak, 2019). In turn, policymakers and curriculum developers are left in the dark about how such integration effectively can be realised. Particularly for curriculum developers in higher vocational education, integrating research into the curriculum is a relatively new endeavour. Research has only become part of European higher vocational curricula after the Bologna Declaration in 1999 (Griffioen & de Jong, 2015; Huisman, 2008).

The curriculum defines what should be taught and how (Barnett, 2009), thus outlining the extent to which research plays a role in students' education and the various ways in which this role is shaped. The integration of research into higher education curricula has received much attention since the introduction of research in applied universities at the start of this century. Higher-education institutes are expected to prepare students for their place in the knowledge society, entailing a need for students to develop competences such as critical thinking, complex problem solving, and the ability to adapt to a rapidly changing society (Brew & Mantai, 2017). Such ambitions have led study programmes worldwide to further strengthen the development of research competences in alumni through their curricula (Brew & Mantai, 2017; Healey, 2005b) as well as to apply research as a didactical tool.

Scholars have proposed various conceptualisations of the research–teaching nexus in relation to the curriculum, although its diversity also resulted in an experienced lack of straightforward definition (Tight, 2016). For example, Brew (1999) stressed that the plurality of the existing complex relationship between teaching and research is dynamic and context driven, as notions of knowledge, research and teaching change over time. She distinguished four conceptions of research among academics' conceptions (Brew, 2001): 'domino', with research as a linear process of 'building block' elements; 'layer', with research as about discovering, uncovering or creating underlying mechanisms, based on data containing ideas and hidden ideas; 'trading', with research focused on trading products, relationships and personal recognition; and 'journey' in which research is a personal journey of discovery that might lead to personal transformation. While the differences between disciplines were expected, Brew did not find an overrepresentation of certain disciplines in particular conceptions. She stated: 'This is consistent with the view expressed earlier that discipline is only one factor influencing the ways research is experienced', which implies that more factors than the discipline likely influences the integration of research in the curriculum (Brew, 2001, p. 284).

A second perspective can be found in Healey's conceptual model of the types of research in education (Healey, 2005a). In this model, four types of research integration on two axes are distinguished, representing the students' involvement as participants or audience on the one hand, and the emphasis on research content versus research processes and problems on the other. The four approaches are often applied as design tools, starting from the presumption that a balanced application of all four approaches presents the student with the best possible benefits from research integration.

A third example intends to reach beyond the divide between research and education. As part of this approach, Annala and Mäkinen (2011) suggest a set of criteria promoting ideal research–teaching integration in the curriculum, as based on interviews with lecturers and students of a research-intensive university. Criteria include using real research projects with partnerships between students, societal stakeholders and faculty staff; space for a diversity of growth in academic expertise; and the integration of labour market expectations without losing sight of the academic research–teaching nexus and curricular ideals. Such an integrated curriculum of research and education would facilitate 'progress in students' inclination, attitude, and commitment to disciplinary wonder' (p. 16).

In addition to a lack of conceptual clarity, research integration in the curriculum also generally lacks a thorough empirical foundation (Griffioen et al., 2019; Verburgh, Schouteden, & Elen, 2012). In their systematic literature review, Griffioen et al. (2019) provide an overview of the body of knowledge on research in the curriculum by categorising the included papers according to the ten curriculum aspects of Van den Akker's (2003) curricular design model, ranging to its rationale (why are they learning?), its aims and objectives (towards which goals are they learning?), to its content (what are they learning?) and grouping (with whom are they learning?). Empirical evidence on research in the curriculum showed to be limited and mainly focused on aims and objectives and on learning activities, while foremost based on single, descriptive case studies. The authors conclude there is a lack of experimental data on the effects of curriculum design and intended learning goals. The highly needed empirical insight into the way research can be integrated with higher education curricula, and ideally in the effects on student learning, is crucial in informing efforts to rightfully design this integration.

This chapter aids in regard to the first. To be able to envision the integration of research in the curriculum and to formulate the necessary steps towards facilitating it, this chapter focuses on research related to learning goals in bachelor's curricula. Therefore, relevant frameworks are described, followed by empirical findings from different perspectives. Adding to this body of knowledge, an extensive case study focused on the integration of research in all bachelor's curricula of Amsterdam UAS at two points in time is reported. By examining changes in research-related learning goals as described in the intended curricula of bachelor's programmes, a comprehensive picture is painted of the integration of research across disciplines. The closing section discusses changes in the curriculum layer and the role of research in monitoring change.

Integration of Research and Teaching in Higher-Education Curricula

The integration of research and teaching can take many forms, and in turn, approaches to studying such integration also vary widely, as was also shown in the previous chapters. In this section, we specifically discuss the various possible perspectives to studying the integration of research in higher education curricula into curricula as intended (Van den Akker, 2003).

Combined, empirical studies about research integration at the curriculum level generally focus on four perspectives: perceptions of research, development of research skills, amount of research-related activities in the curriculum and the purpose of research in the curriculum as a means to solve societal issues. The first and most frequently used perspective is the teachers' and students' perceptions related to research in the curriculum. Several previous studies on the integration of research in the curriculum have examined the teachers' and/or students' perceptions (Brew & Mantai, 2017; Griffioen, 2020; Vereijken, van der Rijst, van Driel, & Dekker, 2018), often through methods of semi-structured interviews (Brew & Mantai, 2017) or questionnaires (Griffioen, 2020; Hu, van der Rijst, van Veen, & Verloop, 2014, 2015; Vereijken et al., 2018; Visser-Wijnveen, van der Rijst, & van Driel, 2015). These mostly target the challenges and barriers to implementing research in courses as the lecturers perceive them (Brew & Mantai, 2017) or students' perceptions on integrating research (Griffioen, 2020; Vereijken et al., 2018). The findings indicate that students' perceptions of current research in teaching correlate with their motivation for research in general (Vereijken et al., 2018), with teachers' beliefs about the ideal role of research in education exceeding actual teaching practices (Hu et al., 2014, 2015) and with how the types of research involvement differ depending on the study year (Griffioen, 2020). Furthermore, studies indicate that how lecturers perceive their own roles can influence the way they integrate research into their education. For example, five profiles for the research–teaching nexus arose from interviews among humanities lecturers, ranging from the teacher as the content-expert to the teacher as a research motivator for students, the teacher as a research role model, as a tutor and provider of research projects and the teacher as collaborating with students in the ongoing research (Visser-Wijnveen, Van Driel, Van der Rijst, Verloop, & Visser, 2010).

Different conceptions with different emphasises on knowledge, acquiring skills, or becoming a scholar can lead to different integrations of research in education, varying from individual uncoordinated skills development for students to integration into the scholarly community, each with different opportunities for further development (Brew & Mantai, 2017). Yet, in both the previous curriculum and the changed curriculum of medical education, students' beliefs about the relevance of research for practice and learning did not change over the course of three bachelor's programme years, though their participation in and motivation for research, perceptions of critical reflection on research findings and familiarity with staff research increased after the change (Vereijken, Van der Rijst, Van Driel, & Dekker, 2020). These findings in perception-based studies illustrate the experiences with research integration of the teachers and/or students directly involved, which limits their scope to the range of the experiences that the questionnaire or interview questions elicited.

 A second perspective of empirical research focuses on teaching the necessary research skills and the related intended and actual learning outcomes. For example, the pattern of research skill development in science graduate students was investigated by analysing written research proposals to evaluate changes in quality over the course of an academic year (Timmerman, Feldon, Maher, Strickland, & Gilmore, 2013). Another example is the narrative account of three teacher educators teaching research methods using a dialogic pedagogy to tailor their instruction to their students' needs in support of them achieving the learning goals (Baxan, Pattison-Meek, & Campbell, 2020). Case study approaches such as these effectively illustrate the gradual development of certain research competences, such as using primary literature or data analysis, across time. However, it does not provide insight into the integration of research across settings or competences at large.

 A third perspective of empirical research considers the balance between research and professional practice in full educational programmes. In this perspective, Baan, Gaikhorst, and Volman (2019) investigated the attitudes towards research as a reflection of its integration in the curricula of one academic and four professional teacher education programmes via a curriculum analysis, survey and interviews. Both types of programmes had integration, but the academic programme addressed more forms of research in a more consistent way and their students were more research-minded. Magnell and Geschwind (2019) used a similar approach and combined labelling activities in the syllabi with staff interviews in an engineering programme. This approach provided a broad insight into the integration of research because the data from the curriculum analysis and the interviews were paired. The purpose was to challenge the perceived incompatibility between research activities and professional practice activities in the curriculum, showing that engineering education in that specific programme could very well host a seamless integration of research and professional practice (Magnell & Geschwind, 2019). Again, both studies analysed only one department of education, thus providing only context-rich conclusions. One exception to the case study approach found was the Verburgh et al. (2012) study in which they investigated forty-five full bachelor's and master's programmes in Flanders. The findings showed a distinction between three types of educational programmes, based on how much attention research had in all of the curriculum's courses: low-research attention type (47 per cent), in which research related learning goals do not seem to be part of the programme main objectives; result-oriented type (35 per cent), in which acquiring knowledge of research is the most important research-related learning goal, though critical thinking, practical research skills and the competence to become a researcher are also mentioned; and critical thinking type (18 per cent), in which there is distinct attention for critical thinking learning goals, complemented by learning goals on practical research skills and developing students to become researchers. No disciplinary differences that would fit Biglan's (1973) categorisation were found between the three types.

A fourth empirical perspective takes a macro approach to investigate how the integration of research at the programme level may contribute to attaining broader societal issues. This was done, for example, through studying the exploration of the interrelation between competences for research and sustainable development in which earlier defined research competences at Leuven University College were related to a framework of competences for sustainable development (Lambrechts & Van Petegem, 2016). Conclusions focused on the relationship between research competences and the competence to handle sustainable development issues. Another example (Pallant, Choate, & Haywood, 2020) is Allegheny College where the Environmental Science and Sustainability Department educates students to solve real-world environmental problems. Throughout the curriculum, students think through, analyse, research and apply components of all seventeen sustainable development goals to local through global challenges, in a core set of scaffolding courses with the flexibility for specialised focus and depth of understanding about topics of student interest. The authors do note that to allow students to solve sustainability problems, the connectivity between the different sustainable development goals and past context, historical events and contemporary opportunities for application requires being explicitly stated and clarified. Pluim, Nazir, and Wallace (2021) stress the diversity in what they call the environmental perspective on education, around a core focus of teaching students to think of the Earth more as a series of interdependent systems of which humans are only one part, compared to the previous more anthropocentric ways of thinking.

While the four empirical perspectives provide distinct viewpoints on integrating research and teaching in the curriculum, what is absent is a focus on a more generic design, or design characteristics that reach beyond individual case studies. By considering research-related learning goals across multiple bachelor's programs, this study aims to at least provide insight on how research in the curriculum changes over time. Future research should focus additionally on these goals' specific designs, as well as their effects in the learning of students as members of society.

Disciplinary Differences

Disciplinary differences are a prominent focus of research–teaching nexus studies, although they hardly connect to the curriculum-level design of this connection. Again, there are different perspectives that, when combined, paint a diffuse picture of the disciplines' influence on the types of research integration.

Some studies did find differences between disciplines, but they focus on very different elements of research–education connections. Gros et al. (2020) studied the students' perceptions on research competences and found that they differed from managing knowledge sources in the Law Department, to a focus on problem-solving skills and teamwork in the Medicine and Engineering departments, while the History Department mainly was unclear about research competences. These findings relate to Healey's (2005b) views that hard sciences focus on building practical skills in a more participatory way; he added that this was also done later in the curriculum than in, for instance, the soft sciences. However, Griffioen (2020) contradicted these notions with the students' experiences across different disciplines in a vocational higher education institution. In this vocational setting, all faculties offered programmes in applied sciences, and a distinction between life (e.g. physical therapy) and non-life (e.g. architecture) programmes appeared prominent. The life faculties showed a trend known from the hard sciences: greater active involvement in research of senior students compared to junior students, also in soft-life studies. The non-life faculties showed similar student involvement across all years. By turning from perceptions to written descriptions of intended curricula, Verburgh et al. (2012) found no clear difference in the prevalence of research-related learning in the soft sciences compared to hard sciences, which they assigned to an overrepresentation of vocational bachelors, who generally are more interdisciplinary in nature. Combined, these studies provide no clear indications of disciplinary differences, leaving curriculum designers on their own accord. The empirical study in this chapter aims to contribute to this disciplinary insight at the curriculum level.

An Instrument to Investigate Change in Research-Related Learning Goals

The empirical study in this chapter aims to bridge the gap between highly focused empirical studies and zoomed out (philosophical) ideas by investigating research integration on a more comprehensive level: written down learning goals in intended curricula. Learning goals provide a clear statement of what outcomes are expected from students as a result of the intended learning experiences in a course over a specific time period. Following Harden (2002), learning goals function for both students and teachers as an effective language to communicate matters of the course curriculum, for sharing appropriate resources and in facilitating a learning environment. Learning goals can be used to map the knowledge and skills intended for students to acquire. In turn, efforts to integrate research competences in higher education can be reflected in the learning goals. By analysing all undergraduate courses of a full university, this study provides a comprehensive image of the intended development of research competences across disciplines in a single university.

One of the issues in monitoring the change process in the university was whether research-related learning goals in the curricula had changed. If such a change occurred, it would be indicative of the shifting views and aims of curriculum developers in the university. Change was expected in the form of increasing or decreasing prevalence of research-related learning goals as a result of developers' shifting attention to and trust in research. Alternatively, a change could be expected in how the content of the learning goals may change, for instance, when increased attention may present itself not only in the increased addressing of research in the curriculum, but also through more in-depth attention to specific steps and skills of doing research. Therefore, the focus of university change in this study is at the level of the research-related learning goals' prevalence as well as their content. Additionally, whether disciplinary differences were found between the different faculties is reported.

Sample and Measurement Instrument

To provide insight into changed prevalence and content as such and between disciplines, nearly 7,000 publicly available study guide texts were collected from the Amsterdam UAS website, from the start year and final year of the strategic programme period (2015–2020). Every study guide text contained information about a single course including its intended learning goals. The research-related learning goals were systematically categorised using an adapted version of the taxonomy Verburgh et al. (2012) developed to adequately consider the change in the position of research in multiple curricula across different faculties. Based on several rounds of coding, the descriptions of the types of research-related learning goals were somewhat broadened to better capture the formulations on research in the Amsterdam UAS learning goals, resulting in the hereafter described six types of research-related learning goals:

Knowledge. Learning goals in this element pertain to integrating research knowledge into the curriculum. The purpose is to acquaint students with research results within their discipline so that they can apply this knowledge in their own professional practice.

Methodology. This goal relates to developing students' understanding of the research process and of how knowledge is produced in the discipline. It has to do with acquiring knowledge about the foundations of research and not learning about the methodology per se. For example, a teacher can aim to develop an understanding of the method's theoretical underpinnings or the impact of it on the results without aiming at learning to apply a research method and interpret the results gained with it.

Instrumental skills. This goal relates to developing instrumental research skills, such as formulating a research question, finding relevant research literature, collecting and analysing data, working with research instruments, formulating a conclusion, and reporting findings.

Critical thinking. This goal relates to developing students' critical attitude towards their professional practice as well as towards information, knowledge and knowledge construction in their discipline. It can be defined as the kind of purposeful, reasoned and goal-directed thinking that an individual needs to solve problems, make decisions, formulate inferences and calculate likelihoods.

Curiosity. This goal pertains to creating willingness and/or interest in students to follow future developments in the field as well as to explore what is still unknown and how the field can evolve.

Research competences. This goal encompasses the previous ones, but enjoins with the long-term value of 'developing researcher-minded attitudes'. The competence to become a researcher implies an 'integrated set of skills, attitudes and knowledge needed to set-up and conduct research' (Elen & Verburgh, 2008, p. 58). As such, it encompasses the ability to engage in all the steps of scientific inquiry (i.e. formulate a problem, find relevant literature, collect and analyse data and formulate a conclusion), and to integrate these steps into a complete research cycle. If separate bullet points mention independent research steps without integration, these are regarded as instrumental skills.

Analysis of Prevalence of Research-Related Learning Goals in Curricula

To assess the prevalence of research-related learning goals, each modular study guide was scored 0, 1 or 2 for each single learning goal of the taxonomy. The goals in every guide received a 'not present' if that goal was not apparent, an 'implicit' (1) if the text only hinted towards the learning goals/element or a 'present' (2) if a research-related learning goal was explicitly stated. This meant that each study guide text received six separate scores representing the learning goals. Additionally, if the guide had no learning goals section whatsoever or the course did not have a study guide available, it received a 'no info' for all goals.

Every study guide was additionally assigned a weighting according to the amount of credits assigned to the course. In the Dutch system, a nominal student receives 60 credits per college year. These weightings per study guide text were reduced relatively if the course was an elective or part of an optional learning trajectory (for instance if there were three courses of 2 credits each to choose from, each course weighted credits were 2/3). The cumulated combination of presence scores and relative weighted resulted in a score for the presence of each learning goal per each faculty at the start as well as at the end of the strategic programme. This percentage was calculated for each of the six goals from the taxonomy and for each possible coding (not present, implicit, present or no info). This outcome is the unit of data used in this study for assessing prevalence.

Analysis of the Content

To assess the content of the research-related learning goals in the curriculum, all quotes from the guides that received an implicit or present score were collected and their content was summarised for all faculties prior to and after the strategic programme.

One of the important issues in monitoring the change process in the university was whether the learning goals of the bachelor's curricula changed. This followed from the chosen content and mechanism of change as explained in Chapters 1 and 2. If a change in learning goals would occur, it would be an important indication that the focus of the bachelor's programmes, and therefore the students' education, changed (enacted and experienced) as well. Possible changes would be an increase of learning goals related to research as well as a shift in the type of learning goals or even a reduction of research-related learning goals. Additionally, there was the question of whether the prevalence in research-related learning goals would differ between the different disciplinary fields. Further, differences in directions of change in prevalence would be possible.

Finding Change in Research-Related Learning Goals across the University

The findings are presented from quantitative to qualitative: First, the prevalence of the learning goals in both time periods at the institutional level is described, followed by changes in the learning goals' content.

Overall Changes in Learning Goal Prevalence over Time

An overview of learning goal prevalence across all seven faculties shows knowledge, instrumental skills and research competence as the most frequent research-related learning goals for all programmes. Next in terms of prevalence were critical thinking and methodology. Lastly, curiosity received the lowest amount of attention in all programmes of the first period. The prevalence of the six types of research-related learning goals in courses as percentages of the faculty study credits containing these goals ranged from zero to twelve. Overall, these numbers illustrate that research-related learning goals are not numerously present. Furthermore, it illustrates the variation of the overall percentages of research-related learning goals between the separate programmes in the first period.

In the second period, knowledge, instrumental skills and research competences again had the highest prevalence across all faculties, with either Instrumental skills or knowledge as the highest prevalence in different faculties. The prevalence of the six types of research-related learning goals in courses as percentages of the faculty study credits containing these goals then ranged from three to sixteen. Overall, the study guide texts show a slight increase in research-related learning goals. The knowledge goals category is the only type with a clear increase in prevalence. Critical thinking, methodology and curiosity were three to four times less frequent than knowledge, instrumental skills and research competences, albeit with some slight variation between the different programmes.

In this quantitative comparison, hardly anything appears to have changed over the years, except for an increase in research knowledge being integrated in the curriculum of more programmes than before. Both periods show a similar pattern of prevalence for six research-related learning goals. At this level of data aggregation, the changes over time are small.

Overall Changes in Learning Goal Content

Changes over time do appear clearer when zooming in on the separate learning goals' content.

Knowledge Goals. Learning goals focused on knowledge serve to acquaint students with theories and research results in their disciplinary field. Reading papers and manuals to learn about recent and relevant scientific research and theories are the most common means to this end, for example, to 'make students aware of the most important psychological theories related to choice behaviour' in a social programme, or to 'receive a broad orientation of concepts and theories in the field of industrial automation' in a technical programme.

This rather passive type of knowledge is sometimes complemented by learning goals on more active types of knowledge, such as applying it in professional practice. The faculty of health heavily focuses on this in both time points, while the technical faculty only did so in the second period, thus moving from teaching research results to having students incorporate them into practice. This application is well exemplified in the medical fields where evidence based practice (EBP) is held in high regard. This means that students are stimulated to continuously search for and incorporate recent findings in their own practices. For instance, in one health programme, students are expected to 'integrate evidence into clinical reasoning'.

Additionally, the faculty of education shows a pattern in which both the focuses of passive knowledge (knowing) and active knowledge (application, doing) are more clearly divided across learning goals. This division follows the set-up of the educational programmes in this faculty, which include the duality of learning to teach and to teach in different fields (e.g. biology, chemistry). Pedagogical knowledge goals usually include applying knowledge ('apply the most relevant theories in pedagogical practice examples'), whereas the subject field-specific knowledge goals are more passive ('read and understand popular scientific articles regarding modern physics research').

Furthermore, where the faculty of health already had a strong focus on EBP in the first period and their research-related learning goals did not show a shift in content in the second, the other faculties showed a change in formulating learning goals, from being very generically formulated learning to more detailed formulations, including specific scientific sources or techniques to use and to what purpose or how to use them.

Methodology Goals. The second goal pertained to acquainting students with the research process. Overall, the content of this goal was concerned mostly with teaching students how to prepare their own research by selecting methods and knowing the different steps in the research process, for instance, 'to understand the process of quantitative analysis'. Overall, this goal was focused on research in general instead of the more field-specific approach that can be found in some other learning goals. An exception was seen in the health faculty where goal formulations were usually related to EBP: '[the student knows] the five steps of evidence based practice'. Other than the faculty of business and economy, which slightly moved towards a stronger focus on being able to explain choices made in research, no meaningful change across time appeared on this learning goal.

Goals for Instrumental Skills. This goal had the largest overall prevalence within the Amsterdam UAS curricula and showed a great diversity of content. In the technical faculty, preparing research was the main focus in both time periods, such as for experiment design, proposal writing or performing aspects or tasks of preparatory research. The faculty of health also positioned research-related instrumental skills as a preparatory tool, in this case for patient care, for instance, 'Identifying uncertainties in a case, regarding cause, diagnosis, therapy and prognosis' or more specifically: 'taking anamneses and identifying relevant items'. This faculty showed a decrease in diversity of content from the first to the second period where mostly 'preparing research questions' was posed. For the faculty of applied social sciences and law, a shift was seen from more 'in-research' skills, such as statistical analysis in the first period; to more preparatory skills, such as devising research questions in the second. The faculty of sports and nutrition combined profession-specific types of research, 'students are introduced to the techniques of ice skating and learn to observe and analyse these techniques and be able to give improvements for a skater's technique' with more generic research skills, such as 'performs a QDA tasting test, imports data into SPSS or Excel, and runs the analyses'. Lastly, for the faculty of education, again a division between overarching pedagogical skills, such as investigating behaviour in the classroom, and more specific skills, such as preparing microbiological experiments for in-class teaching, were found.

Overall, a slight shift was shown from a somewhat narrow focus on detailed and specific steps of research within a research cycle to somewhat zooming out by adding the proposed steps' context or purpose.

Critical Thought and Curiosity. These goals were least prevalent in the course descriptions. Critical thought mostly related to being able to weigh the value and relevance of literature and the professional practice. In only a few descriptions, the general attitude of 'being a critical thinker' was mentioned. Curiosity overall was the least prevalent of all the goals, but had a spike in the medical school in the second period, due to a single quote being systematically reused throughout the nursing programme, namely, 'the nurse works from an ever-present investigative attitude, leading to reflection, evidence based practice and innovation of professional practice', which raises questions about its depth of content.

The lesser prevalence of critical thought and curiosity may be due to the fact that they – especially curiosity – are hard(er) to pin down and create objective examination tools for; therefore, making it preferable not to mention them as an effect of the system for quality enhancement. This does not mean these goals were not strived for in class, rather the document data simply does not provide insight into teaching–learning interactions, but they were not so much discerned in the formal course guides. The content of goals on curiosity and critical thought did not appear to change across time.

Research Competence. Lastly, the more encompassing research competence goal was prevalent across all faculties and usually pertained to students doing their own research by going through all the empirical cycle's steps in some form. The most fitting quotes would list explicitly the entire process of research the students did and made for valuable information, such as 'applying the empirical cycle; formulating problems and goals embed in literature; make a research design; methodically gather data; data-processing; draw conclusions and present'. However, this learning goal also included the vaguest descriptions, but still indicating a full research process, such as 'going through the steps of research' or 'doing research in the field'. In almost all cases, the quotes focused on field research such as organisational research in the business programmes or 'doing research in the school' in the educational programmes. No overall meaningful changes over time emerged.

Faculty-Level Changes

Zooming in further on research-related learning goals within the faculties reveals prevalence patterns that differ from the overall prevalence because the differences include increases as well as decreases of prevalence in the second period. In some instances, these descriptions require simultaneous consideration of the content of the different learning goals to be able to interpret what happened. Some, but not all, changes in prevalence appear to be related to a shift in content. The apparent coincidences of these changes in prevalence and content of research-related learning goals are illustrated with quotes from the study guide texts.

Faculty of Education

With curiosity as the exception (rise from 0 per cent to 1 per cent), all research-related learning goals in the faculty of education dropped in prevalence from the first time period to the second. As previously explained, the findings show that the faculty of education makes a clear distinction between a similar core educational curriculum all teacher education programmes shared and their subject-specific parts of curriculum, such as biology or geography. This distinction is especially evident in the knowledge learning goals, which were first present in 18 per cent of the syllabi and were aimed at acquainting students with subject-specific theories and literature, as well as the knowledge and application of pedagogical and didactic concepts. Knowledge goals changed over time as their prevalence decreased somewhat to 15 per cent, yet their focus changed as the goals reflected the development of a more active approach: from 'the student develops a conceptual framework' in the first time period to 'is able to independently search and process (scientific) literature' in the second. Another example: 'The student acquired knowledge of important theories about communicating with children' changed to 'you [the student] demonstrate that you can master various theoretical perspectives when analysing your own actions in practice'. In instrumental skills, there was a slight shift from practical execution of techniques to more focus on pedagogical-didactical research-based professional action with, for example, 'the student knows several different observational instruments to determine the developmental level of young children and they uses these instruments in the correct manner'. In the first time point is stated that 'you [the student] have insight and skill with observing (individual) students that have specific education needs'.

In the second time point formulations such as 'You base your actions on these observations and your interpretations' were found. Replacing two highly general goals in the first time point on the empirical cycle and 'conducting research in school' by the single 'setting up, conducting and reporting an educational sciences investigation' in all educational programmes in the second time point, appears to explain the decreased prevalence of goals pertaining to the research competence (from 7 per cent to 5 per cent). Resulting from often repeated goals across the programmes in this faculty, methodology first included a strong orientation towards broad research processes: 'Application of the empirical cycle: formulation of proposal, gathering of data methodologically, processing of data, drawing conclusions and presenting'. However, as the prevalence decreased over time, its focus also shifted to the independent set-up of educational research, focusing stronger on the disciplinary context: 'You [the student] can pick the right research method and the accompanying measurement instruments, based on the literature review'. Methodology (3 per cent to 2 per cent) and critical thinking (5 per cent to 2 per cent) goals dropped in prevalence over the years from slightly present to hardly present.

Faculty of Applied Social Sciences and Law

This faculty includes educational programmes such as public administration, law and social work. As the prevalence of knowledge goals decreased (from 15 per cent to 10 per cent), its focus became slightly more specific. First, it mainly concerned knowing theories and the programme's background, which mostly have become obtaining knowledge of relevant theories over time. The learning goals were rather abstract in the first time period, for instance, 'The student has knowledge of psychological theories, methods and techniques on processes of change and intervention within organisations'. In the second time period, more learning goals were formulated as professional actions and specify what knowledge is required in what way; 'You can analyse a neighborhood based on urban sociology theories and concepts'.

Little change appears to have occurred for the prevalence (9 per cent to 10 per cent) and scope of instrumental skills goals, which continue to have a broad perspective of research: 'independent performance of statistical analysis' and 'know how to perform a literature search'. In addition to this broad perspective, some faculty-specific methods were explicitly mentioned. For example, 'can extrapolate results from the neighborhood research and translate these results to professional advice' and 'research the administrative theme "social entrepreneurship" by means of desk research and interviews and write a paper on it'. Yet a few goals in the second time period suggest a movement from general and field-specific research skills to more holistic descriptions of applying those general and field-specific research skills. 'The applied psychologist can systematically and methodically interpret data relating to behavioral issues that arise on the group and organisational level' to 'Can identify, analyse and creatively tackle a complex question or developmental need in a changing context, including international ones, by identifying and using psychological knowledge and data to arrive at behavioral interventions and/or advice'. Research competences drop slightly in prevalence (10 per cent to 8 per cent), while goals containing methodology (steady at 3 per cent) and critical thinking (steady at 6 per cent) continue to have the same prevalence. Curiosity hardly appears at all in the study guides.

Faculty of Business and Economics

Educational programmes that fall under the Faculty of Business and Economics are programmes such as human resource management, economics and accountancy, of which all cumulated learning goals present in the study guide texts have increased over time, with knowledge from 6 per cent to 12 per cent, instrumental skills from 12 per cent to 21 per cent and research competence from 8 per cent to 15 per cent. Between the time periods, a content shift appears where the knowledge goals first focused on theoretical knowledge applicable for the professional practice: 'Ability to apply culture-theoretical models', to an addition of knowledge supplementary to conducting research: 'Examine relevant business theories, in relation to the main research question, to formulate and justify sub question'. A change towards using theories and other knowledge to giving arguments and underpinnings, beyond understanding or general 'application' appears to have been made. Another slight content shift occurred in the learning goals covering methodology (prevalence from 3 per cent to 4 per cent) and instrumental skills, which were focused on concretising narrowly defined research skills and understanding related to the professional practice and have become more focused on higher-order research competences. For example, 'Translate a specific business problem into concrete and (partly) measurable research questions' in the first period to 'Analyse a complex business problem in an international business setting with use of an adequate research design, resulting in an evidence based feasible solution' in the second. Also, a focus on collecting, handling and analysing data is extended with interpretation of findings (into practical solutions). 'You [the student] edit the Excel dataset and organise it according to patterns and trends that are relevant to the complex request for advice' to 'You [the student] can make mathematical, statistical and financial models in Excel and interpret the (business) economic results'. The other goals remain unchanged, such as the research competences goals related to both programme-specific research and more broad goals, such as 'Independent set-up and conducting of a questionnaire-study, followed by performing a quantitative analysis'. Curiosity went from hardly present in the first period, to slightly more present in the second period (1 per cent) and critical thinking also shows a slight increase in prevalence (3 per cent to 4 per cent).

Faculty of Health

The Faculty of Health includes educational programmes to educate paramedical professionals, such as physical therapists and nurses. Knowledge learning goals, whose prevalence more than doubled over time (from 16 per cent to 45 per cent), reflected the faculties' orientation as they revolved around applying relevant knowledge in the field of health sciences. Over time, the focus changed slightly towards applying scientific knowledge and especially establishing patient needs in EBP, mostly found in the syllabi of the nursing programme.

Instrumental skills dropped in prevalence and its content, and became slightly more focused on EBP. More specific, a small focus shift from instrumental skills related to diagnostics to the research part of EBP is visible: from 'Independent and systematic searching, selecting and evaluation of relevant scientific literature' to 'find, choose and use relevant (scientific) literature to substantiate choices'. In addition to instrumental skills and knowledge goals, research competences also demonstrate a focus on specified research situated at the core of the faculty and have augmented enormously (from 5 per cent to 20 per cent), which can be traced back to learning goals that are repeated in multiple study guide texts belonging to the nursing programme, such as

> The nurse works continuously to develop and promote the nursing profession. Her[sic] own expertise and that of her [sic] direct (future) colleagues is continuously improving by actively searching and sharing (different types of) knowledge, and, if applicable, in practice orientated research.

Critical thinking dropped from 8 per cent to 3 per cent prevalence, methodology from 4 per cent to zero and curiosity went from zero to a high (18 per cent) prevalence of which the latter is again connected to recurring quotes from the nursing programme. This illustrates that for some goals, the augmentation does not equally reflect an increased amount of research-related learning goals for all programmes belonging to this faculty. Overall, the different learning goals together demonstrate that research in the faculty of health is driven by patient-centred EBP, as skills are patient-centred and aimed at obtaining knowledge to choose the best treatment.

Faculty of Technology

This faculty includes educational programmes such as applied math, engineering and architecture. It shows small increases in knowledge (5 per cent to 7 per cent), in instrumental skills (15 per cent to 19 per cent), in critical thinking (2 per cent to 4 per cent), and in research competence goals (11 per cent to 13 per cent). A few curiosity goals are present (2 per cent) before they disappear from the syllabi in the second time point. Methodology remains the same at 3 per cent. The content of the goals shows little change over time, although some goals are described in more detail in the first time point than in the second, for instance, 'Integrally applying previously acquired theoretical knowledge' to 'You [the student] can acquire and build on existing knowledge, and if necessary adjust the process and design based on predetermined sources besides Google (companies, articles and research institutions)'. The rich diversity of programmes housed in this faculty is mostly reflected in the variety of instrumental skill goals that pertain to relative complex skills, such as 'the right skills to design experiments to assess the impact of variability within a system' as well as purely research-orientated skills: 'Ability to research several (frequent) traces and apply several simple research methods'. Between the time points, the scope broadens to more learning goals on research design besides learning goals on measurements and data handling, although this reaches its dominance through two educational programmes.

Research competence goals mainly involve conducting practice-oriented research, of which the content differs greatly within the faculty, especially in the first period, such as 'Conduct urban typological research on city plans, building typology and public space', 'You [the student] can develop a design vision for the redesigned product based on user research', and 'You [the student] learn to conduct practice-oriented research in a team in the field of digital automation with nautical applications'. As for the other research-related learning goals in the second period, most goals are broader formulated, such as 'demonstrate competency by showing a solid research approach and by making a clear distinction between primary and secondary issues'.

Faculty of Sports and Nutrition

This faculty includes sports-related programmes and nutrition and dietetics. In this faculty, the goals containing knowledge (6 per cent to 14 per cent), critical thinking (2 per cent to 6 per cent), instrumental skills (5 per cent to 7 per cent), and research competences (2 per cent to 5 per cent) increased from the first time point to the second, whereas methodology did not change in prevalence (2 per cent) and curiosity was absent in both time points. A shift in the orientation of the knowledge goals indicates the students are encouraged to become more actively engaged with academic knowledge related to the programme; 'Bases their actions on a multitude of (evidence-based) theories and connects these to each other', where before it was mostly aimed to gain a theoretical background related to the professional practice, such as 'You [the student] know what the discussed psychological theories mean'. Also illustrated by a more active use of scientific papers in the second time point: 'the student has a good knowledge and understanding of the theories of Hofstede, Schwartz, Trompenaars, Hall and Pinto and is based on this knowledge and understanding able to explain and to predict the behavior of people belonging to different cultures', compared to the first time point which aimed to: 'combine the results of scientific papers and come to an overall conclusion, considering the quality of these papers'. While the prevalence of methodology goals was stable over time, the goals have become more specific to understanding faculty-specific research methods, such as 'Can describe the various forms of market research and knows which research method to apply'. Critical thinking is less orientated to the student's own practice in both time points: 'assess the quality of scientific papers'. With limited changed prevalence, instrumental skills are in the first time point focused on learning to use specific methods, such as focus groups and instruments, that measure children's movement development. In the second time point, the instrumental skills learning goals sometimes mention the purpose of using the methods, for example 'You [the student] draw up the dietetic diagnosis, goals and advice and coordinate this with the dietetic research'. The research competences relate mostly to the professional practice, such as 'the student conducts a consumer and sensory research on the developed product and provides a summary of the research objectives, methods, results, conclusion and recommendations in the business plan'.

Faculty of Digital Media and Creative Industries

This faculty includes programmes such as Amsterdam Fashion Institute, IT, Communication and Multimedia Design. This faculty shows a decrease in the prevalence of research-related learning goals between the two time points, except for knowledge goals (6 per cent to 8 per cent). Knowledge goals pertain to both understanding and applying scientific knowledge, and obtaining knowledge from specific types of research: 'To understand what fashion theories are and how they play a role within the field of fashion research'. In the second time point, a larger number of learning goals related to knowledge are formulated in a more detailed manner, for instance: 'apply scientific knowledge' to 'develop, test and present concepts, based on research offered by the lecturer'. A dual approach of broad research skills, but with a practice-specific focus, such as 'the investigation of the functionality and quality of a tool', is reflected in the research competences (9 per cent to 6 per cent) and in instrumental skills goals (13 per cent to 11 per cent). In addition, there is a range of instrumental research skills related to the faculty's specific programmes, such as the design of a research project around an IT problem. In prevalence, methodology learning goals went from 8 per cent to 4 per cent. Curiosity, despite having a low prevalence (less than 1 per cent), shows a changed content and is conceptualised as students' active attitudes where before it was a more general outlook to the field – from 'I and the field: You show a curious, critical and inquiring attitude' to 'Learning how to learn: At the end of this course, students must be able to self-learn a new blockchain architecture and design framework, by exploring the scientific and industrial literature (professional databases, sites, and journals)'. The point of attention for learning goals related to critical thinking (6 per cent to 3 per cent) moved away slightly from theories towards research.

To Conclude: Changes at the Curriculum Layer

As a core case in this book, a strategic programme aimed to create awareness of the value of integrating research in the curriculum and stakeholders' desire to realise such integration at all faculties and programmes. In this monitoring study, in a timespan of four years, the development across the university led to an increase in the prevalence of research-related learning goals in undergraduate curricula and a small but meaningful conceptual shift in formulating these goals. However, differences between the faculties are also more apparent, where programme managers and teaching teams become more aware of the possible viewpoints on research in education and over the years have started to make more deliberate decisions on what to aim for in courses. Developing the faculty-wide vision documents on the role of research in professional practice and in the curriculum are additional evidences of these developments. Apparently, the changes in vision rationales discussed in Chapter 5 have been parallel to changes in learning goals.

Although the changes found are mostly rather subtle, the learning goals do reflect a change in perceptions from fuzzy to more focus, sometimes professionally oriented in its application, sometimes academically oriented as far as sources are concerned; in other programmes, both orientations can be found. In backward curriculum design, and together with the rationale, the learning goals provide direction for designing the full curriculum. Therefore, the somewhat more precise learning goals provide a clearer path for curriculum developers. Some goals almost prescribe certain learning activities, for example 'After this module you can run a regression analysis in Excel and choose the best model in an economic application'. Other learning goals provide more space for design and teaching, such as 'demonstrate professional competency as a starting applied researcher by creating a research abstract, poster, presentation and paper using communication standards and showing critical thinking and reflection'.

While precisely formulated goals provide a clear orientation for design and teaching, they also include the risk of positioning research in the curriculum only in an instrumental manner of learning tricks. In that case, it is clear what trick should be learned, but why it is learned is unclear. In turn, too general learning goals create the chance of a lack of clarity in terms of direction among curriculum designers, teachers as well as students who do not know towards what they are expected to work. Therefore, the level of detail in learning goals needs to be balanced to include a clear content as well as provide space for including the spirit of the rationale at the level of the learning goal. If the what (learning goal) and the why (rationale) are connected, there is clarity in the choices made in design as well as about the choices to be made in teaching–learning interactions.

From a research perspective, this is an important study to understand how scientific underpinnings are needed for sound monitoring of change. Just as in scientific research, decisions on methods in monitoring determine what type of insight are found and what is left out by design. As the case showed, quantitative and qualitative operationalisations of change led to different findings. Different operationalisations of change within a quantitative approach can also lead to different interpretations of the same data. The changes in prevalence of the learning goals in percentages within the faculties appear small at first sight because the relative percentages are low. However, this study has shown that additional qualitative insights into the changes are clearer on the changed positioning of research in undergraduate curricula over time. Therefore, combining measures and making the effort to gather data that can confirm or oppose the proposed changes is an important instrument for change agents in universities.

References

Annala, J., & Mäkinen, M. (2011). The research-teaching nexus in higher education curriculum design. *Transnational Curriculum Inquiry, 8*(1), 3–21.

Baan, J., Gaikhorst, L., & Volman, M. (2019). Stimulating teachers' inquiring attitude in academic and professional teacher education programmes. *European Journal of Teacher Education, 43*(3), 352–67. doi:10.1080/02619768.2019.1693994

Barnett, R. (2009). Knowing and becoming in the higher education curriculum. *Studies in Higher Education, 34*(4), 429–40. doi:10.1080/03075070902771978

Baxan, V., Pattison-Meek, J., & Campbell, A. B. (2020). Dialogic pedagogy in graduate teacher education research advisement: A narrative account of three teacher educators. *Dialogic Pedagogy: An International Online Journal, 8*, SA60–SA84. doi:10.5195/dpj.2020.308

Biglan, A. (1973). Subject matter in different academic areas. *Journal of Applied Psychology, 57*(3), 195–203.

Brew, A. (1999). Research and teaching: Changing relationships in a changing context. *Studies in Higher Education, 24*(3), 291–301. doi:10.1080/03075079912331379905

Brew, A. (2001). Conceptions of research: A phenomenographic study. *Studies in Higher Education, 26*(3), 271–85. doi:10.1080/03075070120076255

Brew, A. (2010). Imperatives and challenges in integrating teaching and research. *Higher Education Research & Development, 29*(2), 139–50. doi:10.1080/07294360903552451

Brew, A., & Mantai, L. (2017). Academics' perceptions of the challenges and barriers to implementing research-based experiences for undergraduates. *Teaching in Higher Education, 22*(5), 551–68. doi:10.1080/13562517.2016.1273216

Elen, J., & Verburgh, A. (2008). *Bologna in European research-intensive universities. Implications for bachelor and master programs*. Antwerp: Garant.

Griffioen, D. M. E. (2020). Differences in students' experiences of research involvement: Study years and disciplines compared. *Journal of Further and Higher Education, 44*(4), 454–66. doi:10.1080/0309877x.2019.1579894

Griffioen, D. M. E., & de Jong, U. (2015). Mapping Dutch Higher education lecturers' discourse on research at times of academic drift. *Scottish Journal of Arts, Social Sciences and Scientific Studies, 26*(1), 81–94.

Griffioen, D. M. E., Ashwin, P., & Scholkmann, A. (2021). Who ensures that society has the professionals it needs? Differences in the policy directions of three European countries. *Policy Reviews in Higher Education* (February), 1–16. doi:10.1080/23322969.2021.1880290

Griffioen, D. M. E., Groen, A., & Nak, J. (2019). The integration of research in the higher education curriculum: A systematic review. *The Higher Education Journal of Learning and Teaching, 10*(1). doi:10.24384/vhs6-1j85

Gros, B., Viader, M., Cornet, A., Martínez, M., Palés, J., & Sancho, M. (2020). The research-teaching nexus and its influence on student learning. *International Journal of Higher Education, 9*(3), 109–19. doi: 10.5430/ijhe.v9n3p109

Harden, R. M. (2002). Learning outcomes and instructional objectives: Is there a difference? *Med Teach, 24*(2), 151–5. doi:10.1080/0142159022020687

Healey, M. (2005a). Linking research and teaching to benefit student learning. *Journal of Geography in Higher Education, 29*(2), 183–201. doi:10.1080/03098260500130387

Healey, M. (2005b). Linking research and teaching: Exploring disciplinary spaces and the role of inquiry-based learning. In R. Barnett (Ed.), *Reshaping the University: New Relationships between Research, Scholarship and Teaching* (pp. 67–78) McGraw Hill: Open University Press.

Hu, Y. J., Van der Rijst, R., Van Veen, K., & Verloop, N. (2014). 'And never the two shall meet'? Comparing Chinese and Dutch university teachers about the role of research in teaching. *Higher Education, 68*(4), 607–22. doi:10.1007/s10734-014-9734-0

Hu, Y. J., Van der Rijst, R., Van Veen, K., & Verloop, N. (2015). The role of research in teaching: A comparison of teachers from research universities and those from universities of applied sciences. *Higher Education Policy, 28*(4), 535–54. doi:10.1057/hep.2014.19

Huisman, J. (2008). Shifting boundaries in higher education: Dutch Hogescholen on the move. In J. S. Taylor, J. Brites Ferreira, M. de Lourdes Machado, & R. Santiago (Eds.), *Non-university Higher Education in Europe* (pp. 147–68). Dordrecht: Springer.

Jenkins, A., Healey, M., & Zetter, R. (2007). *Linking teaching and research in disciplines and departments*. Retrieved from York: http://www.heacademy.ac.uk/assets/York/documents/LinkingTeachingAndResearch_April07.pdf.

Lambrechts, W., & Van Petegem, P. (2016). The interrelations between competences for sustainable development and research competences. *International Journal of Sustainability in Higher Education, 17*(6), 776–95. doi:10.1108/ijshe-03-2015-0060

Magnell, M., & Geschwind, L. (2019). Higher education research & development a seamless blend of research and professional practice: Dual coupling in engineering education. doi:10.1080/07294360.2019.1581141

Pallant, E., Choate, B., & Haywood, B. (2020). How do you teach undergraduate university students to contribute to UN SDGs 2030? In W. Leal Filho, A. L. Salvia, R. W. Pretorius, L. L. Brandli, E. Manolas, F. Alves, U. Azeiteiro, J. Rogers, C. Shiel, & A. Do Paco (Eds.), *Universities as living labs for sustainable development: Supporting the implementation of the sustainable development goals* (pp. 69–86) Cham: Springer.

Pluim, G., Nazir, J., & Wallace, J. (2021). Curriculum integration and the semicentennial of Basil Bernstein's classification and framing of educational knowledge. *Canadian Journal of Science, Mathematics and Technology Education, 20*, 715–35. doi:10.1007/s42330-021-00135-9

Ruzafa-Martínez, M., López-Iborra, L., Barranco, D. A., & Ramos-Morcillo, A. J. (2016). Effectiveness of an evidence-based practice (EBP) course on the EBP competence of undergraduate nursing students: A quasi-experimental study. *Nurse Education Today, 38*, 82–7.

Taylor, R., & Canfield, P. (2007). Learning to be a scholarly teaching faculty cultural change through shared leadership. In A. Brew & J. Sachs (Eds.), *Transforming a university. The scholarship of teaching and learning in practice* (pp. 233–47). Sydney: Sydney University Press.

Tight, M. (2016). Examining the research/teaching nexus. *European Journal of Higher Education, 6*(4), 293–311. doi:10.1080/21568235.2016.1224674

Timmerman, B. C., Feldon, D., Maher, M., Strickland, D., & Gilmore, J. (2013). Performance-based assessment of graduate student research skills: Timing, trajectory, and potential thresholds. *Studies in Higher Education, 38*(5), 693–710. doi: 10.1080/03075079.2011.590971

Van den Akker, J. (2003). Curriculum perspectives: An introduction. In J. Van den Akker, W. Kuiper, & U. Hameyer (Eds.), *Curriculum landscapes and trends* (pp. 1–10). Dordrecht: Kluwer Academic Publishers.

Van Laar, E., Van Deursen, A. J. A. M., Van Dijk, J. A. G. M., & de Haan, J. (2017). The relation between 21st-century skills and digital skills: A systematic literature review. *Computers in Human Behavior, 72*, 577–88. doi:10.1016/j.chb.2017.03.010

Verburgh, A. L., Schouteden, W., & Elen, J. (2012). Patterns in the prevalence of research-related goals in higher education programmes. *Teaching in Higher Education, 18*(3), 298–310. doi:10.1080/13562517.2012.719153

Vereijken, M. W. C., Van der Rijst, R. M., Van Driel, J. H., & Dekker, F. W. (2018). Student learning outcomes, perceptions and beliefs in the context of strengthening research integration into the first year of medical school. *Advances in Health Sciences Education, 23*(2), 371–85. doi:10.1007/s10459-017-9803-0

Vereijken, M. W. C., Van der Rijst, R. M., Van Driel, J. H., & Dekker, F. W. (2020). Authentic research practices throughout the curriculum in undergraduate medical education: Student beliefs and perceptions. *Innovations in Education and Teaching International, 57*(5), 532–42. doi:10.1080/14703297.2019.1674680

Visser-Wijnveen, G. J., Van Driel, J. H., Van der Rijst, R. M., Verloop, N., & Visser, A. (2010). The ideal research-teaching nexus in the eyes of academics: Building profiles. *Higher Education Research & Development, 29*(2), 195–210. doi:10.1080/07294360903532016

Visser-Wijnveen, G. J., Van der Rijst, R. M., & Van Driel, J. H. (2015). A questionnaire to capture students' perceptions of research integration in their courses. *Higher Education, 71*(4), 473–88. doi:10.1007/s10734-015-9918-2

7

Changes in Academics' Job Profiles

Sanne R. Daas, Didi M. E. Griffioen, Chevy M. van Dorresteijn and Indira N. Z. Day

Introduction

During the last decades, there has been a tendency of 'academic drift' within higher education (Lourdes Machado, Ferreira, Santiago, & Taylor, 2008; Harwood, 2010), with a potential to staff drift in which lecturers in applied universities become more 'academic' through the addition of research responsibilities (Griffioen & De Jong, 2013; Kyvik, 2007; Neave, 1978). New universities in mainland Europe moved away from a teaching-only practice to more engagement with research, whereas old universities (i.e. research-intensive institutions) attempted to improve their teaching capacity (Huisman & Kaiser, 2001; Kyvik & Skodvin, 2003). Within the Netherlands, the Ministry of Education, Culture and Science emphasised the connection between research and teaching within universities (2015), following the general positive–normative view on research integration (Trowler & Wareham, 2008).

The most often applied research–education connection is within the work of academics. Some consider researchers with teaching responsibilities or lecturers with research responsibilities as the underpinnings of universities (Handal & Herrington, 2003). There are multiple presumed benefits of embracing an integrative role of academics in higher professional education institutions. It is not just one group of stakeholders, such as students, that could benefit, but integrating research and teaching in the academic leads to all types of positive effects: First, skilled, up-to-date researchers are able to teach students the latest ideas, innovations and methods of their own discipline (Turner et al., 2008). Second, academics working in education and research provide a line of communication and of knowledge between research programmes and curricula, which leads to faster integration of research in the curriculum as well as provides opportunities to involve students in research projects. Third, students might be enthused if lecturers discuss their own research projects: Getting to know the 'research cycle' by hearing first-hand experiences is insightful in many ways, and is a very different learning experience from 'just' reading or hearing about the outcome of such research (Healey et al., 2005; Hunter et al., 2007). Vice versa, lecturers are offered a unique moment of reflection and of feedback by discussing their ongoing research with groups of future professionals. This might strengthen the research (Fung, Besters-Dilger, & Van der Vaart, 2017). At the same time, some systematic quantitative studies do not show any cross-quality effects between research and education (Hattie & Marsh, 1996), and others show that integrating 'education' and 'research' could result in different results, depending on the indicators applied, such as master grade of students or student satisfaction (Palali, Van Elk, Bolhaar, & Rud, 2017).

However, an important element in higher education change are the people who personify that change and one important aspect is the personification of the lecturer. Especially when changes are made while executing primary processes, the academics involved need to be able and willing to become part of the intended changes. Additionally, they need to be willing and able to do so collectively (Ashwin, 2006). Being willing and being able to are two rather different elements in organisational change. Willingness to change refers to one's perceptions of the changes proposed, the interaction with these changes and one's professional identity, as well as the practice's level of improvement one assigns to the proposed changes. These notions interfere with one's ability to change, in particular one's self-evaluated ability, also called self-efficacy (Bandura, 2006). Lecturers' beliefs about their ability to perform the new tasks influence their performance, as lecturers to students in research aspects, but also their own performance as (new) researchers' (Griffioen, De Jong, & Jak, 2014, p. 25). Therefore, lecturers' trust in their own capabilities influences the integration of research across the university (Griffioen et al., 2014; Runhaar, Sanders, & Yang, 2010).

However, changing academic's belief and identity to include research is not an easy endeavour, even if it has multiple benefits for lecturers and research itself. Following Becher (1989), Trowler (1998, p. 57) explains:

> [T]he way groups of academics organise their professional lives and nature of the professional task on which they are engaged 'would seem to be inseparately intertwined'. Their offices are bedecked with artefacts that symbolise their disciplinary allegiance. The very language they use is structured by their

discipline, conditioning the modes in which arguments are generated, developed, expressed and reported.

As with other proposed research–education connections, it would request a mechanism to alter the balance between both in academics' practices. Changing practices in this regard easily needs to result in changing academics' capacity. Generally, universities have two essential strategy options for changing their personnel's capacity: professionalisation and hiring (Griffioen, 2018). This chapter focuses on the latter: to hire a newly defined body of employees with new capabilities to fulfil new tasks. Combined, the two strategies can assist in building the university's capacity for research as well as for research integration. Building research capacity is 'a process of individual and institutional development that leads to higher skill levels and greater ability to perform useful research' (Grange, Herne, Casey, & Wordsworth, 2005, p. 32).

There are some examples of universities making an institutional shift from approaching their academic staff as lecturers to approaching and changing how their own roles as academics are understood, without undermining the intrinsic motivation of such staff members (e.g. Hunt, 2016). However, this is difficult to achieve in large higher education institutions. Furthermore, it is a costly and time-consuming endeavour and does not always deliver a structural solution. professionalising academics might lead to more knowledge about research or education in the short term, but does not account for direct experience with one of the two disciplines, thus risking the acquired knowledge during such courses to fade over time. The other way to change the sole focus on teaching activities to including a stronger emphasis on research, or the combination of research and teaching, is to hire new lecturers with stronger research competences.

However, hiring strategies are not straightforward either (Griffioen, 2020). Dutch applied universities do not specifically aim for an increase in research output that one would expect when universities raise their research capacity (Levine, Russ-Eft, Burling, Stephens, & Downey, 2013). Dutch applied universities aim for 'a functional balance between didactical competencies, professional competencies, and research competencies in lecturers that go beyond a lecturer's formal educational level' (Griffioen, 2018, p. 350). While this balance is more relevant for the proposed research integration strategies explained in this book, its diffuse message makes changing hiring practices more difficult. Moreover, hiring new staff in universities is generally the responsibility of lower management, yielding that changing hiring practices implies changing beliefs and competences among lower management as a prerogative (Griffioen, 2018).

The Dutch Ministry of Education presented clear aims for applied universities to increase the research–education connection in their consecutive Strategic Agendas, with the clearest quote in 2015: 'The ambition of 2025 is that [all] institutes for higher education have connected research, teaching and practice on all levels' (Ministry of Education, 2015, author's translation).

In line with the Dutch national governing structure (Griffioen, Ashwin, & Scholkmann, 2021), and the following national debates about research integration (Griffioen, 2013), smaller or larger change efforts in all Dutch applied universities were seen. Therefore, these universities could be expected to shift in the profiles of employees sought to add to their capacity of employees.

Although the scale of analysis of the individual employee has – indirectly – played a part in several of the chapters, here we consider the academic further, employees that are hired for their academic expertise. Researching the proposed role of academics working in higher professional education in job openings leads to knowledge on the practicalities of the research–teaching nexus: How are these two realms united in the individual academics' responsibilities? Do research and teaching tasks and competences complement each other, or are these two self-contained fields of expertise?

In the light of changing the integration of research and education in the academic, coping strategies among professional academics in adding the task of research through professionalisation or new employment become relevant. Therefore, this chapter first considers the coping strategies of lecturers who include research tasks and competences to their responsibilities through professionalisation or hiring. Then, the changes in tasks and lecturers' competences as the universities request are presented through a national longitudinal study between 2015 and 2019. The found shifts indicate whether the universities' ambition to change their practices to include research has resulted in the ground-floor ambition to hire a new type of personnel. Where changes in core strategy are relatively easily made, these ground-floor changes can indicate shifts in university practice.

The Academic's Coping Strategies in the Research–Teaching Nexus

Historically, lecturers' initial role in applied universities was described as a purely teaching-focused job, with a great perceived distance between the teaching responsibilities and the latest developments in the discipline (e.g. Santos, Pereira,

& Lopes, 2021). Developments in professionals' fields were deemed important and therefore more actively followed. Just before the turn of the century, the lecturer's role was changing: More than before, lecturers in applied universities were expected to share up-to-date knowledge about developments and innovations in their discipline, both in a sense of 'new knowledge' and of new methods or techniques (Griffioen, 2013). The notion of professionalism changed from a high trust in experienced action to the need for providing more systematic underpinnings and evaluating practice as part of accountability cultures (Fook, 2004). Professionals were trusted more if research results confirmed their actions. This goes hand in hand with a stronger emphasis on lecturers taking on research tasks themselves as well – from being informed about research, to being active researchers. Research was expected to become part of their professionalism, knowledge, identity and action, while before professional expertise and didactical skills were considered sufficient (Griffioen, 2013; Griffioen et al., 2014).

Additionally, from a pedagogy perspective, in the last decades, a shift occurred from knowledge as something that is produced in research or professional practice and was then transferred to learners, to a more complex understanding of processes of knowledge circulation, also including students in different pedagogical roles (Kamp, Dolmans, Van Berkel, & Schmidt, 2011). Knowledge is made by practice and actions, and the practices changed (e.g. Felicja, Servant, Norman, & Schmidt, 2019). This is presumed for scientific knowledge (Shapin & Schaffer, 1985) and can be applied for professional knowledge. Knowledge building occurs via collaborations and exchanges, even when the dominant disciplinary perspective focuses more on objectivity (Brew, 2001). Therefore, the lecturer's role is diversified as well and students and lecturers are more collectively building knowledge structures. Healey's (2005, p. 13) typology of research–teaching relationships offers a helpful structuring device to recognise such activities. In this, he identifies four types of research implementation in education: Research-tutored students are positioned as participants, and the focus is on learning about research content. The research-based variation views students as participants, and teaching and learning focus on research processes and problems. Research-led students participate more like an audience, learning about content that follows from research. Finally, research-oriented implementation shapes students as an audience, but then focuses on research processes and problems. Each of these four types are expected to rely on a different set of skills for every type. To deliver 'research-based' teaching activities, for instance, a lecturer should have solid research experience and competences as well as research-specific didactical skills. Thus, already the integration of research within a teaching role suggests different competences needed.

This yields for changed expectations for lecturers' roles and competences. At a systems level, the Dutch national government stated that all lecturers should at least have a master's degree (Ministry of Education, 2015). At the time, a large part of the body of lecturers was employed based on a bachelor's degree and extensive professional experience (Griffioen, 2013), a system previously relying on experience and not degrees. Such broad strokes of change often also result in perverse effects, in this case groups of lecturers striving for the 'easiest' master's degree to be able to get permanent positions, and very young academics without professional experience being hired because they did have a master's degree while lacking pedagogical expertise. 'Research competences' and 'master's degree' were made mutually equal, often not resulting in the requested competences or experience (Heest, 2018). Currently, most of these perverse effects are reduced, although the choice of salary scales for lecturers is still partly based on 'having a master's degree', and not fully on the competences implied by such a degree. These broad stroke changes can create large changes quickly, but they need to be combined with the tuning of these changes related to specific contexts.

The changed expectations also resulted in new coping strategies among lecturers, now balancing different responsibilities within their educational role and increasingly taking on research roles. A few scholars have studied these changes in lecturers of an applied university. The first perspective found in the literature focuses on the change seen in the professional identities of lecturers in these situations, for instance, among new nurse-educators and teacher-educators in Portuguese and English professional higher education (Lopes, Boyd, Andrew, & Pereira, 2014). This study showed disciplinary differences in identity. Nurse-educators identified as nurses educating other nurses, in which they also needed to share with their students an – what they saw as – 'underdeveloped type of nurse research which was more related to reflection' (p. 179). However, the teacher-educators did not identify as school teachers (anymore). For them, research was one of their academic roles. Therefore nurse-educators and teacher-educators have shown to have a different type of dual identity due to their difference in ties to the professional field. Where research did not empower the nurse-educators' identity as nurse and educator, it did empower the teacher-educators' identity as academic and educator.

A second focus is on the more experienced lecturer taking on an active research role (Winkel, Van der Rijst, Poel, & Van Driel, 2016). In a Dutch applied university, six coping strategies related to the lecturers' identity were found. The 'continuous learner' considered research an addition to teaching because it adds knowledge to teaching or because teaching no longer provides new learning opportunities. The 'disciplinary expert' aimed to increase their knowledge or their authority as the knower of the discipline through research. The 'skilled researcher' wanted to understand how research worked, of which some enjoy the craftmanship and others like the potential of innovation. The 'evidence-based teacher' aimed to be a role model for students as evidence-based professionals or to provide a more solid foundation under the teaching role. The 'guardian' was mainly working on sustaining boundaries, such as time to their research work, while the 'liaison officer' aimed to cross boundaries as a broker and developer across education, the professional field, or the scientific field.

A third focus was on the combined lecturers' roles in applied higher education, therefore more connected to the systems level of academic work. A study in health education (Boyd & Smith, 2011) shows how a large proportion of lecturers cope with the combined roles by subverting research activities and their research identity, even while research is highly regarded in their university: 'These academics are choosing or being directed to pursue identity trajectories that emphasise knowledge exchange, leadership or teaching and are overturning the privilege given to researcher identity in the higher education sector' (p. 693).

Smaller proportions of lecturers lead to resonance, dissonance and rejection of research. Additional analysis (Smith & Boyd, 2012) has shown that the group of lecturers rejecting research generally 'are strongly motivated to contribute to the development of student practitioners. They tend to hold on strongly to their identity as a clinical practitioner rather than quickly embracing new identities of scholar and researcher' (p. 63).

Where Henkel (2005, p. 164) stated that the academics' 'research reputation' was the strongest currency in higher education, this shortlist of studies of the small field of academic identity and coping strategies in applied universities depicts a more nuanced picture of lecturers in applied higher education – to say the least. For some lecturers, their identity is based more on their professional role, for others research is a part of their core identity, some cope wonderfully while others struggle massively. However, it is clear that the different roles request at least some juggling, and this can result in a shifting identity when research is embraced as a new task and/or learned as a new set of competencies.

Who to Hire to Enact organisational Change

The focus on implementing research in applied universities from the perspective of the lecturer's identity and coping strategies has enriched the insight into the possible responses a change agent can expect when adding 'research' to the mix of roles and competences. However, it does not provide insight into the type or types of lecturers or academics that applied universities intend to appoint when searching for new employees.

As the multiple roles in the lecturers' coping strategies have demonstrated, it is hard to recognise a clearly defined conception of 'the' academic in higher professional education. With the historical changes from teaching-only institutions to universities of research and education, combining research and teaching activities and responsibilities in the role of individual academics within the organisation meant that job profiles had to become more varied, specific and explicit:

> In the process of transferring powers and responsibilities from the government to universities and *hogescholen*, a trend can be identified—movement away from uniformity in dealing with staffing issues, and towards the devising of personnel management systems that allow for individual, subject, or market differences and flexible reward systems. An important development is the current implementation of a new system of job profiles for academic staff at universities. This system aims at making explicit the various roles, tasks, and responsibilities that must be carried out to achieve the stated objective. Individual development plans become possible, in which different staff roles are to be acknowledged, both vertically and horizontally within the same ranks. Individual staff members can apply for specific roles on the basis of an assessment of their qualifications—for example, to be more involved in either teaching or research. Teaching activities are classified into four specified tasks, such as teaching, curricular development, counselling student projects, and evaluation. Research activities consist of coordination, acquisition of contract research, and participating in research working groups and committees.
>
> (Huisman, 2008)

The remainder of this chapter considers the content of 'future' academic employees of Amsterdam UAS, in line with a more divided human resources system, and as indicating the changes that take place at the staff level between 2016 and 2019. By formulating tasks and competences in job profiles, the changing relationship between teaching activities and research activities as it is united in the individual academics' responsibilities can be revealed. Potentially, the shifting roles of lecturer and researcher result in a more integrated variation of that role. However, it is also likely that the more uniform roles of lecturer and researcher are found, which indicates team managers' confirmation of the existing division between both primary processes and therefore an (implicit) resistance to an increased organisational hybridity, as explained in Chapter 1

(Bystydzienski, Thomas, Howe, & Desai, 2016; Quirke, 2013). Therefore, studying these roles means exploring how, and to what extent, different tasks and competences related to education and research are distinguished in the job description, and what 'weight' is given to every element.

A Nationwide Perspective to Change in Job Profiles

The potential changes in the job profiles of newly hired staff in Dutch applied universities were studied parallel to the Amsterdam strategic programme by analysing job openings. In the same week (around June 28) between 2016 and 2019 annually, all publicly announced job openings were gathered from the main Dutch online job board for Dutch universities of applied sciences (http://www.werkenbijhogescholen.nl). Only openings related to the primary processes of research and teaching were collected, leaving out openings related to management or supporting staff positions. The data gathering resulted in a sample of N=474 job openings (2016: n=124; 2017: n=87; 2018: n=168; 2019: n=95) coming from twenty Dutch universities of applied sciences. We chose this timing at the end of the college year because of its annual peak in the number of job openings aimed to complete the staffing for the next college year.

The job opening texts were analysed in line with the methods of Pitt and Mewburn (2016) and Griffioen (2018), who also analysed job openings and their coding scheme for the competences were both inspired by the Researcher Development Framework (RDF; Vitae, 2010). Yet, because the RDF is primarily researcher-focused, we adapted the RDF and created some extra categories that were more education-focused to distinguish and give more weight to specific teaching competences.

A coding scheme was created to discern two main facets in job openings: competences and tasks. Competences were concerned with personal characteristics or skills prospective employees had to possess to qualify for the job. Tasks indicated the activities/jobs the prospective employees were expected to do.

The competences were codes based on RDF by Vitae (2010). Inductively and as an expansion of the RDF, three types of educational competences were discerned: 'teaching knowledge', 'educational developmental abilities' and 'teaching experience', which in some way were the counterparts of 'research knowledge', 'research developmental abilities' and 'research experience'. The code group 'resources and finances' was initially added as neither research-focused nor education-focused, but ultimately turned out to be a research-focused competence because it only concerned applying for research grants.

The tasks were coded using Griffioen's (2018) coding scheme, which was originally inductively developed through an open coding content analysis of job openings (Joffe & Yardley, 2004). Before and during our coding process, we found no reason to deviate from this coding scheme. A list of all tasks and competences can be found in Table 7.1, including some example quotes.

Table 7.1 Overview of all tasks and competencies including example quotes

	Code	Example quotes (translated by authors)
	Competences	
Education-focused	Teaching in higher education knowledge (TiHEK)	*You have knowledge about didactical skills*
	Educational development abilities (EA)	*You are able to translate research results into relevant building blocks for the education*
	Teaching experience (TE)	*Experience in supervising/guiding students*
Research-focused	Research knowledge (RK)	*Knowledge of research skills and practice-based research*
	Research development abilities (RA)	*As a visionary, you have a clear view on the research theme, which you can translate into research questions in an excellent manner*
	Research experience (RE)	*You have published in scientific and professional outlets*
	Resources and finances (RF)	*You can obtain project grants and other external sources of funding*
	Tasks	
Education-focused	Educational development (ED)	*Part of your responsibilities will be the maintenance and continuous development of educational programmes*
	Examination (EX)	*You will grade exams*
	Lecturing (LE)	*You will teach students*
	Supervision (SU)	*You will provide students with feedback and feedforward that the student can apply to projects in the programme, during internships or during work*
Research-focused	Acquisition (AQ)	*You will use your professional network for acquiring research assignments*
	Dissemination (DS)	*You will publish your findings in scientific and professional journals*
	Research (development) (RD)	*You will be involved in conducting practice-based research together with students*

Samples from each year were separately coded in Atlas.ti8 by two researchers. One researcher coded the complete sample and the other performed a 10 per cent cross-check of the sample. The codes were then individually compared and all coding differences were discussed between the two researchers until consensus was reached. The codes given to individual job openings were then transformed in a binominal score of present/not present.

Conceptually, (2^4 =) 16 job profiles were possible, based on the binomial occurrence of teaching-focused and research-focused competences and teaching-focused and research-focused tasks in the job openings. All job openings were analysed to assess whether they contained any competence or task related to either teaching or research. In the following sections the findings of this study are explicated.

Combinations of Research and Education that Dutch Applied Universities Look for in Academics

Academics' jobs can depict different combinations of research and education, as was also shown in Section 7.2. The analysis of job openings in applied universities between 2016 and 2019 indicated that out of the conceptually sixteen potential different types of profiles, four profiles covered over 80 per cent of the job openings, with all other profiles covering only 1–3 per cent of the job openings. These four profiles can be depicted as the 'teacher', 'teacher-researcher without research competencies', 'teacher with dual competencies' and the 'teacher-researcher', and are hereafter explained. Quotes from the job openings are referred to in-text by a number that refers to the particular job opening and the year, and are translated from Dutch to English by the authors.

Profile 1: 'teacher'

The findings show that one of the four most prevailing job profiles that applied universities intended to hire between 2016 and 2019 can be depicted as the 'teacher'. The job openings in this profile only contain competences and tasks focused on teaching. Considering the competences that were mentioned in these job openings, prospective employees were required to be experienced in teaching and educational development, and possess knowledge of teaching in higher education. Experience with teaching was mentioned both explicitly (e.g. 'teaching experience as a language teacher is a requirement', 2017, d. 38)

Table 7.2 Relative occurrence of research- and teaching-related competences and tasks (percentage of profile totals)

Profiles → Categories ↓	Teacher	Teacher-researcher without research competences	Teacher with dual competences	Teacher-researcher
Teaching in higher education knowledge	62%	70%	72%	61%
Educational development abilities	40%	30%	43%	40%
Teaching experience	86%	70%	89%	68%
Research knowledge	-	-	62%	64%
Research development abilities	-	-	-	14%
Research experience	-	-	46%	74%
Resources and finances	-	-	10%	17%
Acquisition	-	14%	-	17%
Dissemination	-	8%	-	32%
Research (development)	-	88%	-	96%
Lecturing	94%	82%	83%	75%
Supervision	88%	84%	86%	82%
Examination	19%	10%	28%	14%
Educational development	76%	78%	82%	88%

and implicitly (e.g. 'you are able to teach a range of sports', 2018, d. 79). With regard to teaching in higher education knowledge, openings were looking for candidates who had 'affinity for working with young adults' (2018, d. 140) or were 'interested in pedagogy and the learning process of young upcoming professionals' (2019, d. 101). Furthermore, it was important for prospective teachers to have educational development abilities (2018, d. 4): 'you know how to translate developments in the field to good and challenging design education'. In line with this, practical experience was often asked: 'relevant working experience (minimum of 5 years) at a production company and/or design company as a designer or engineer' (2016, d. 36), sometimes of multiple years. Some openings also stated candidates should have a professional network that could be used during 'designing and the execution of education' (2019, d. 84). In regard to the required degree, most openings stated candidates should have a master's degree. However, some stated a bachelor's degree was sufficient.

In regard to the tasks, candidates applying for openings in this profile were mostly expected to contribute to lecturing and supervising students, as in the following example: 'you will give lectures and tutorials and supervise students during projects and their graduation research' (2017, d. 28). Next to supervising students during projects, some openings expected candidates to contribute to coaching students – for example in their competence development (2018, d. 123), or in their development towards independent professionals with an inquiring mind (2017, p. 58). In addition, candidates were often asked to participate in educational development by, for example, 'actively participat[ing] in the continuous improvement of our education' (2018, d. 12). Sometimes, candidates were asked to link practice to educational programs by 'identif[ying] relevant developments in practice and translat[ing] these to the educational programmes together with the team' (2018, d. 46). Lastly, a small proportion of the openings asked candidates to contribute to examination through conducting tests or examining graduation projects.

Profile 2: 'teacher-researcher without research competencies'

A second job profile found among a considerable amount of job openings was the 'teacher-researcher without research competencies'. This job profile requested prospective candidates to both execute teaching and (possibly) research tasks, but in regard to the competences, only expected candidates to possess teaching-related competences. Research-related competences were not mentioned in these job openings. Regarding the competences, candidates were required to have expertise and practical experience in the relevant discipline. Additionally, candidates needed to possess up-to-date knowledge about developments in practice: 'you are informed about and follow the recent developments and research in your field of expertise' (2016, d. 16). Furthermore, prospective candidates were mostly not expected to demonstrate experience with teaching. Instead, 'a drive to educate students' (2019, d. 31) and a preference for candidates who had teaching experience or who were willing to professionalise themselves in teaching were asked. Affinity or (in some cases) experience with developing education was also asked in the openings. Job openings in this profile largely required candidates to have a master's degree, but a few stated that a UAS bachelor's degree was also sufficient. Additionally, some candidates are asked to have a relevant professional network and work experience in professional practice.

Considering the tasks, candidates were mainly required to contribute to teaching: 'the core of your work as a lecturer is the execution of teaching within the educational program' (2019, d. 2). In addition, tasks such as supervising students and contributing to educational development were asked: 'In addition, you supervise and examine students during their internship, graduation or in doing practice-based research' (2019, d. 70). Educational development was mainly concerned with integrating recent developments in course programs: 'Analysing developments in the discipline and professional practice and integrating the results in educational programs' (2018, d. 30) and 'enhancing the educational quality' (2017, d. 27). A few job openings mentioned conducting research as a compulsory task, but most candidates had the option to contribute to conducting research: 'participating in innovative research projects may become part of your tasks, depending on preference, ability and availability' (2019, d. 49). Other research-related tasks mentioned were: 'writing and publishing research papers with students and colleagues' (2018, d. 24) and 'acquisition of assignments for the knowledge centre' (2018, d. 30). Additionally, a few candidates were asked to 'maintain connections with the professional field and other relevant institutions, so that you are informed about the recent developments in your domain' (2017, d. 27).

Profile 3: 'teacher with dual competencies'

A third profile that appeared as one of the most prevailing job profiles applied universities looked for was the 'teacher with dual competences', which encompassed job openings that included teaching competences and tasks and additionally required prospective candidates to possess research competences. Unlike the 'teacher without research competences', the job openings that requested this profile did not mention executing research tasks, but did request research competences. In regard to the competences, prospective employees were expected to have experience with research and teaching, and in some job openings, candidates were even expected to have multiple years of experience with mostly teaching: 'With some years of teaching experience and additionally research experience, for example through a PhD research in the biomedical/biotechnological area' (2017, d. 42). Additionally, prospective employees were asked to be able to 'signal relevant developments in the professional field and use these to propose adjustments to the educational program' (2016, d. 22). In line with this, some candidates were expected to be experienced in developing educational programmes, but none were asked to have experience with developing research projects. Unique to this profile was the focus on more specified and detailed knowledge about teaching, such as knowledge about what makes content meaningful and effective, and knowledge about a diverse range of didactical working methods. In addition, openings in this profile were the only ones that mentioned prospective candidates should have 'a research-minded attitude': 'you have a learning, reflective and research-like attitude and are able to guide students in achieving this' (2019, d. 78). Furthermore, many openings in this profile asked for professional experience relevant to the opening's related discipline as well as a relevant network and the ability to easily make connections within and outside the organisation. In general, candidates in this profile were expected to have a master's degree, but some openings stated a bachelor's degree was also sufficient. A few openings stated a PhD was compulsory.

Considering the tasks, prospective candidates in this profile were mostly expected to give lectures, coach students (during internships and graduation projects) and contribute to educational development. In this profile, educational development was not solely concerned with integrating the latest developments in courses, but was also described as enhancing the educational quality and 'contributing to the development of innovative course programs' (2018, d. 113). In addition, some were expected to contribute to managerial tasks, which seems to be an extension of their educational development tasks, such as: 'contributing to quality assurance of the educational program' (2017, d. 24), or 'outlining the course of the minor entrepreneurship' (2019, d. 17). Candidates in this profile were also expected to maintain an active network within their professional field, which in turn should lead to a better integration of professional practice in educational programs.

Profile 4: 'teacher-researcher'

Finally, the fourth most prevailing job profile applied universities looked for was the 'teacher-researcher', which encompassed research-related competences and tasks as well as education-related competences and tasks. Concerning the competences, after disciplinary knowledge, knowledge of or affinity with research methods was required most often. Specific knowledge of teaching methods was not necessarily required, but applicants did need to have affinity or in most cases experience with educating students and giving classes: 'knowledge of and experience with education and research' (2016, d. 102). Unique to this profile were the competences asked regarding acquiring research projects, or having a vision on something: 'you have a clear vision on the current challenges in the logistics and role of the professorship' (2019, d. 104). In addition, similar to employees in 'teacher with dual competencies', employees in this profile were expected to have managerial qualities. However, whereas profile 3 mainly stated candidates should have 'organisational qualities', profile 4 stated candidates should be able to 'manage projects' (2017, d. 5) and 'be an inspirational leader' (2018, d. 3). It seems these managerial qualities were not just for the benefit of organising certain projects, but rather for the leadership over other employees. As such, some candidates were asked to be able to 'take on a diversity of roles, such as the disciplinary expert, researcher, project manager, and mentor' (2017, d. 26). Profile 4 was also the only profile that expected candidates to have experience with publishing scientific articles: 'you have written at least one publication' (2016, d. 54). Most of the openings mentioned candidates should have research experience; however, some of these mentioned it as an 'advantage' rather than a requirement: 'As it is expected [...] to also conduct research, affinity and/or experience with conducting research is considered an asset' (2019, d. 91). In most cases, experience in the professional field was required: 'some years of working experience in the field' (2016, d. 79). Many candidates were expected to have a relevant network, for the benefit of integrating research into educational programs, for acquiring research assignments and for the purpose of raising publicity for the research group. Interestingly, while the other profiles mainly expected candidates to use a professional network to acquire knowledge from professional practice, candidates in this profile were also expected to return knowledge to professional practice: 'through your large and relevant network, you effortlessly create an interaction between science, education and practice. You do this through raising publicity for your research results in publications, readings, demonstrations and forms of education' (2018, d. 3). In some cases, candidates were expected to be 'an authority in your discipline' (2018, d. 3). Considering the required degree, most of the openings stated a master's degree was sufficient, but a considerable amount of openings stated a PhD was compulsory.

Considering the tasks, candidates in the teacher-researcher profile were expected to contribute to both teaching and conducting research as well as innovating and developing these two disciplines in their field: 'together with an enthusiastic team, you contribute to educational innovations' (2016, d. 100). Unique to this profile was that multiple candidates were expected to contribute to acquisition, often in terms of finances for research projects: 'you acquire externally financed project that fit in to the context of the education and research' (2017, d. 57). Whereas the profile 'teacher-researcher without research competences' in some cases asked candidates to disseminate knowledge mainly to the professional field, the current profile expected candidates to disseminate knowledge to the scientific field as well as the professional field in various ways: scientific publications (2016, d. 117), MOOCS (2018, d. 80), readings (2018, d. 3) or presentations (2019, d. 29). Moreover, multiple candidates in this profile were required to manage a team: 'you will create a team [knowledge circle] with teacher-researchers and provide them with coaching' (2016, d. 61).

Comparing Hiring Profiles

As these four profiles encompass approximately 80 per cent of all job openings analysed between 2016 and 2019, they give a good impression of the hiring practices of Dutch applied universities in terms of looking for candidates who are expected to work in jobs related to teaching as well as research. One of these profiles is merely focused on teaching, while three profiles could be considered more research–education integrated job profiles, as they request both teaching and research competences and/or tasks.

An important resemblance between all four profiles is the expectation that new employees would fulfil the same combination of tasks: to teach, to supervise students and to develop education, and therefore include the newest developments of the professional field in educational programmes. The differences between the profiles is mainly found within the research tasks and research competences, and therefore excluding the 'teacher' profile, which does not include research as such. For example, within the research tasks, there is a difference in prominence in conducting research, ranging from research as optional to research as a core responsibility. Additionally, considering the acquisition of research projects, responsibilities range from raising financial resources for these projects to just organising partnerships for research projects. Another difference is the amount of experience in research as well as education, and not being specific in terms of asking to engage with certain research methods or educational experience.

When unpacking the differences between profiles a bit further, it becomes clear that the connotation of research and education can differ between profiles as well. For instance in 'the teacher-researcher without research competences' not only research competences are left out, but also the educational competences requests are rather unspecified. In other profiles, educational experience is positioned with much more prominence. However, on a content level, for the 'teacher with dual competences', much more often specific didactics, ICT skills in education and blended learning experiences are requested.

Another difference is that 'the teacher-researcher' profile more often requests for a personal vision about the professional field or research strand, managerial competences and tasks and 'being an authority in the field'. Furthermore, research and education are much more often mentioned as two parts of a whole, for instance, 'one has experience in research and education'. Interestingly, for the lecturers with a higher research prominence in 'the teacher-researcher profile', having a research-minded attitude is not mentioned, while this is mentioned frequently for 'lecturers with dual competencies'. It seems as if this attitude was already included in the task of research and related experience in conducting research, while its absence requests for the need to mention a particular attitude. For 'the teacher-researcher' profile, in about half of the cases, a PhD is requested, while the other profiles mostly request master's degrees and in some cases a bachelor's degree is sufficient.

Another particularity is the reference of active connections to the related professional field. For the first three profiles, it is often stated that candidates should maintain a network with professional practice to stay up-to-date. For the 'teacher-researcher' profile, this request is added with a statement that candidates should (be able to) bring this knowledge back into practice and acquire research projects.

Thus, not only differences between the prominence of research tasks and competences can be seen between the four different profiles, also the connotation of the content differs between them.

Conclusion: The Changing Dominance of Job Profiles

To consider change in hiring practices in the Dutch applied universities over time, this section considers whether the prevalence of the four most prominent job profiles changes between 2016 and 2019. Then, similar to the previous section, also the differences in connotation in each profile between the years is described (for an overview see Table 7.3).

The findings show the most prevailing job profile that applied universities intended to hire in all years between 2016 and 2019 is the 'teacher', which ranged between 44 per cent and 51 per cent of all job openings. This slight increase is interesting when remembering this book is about studying applied universities changing from teaching-only institutions to research-and-teaching institutions.

Similarly, 'the teacher without research competences' decreases somewhat from 10 per cent to 8 per cent after first gaining prominence. The 'teacher with

Table 7.3 Frequencies of four most occurring job profiles. Relative occurrence between brackets

	2016	2017	2018	2019	Total
'teacher'	55 (44%)	39 (45%)	85 (51%)	47 (49%)	226 (48%)
'teacher without research competences'	12 (10%)	11 (13%)	19 (11%)	8 (8%)	50 (11%)
'teacher with dual competences'	15 (12%)	10 (11%)	25 (15%)	18 (19%)	68 (14%)
'teacher-researcher'	24 (19%)	17 (20%)	22 (13%)	7 (7%)	70 (15%)
Total	124	87	168	95	474

dual competencies' becomes somewhat more prominent from 12 per cent to 19 per cent, and 'the teacher-researcher' profile has a sharp reduction after 2017 from 19 per cent to only 7 per cent in 2019.

Not much content change was found within the profiles between the different years. Formulations showed to be rather similar. There seems to be a slight change in 'the teacher' profile from requesting 'experience in teaching' in 2016 to asking for 'affinity with teaching' in 2019. This possibly is the consequence of a shortage of lecturers in educational programmes, resulting in less requirements to broaden the chance for the educational programmes to find a candidate.

Changing employee profiles as part of an organisational change programme is no easy endeavour. Actual changes – if any – are often hidden underneath employees' formal roles, resulting in false-positive or false-negative results. This chapter has shown what a more sophisticated, though more time-consuming, perspective to similar changes can result in.

The object of study in this chapter were Dutch universities of applied sciences during a time in which Amsterdam UAS had a purposeful change programme to further connect research and education. During this period, many other applied universities in the same country had set in place their own change instruments to achieve similar goals. Despite these efforts, the differences found in job profiles are slim. A decrease of the 'teacher-researcher' profile even contradicts the effort to increase the number of people working in research. The increase in the 'teacher' profile implies the same. It is known from the shop-floor level reality of these universities that individual lecturers have a hard time gaining a research position, and more in general combined positions of teaching and research are difficult to register in the administrative system. Further, different managers are responsible for the education budgets or the research budgets. Lecturers are generally hired by the educational programme as an organisational unit, while research activities take place in different organisational units, which often craft their own, independent job profiles for future employees. Previous research (Daas, Day, & Griffioen, 2019; Jenkins & Healey, 2005; Jenkins, Healey, & Zetter, 2007) suggested that organisational consistency, and in particular bringing managerial responsibilities of research and education in a single hand, would increase the potential for research–education connections. In that regard, it is likely that the changes in educational programmes have been a sufficient start to take more seriously research competences in future employees, as indicated by the reduction of 'the teacher without research competences' profile, and the increase in 'the teacher with dual competences profile'. However, it is likely that an adaptation of organisational structures – where research and education become part of single departments – is needed to increase the hiring of the 'teacher-researcher' profile.

An additional difficulty is the level of expertise sought in future employees, rated from their potential pay scales. As the findings have shown, generally the lecturers sought in these universities are rather experienced professionals with a high potential for teaching. This results in a relatively high pay scale. The number of potential candidates that additionally can bring research expertise to suit that high pay scale is often low. Therefore, for a research department to co-hire a teacher-researcher with an educational department implies that the difference in competency between research and education needs to be balanced out in the pay scale via taking the average which fits the academics' competencies on neither side. Therefore, a separated hiring strategy is likely to be much easier and results in the best value-for-money at both ends, at least as long as the research–education connections in personnel is not viewed as an added value for the university. It still is difficult to put this added value into words, let alone into quality indicators. In that regard, it is not sufficient for change agents to be normative-positive as Trowler and Wareham (2008) characterised; it is essential that change agents request administrators to clearly formulate the expected benefits of the connection, as well as what that is worth. Then organisational changes and budget responsibilities can be positioned in line with the universities' ambition and changes at the personnel level can be more easily achieved.

References

Ashwin, P. (2006). Interpreting the developments. Possible futures for learning and teaching in higher education. In P. Ashwin (Ed.), *Changing higher education. The development of learning & teaching* (pp. 125–34). London: Routledge.

Bandura, A. (2006). Guide for constructing self-efficacy scales. In F. Pajares & T. Urdan (Eds.), *Self-efficacy beliefs of adolescents* (pp. 307–37). USA: Information Age Publishing.

Boyd, P., & Smith, C. (2011). *Being a university lecturer in a professional field: Tensions within boundary-crossing workplace contexts*. Paper presented at the Society for Research into Higher Education, Newport.

Brew, A. (2001). Conceptions of research: A phenomenographic study. *Studies in Higher Education, 26*(3), 271–85.

Bystydzienski, J., Thomas, N., Howe, S., & Desai, A. (2016). The leadership role of college deans and department chairs in academic culture change. *Studies in Higher Education, 42*(12), 2301–15.

Daas, S. R., Day, I. N. Z., & Griffioen, D. M. E. (2019). *The intended synergy between research and teaching of universities of applied sciences in the Netherlands*. Paper presented at the Higher Education Conference 2019, Amsterdam.

Fung, D., Besters-Dilger, J., & Van der Vaart, R. (2017). Excellent education in research-rich universities. In LERU (Ed.). Brussels: LERU.

Felicja, V., Servant, C., Norman, G. R., & Schmidt, H. G. (2019). A short intellectual history of problem-based learning. In M. Moallem, W. Hung, & N. Dabbagh (Eds.), *The Wiley handbook of problem-based learning* (pp. 3–24). Hoboken: Wiley-Blackwell.

Fook, J. (2004). What professionals need from research. Beyond evidence-based practice. In D. Smith (Ed.), *Social work and evidence-based practice* (pp. 29–46). London: Jessica Kingsley Publishers.

Furusten, S., & Alexius, S. (2019). Managing hybrid organisations. In S. Furusten & S. Alexius (Eds.), *Managing hybrid organisations. Governance, professionalism and regulation* (pp. 333–60). Cham: Palgrave Macmillan.

Grange, A., Herne, S., Casey, A., & Wordsworth, L. (2005). Building research capacity. *Nursing Management, 12*(7), 32–7.

Griffioen, D. M. E. (2013). Research in traditional universities and higher professional education: Not in its genes. In D. M. E. Griffioen (Ed.), *Research in higher professional education: A staff perspective* (PhD) (pp. 25–44). Amsterdam: University of Amsterdam.

Griffioen, D. M. E. (2018). Building research capacity in new universities during times of academic drift: Lecturers professional profiles. *Higher Education Policy, 33*, 347–66. doi:https://doi.org/10.1057/s41307-018-0091-y

Griffioen, D. M. E. (2020). Building research capacity in new universities during times of academic drift: Lecturers professional profiles. *Higher Education Policy, 33*, 347–66. doi:https://doi.org/10.1057/s41307-018-0091-y

Griffioen, D. M. E., & De Jong, U. (2013). Academic drift in Dutch non-university higher education evaluated: A staff perspective. *Higher Education Policy, 26*, 173–91.

Griffioen, D. M. E., De Jong, U., & Jak, S. (2014). Research self-efficacy of lecturers in non-university higher education. *Innovation in Education and Teaching International, 50*(1), 25–37.

Griffioen, D. M. E., Ashwin, P., & Scholkmann, A. (2021). Who ensures that Society has the professionals it needs? Differences in the policy directions of three European countries. *Policy Reviews in Higher Education*. doi:https://doi.org/10.1080/23322969.2021.1880290

Handal, B., & Herrington, A. (2003). Mathematics teachers' beliefs and curriculum reform. *Mathematics Education Research Journal, 15*(1), 59–69.

Harwood, J. (2010). Understanding academic drift: On the institutional dynamics of higher technical and professional education. *Minerva, 48*, 413–427.

Hattie, J., & Marsh, H. W. (1996). The relationship between research and teaching: A meta-analysis. *Review of Educational Research, 66*, 507–42.

Healey, M. (2005). Linking research and teaching: Exploring disciplinary spaces and the role of inquiry-based learning. In R. Barnett (Ed.), *Reshaping the university: New relationships between research, scholarship and teaching* (pp. 67–78). McGraw Hill: Open University Press.

Heest, F. v. (2018, 23 May). Hbo hecht weinig waarde aan onderzoeksvaardigheden van docenten. *ScienceGuide*. Retrieved from https://www.scienceguide.nl/2018/05/hbo-onderzoeksvaardigheden-docenten/

Henkel, M. (2005). Academic identity and autonomy in a changing policy environment. *Higher Education, 49*, 155–76.

Huisman, J. (2008). Shifting boundaries in higher education: Dutch Hogescholen on the move. In J. S. Taylor, J. Brites Ferreira, M. De Lourdes Machado, & R. Santiago (Eds.), *Non-university higher education in Europe* (pp. 147–68). Heidelberg | New York: Springer.

Huisman, J., & Kaiser, F. (2001). *Fixed and fuzzy boundaries in higher education. A comparative study of (binary) structures in nine countries*. Retrieved from https://www.researchgate.net/publication/254858253_Fixed_and_Fuzzy_Boundaries_in_Higher_Education_a_comparative_study_of_binary_structures_in_nine_countries?msclkid=a98a03d1d13211ec9b5aff7655224e6a

Hunt, C. (2016). 'Teachers' to 'academics': The implementation of a modernisation project at one UK post-92 university. *Studies in Higher Education, 41*(7), 1189–202.

Hunter, A., Laursen, S. L., & Seymour, E. (2007). Becoming a scientist: The role of undergraduate research in students' cognitive, personal, and professional development. *Science Education, 91*(1), 36–74.

Jenkins, A., & Healey, M. (2005). *Institutional strategies to link teaching and research*. Retrieved from York: http://www.heacademy.ac.uk/assets/York/documents/resources/resourcedatabase/id585_institutional_strategies_to_link_teaching_and_research.pdf

Jenkins, A., Healey, M., & Zetter, R. (2007). *Linking teaching and research in disciplines and departments*. Retrieved from York: http://www.heacademy.ac.uk/assets/York/documents/LinkingTeachingAndResearch_April07.pdf

Joffe, H., & Yardley, L. (2004). Content and thematic analysis. In D. F. Marks & L. Yardley (Eds.), *Research methods for clinical and health psychology* (pp. 56–68). London: Sage.

Kamp, R. J. A., Dolmans, D. H. J. M., Van Berkel, H. J. M., & Schmidt, C. P. (2011). Can students adequately evaluate the activities of their peers in PBL? *Medical Teacher, 33*, 145–50.

Kyvik, S. (2007). Academic drift - A reinterpretation. In The officers and crew of HMS Network (Ed.), *Towards a cartography of higher education policy change. A festschrift in honour of guy neave* (pp. 333–8). Enschede: Universiteit Twente.

Kyvik, S., & Skodvin, O.-J. (2003). Research in non-university higher education sector-Tensions and dilemmas. *Higher Education, 45*(2), 203–22.

Levine, R., Russ-Eft, D., Burling, A., Stephens, J., & Downey, J. (2013). Evaluating health services research capacity building programs: Implications for health services and human resource development. *Evaluation and Program Planning, 37*, 1–11.

Lopes, A., Boyd, P., Andrew, N., & Pereira, F. (2014). The research-teaching nexus in nurse and teacher education: Contributions of an ecological approach to academic identities in professional fields. *Higher Education, 68*, 167–83.

Machado, M.d.L., Ferreira, J.B., Santiago, R., Taylor, J.S. (2008). Reframing the non-university sector in Europe: Convergence or diversity?. In: Taylor, J.S., Ferreira, J.B., Machado, M.d.L., Santiago, R. (Eds.), *Non-university higher education in Europe. Higher education dynamics*, vol 23 (pp. 245–61). Springer, Dordrecht.

Ministry of Education. (2015). *De waarde(n) van weten. Strategische Agenda Hoger Onderwijs en Onderzoek 2015-2025*. Den Haag.

Neave, G. (1978). Polytechnics: A policy drift? *Studies in Higher Education, 3*(1), 105–11.

Palali, A., Van Elk, R., Bolhaar, J., & Rud, I. (2017). Are good researchers also good teachers? The relationship between research quality and teaching quality. *Economics of Education Review 64*, 40–9.

Pitt, R., & Mewburn, I. (2016). Academic superheroes? A critical analysis of academic job descriptions. *Journal of Higher Education Policy and Management, 38*(1), 88–101.

Quirke, L. (2013). Roque resistance: Sidestepping isomorphic pressures in a patchy institutional field. *Organizational Studies, 34*(11), 1675–99.

Runhaar, P., Sanders, K., & Yang, H. (2010). Stimulating teachers' reflection and feedback asking: An interplay of self-efficacy, learning goal orientation, and transformational leadership. *Teaching and Teacher Education: An International Journal of Research and Studies, 26*(5), 1154–61.

Santos, C., Pereira, F., & Lopes, A. (2021). Research, teaching and publication: The challenges of academic work. In I. Huet, T. Pessoa, & F. Sol Murta (Eds.), *Excellence in teaching and learning in higher education: Institutional policies and practices in Europe* (pp. 199–216). Coimbra: Coimbra University Press.

Shapin, S., & Shaffer, S. (2011 [1985]). *Leviathan and the airpump. Hobbes, Boyle and the experimental life*. Princeton: Princeton University Press.

Smith, C., & Boyd, P. (2012). Becoming an academic: The reconstruction of identity by recently appointed lecturers in nursing, midwifery and the allied health professions. *Innovation in Education and Teaching International, 49*(1), 63–72.

Trowler, P. (1998). *Academics responding to change. New higher education frameworks and academic cultures.* London: The Society for Research into Higher Education & Open University Press.

Trowler, P., & Wareham, T. (2008). *Tribes, territories, research and teaching: Enhancing the teaching research nexus.* Retrieved from York: https://www.heacademy.ac.uk/resource/tribes-territories-research-and-teaching-enhancing-teaching-research-nexus-literature#sthash.5NK7FyDy.dpuf

Turner, N., Wuetherick, B., & Healey, M. (2008). International perspectives on student awareness, experiences and perceptions of research: Implications for academic developers in implementing research-based teaching and learning. *International Journal for Academic Development, 13*(3), 199–211.

Vitae. (2010). *Researcher development framework.* Retrieved from Cambridge: https://www.vitae.ac.uk/researchers-professional-development/about-the-vitae-researcher-development-framework

Winkel, M., Van der Rijst, R. M., Poel, R., & Van Driel, J. H. (2016). Identities of research-active academics in new universities: Towards a complete academic profession cross-cutting different worlds of practice. *Journal of Further & Higher Education, 42*(4), 539–55. doi:10.1080/0309877X.2017.1301407

8

Reflections on the Multiple Layers of Organisational Change

Didi M. E. Griffioen

Introduction

The developments that have led to this book were more practical than theoretical: The many conversations over time about this single, large change programme in an applied university resulted in the awareness that a thorough and systematic body of knowledge that could underpin such changes was lacking. Many in the Amsterdam university as well as from outside of it reached out to the change team for support, asking for insights and ideas about how to get a university moving towards a change in research–education connections. Asking for proof about what would work in their change process. Obviously, the option of change already had entered these colleagues' minds, but many others were made aware of these possibilities, often by pointing out an opportunity for improvement just placed in between the lines of conversations about other topics. This awareness of potentially large effects of simple efforts sparked the idea that telling our change story in a book, positioned in the context of the current body of literature on change management and the body of knowledge on the research–teaching nexus, could assist many in seeing new options for change in their own setting. Hopefully, others are also willing to systematically share their experience, so a collective body of knowledge about changing research–education connections is brought to life.

By way of conclusion, this chapter offers a reflection on all previous chapters, lightly touching on what has not yet been stated, but more so integrating the different perspectives of the previous chapters. First, the actual changes in the Amsterdam setting are considered through the lens of successes of change programmes. Second, the combined findings of the different monitoring instruments are examined. Finally, this results in a reflection on the usability of the multi-layered model for change presented in this book.

Success of Changing Research–Education Connections

There is not much systematically known about the success of change programmes in higher education. Only very few scholars have contributed to this field of successful change. Mostly found are the reflections of former presidents, generalisations of instruments, change instruments as isolated actions due to the lack of theoretical frameworks and a lack of detail for choosing quantitative measures. Kezar and Eckel (2002) did empirically study the change process of multiple higher-education institutes. Based on six of these higher education institutes and following a teleological framework, they identified five common core instruments across all six institutes: senior administrative support, collaborative leadership, robust design, staff development, and visible action. The Amsterdam programme is here reflected upon based on these five factors.

The first factor to consider is senior administrative support, which implies that the senior administrators take ownership of the change process, including launching the initiative, chairing discussions, providing financial resources, creating new structures, and actively valuing of what is going well. The senior administration takes full responsibility for the change programme, although there also is a visible division between the different administrators. At the top level, not all easily follow the path of sensemaking and the stages of awareness and desire. Often, top administrators are asking for interventions that resonated more with ADKAR's stage of reinforcement, such as imposing definitions of research, or making judgements about changes made in individual educational programmes instead of providing the individuals in the organisation with the time to create their own definitions and become owners of the new research–education connections. Top management and their secretaries need to become aware of the potential that could be unleashed if stakeholders are put into motion without initial restrictions, obviously to provide guidelines and therefore implicit later on in the developments. At the programme level, the dean responsible for the strategic programme played his public role well, making time to chair sessions and discuss strategy frequently and very publicly. However, with a structure of making the faculty deans each responsible for a different strategic programme, the other faculty deans differed a lot in their investment in this particular strategic programme, ranging from almost co-partnering to being almost fully absent from the public eye on this topic.

As explained in Chapters 1 and 2, the Amsterdam programme very much leaned on collaborative leadership, also Kezar and Eckel's (2002) second factor of success, which yields to 'creating avenues for involvement through workshops, symposiums and roundtables, open invitations throughout the process' (p. 312). They explain how examples also show central administrators providing the autonomy to develop their own change results and craft their own new system.

The difficulty of the programme being heavy on collaboration and autonomy reduced its success on the visible action factor, which consists of both visible and active participation in change activities and the visible (intermediate) effects of the change process. Forums, newsletters, various groups' presentations and visible pilot projects can be part of this instrument. The collective activities of the programme were very visible, also because visibility across the university was part of the programme's mechanism for change: To see change makes wanting to be in the change. However, its foundation in collaborative leadership made it difficult to scale up or even capture changes, and it was therefore not easy to make successes visible, while there were so many successes. Administrators and policy officers often asked for examples of some specific development for formal reports and often find the changes too subtle and only context relevant. Furthermore, the programme team was strategically reluctant to present 'best practices' because it would result in copying behaviour and/or a reduction of the autonomy the educational teams needed for their sensemaking processes. This reduced the changes' formal visibility across the university. Thus, where the programme execution was very visible, its success is not so easy to show or see.

The next factor of success is a robust design that focuses on the results of the change process, including a direction to move forward and a flexible plan to guide institutional actions. As explained in Chapter 1, a design for change can rise from long-term debate of grassroots development, or be planned, but it is important for the plan's content to be embraced by the wider group of colleagues, therefore making the change programme more formal. The Amsterdam programme was very much based on planned change, but was only thinly defined. This strategy provided the firmness derived from top management's involvement, combined with the space needed to be flexible. However, due to having limited planning on paper, the Amsterdam programme very much leaned into the strategic choices made between the programme-owning dean and the programme leader, which was backed by the university's chairman. With this approach of feeling where to go next, not many strategic choices could be delegated, as was difficult for giving workshops and masterclasses. Therefore, the increase in competency was placed within very few colleagues and the increase of activities across the university provided a risk to its quality. Efforts to transfer the insights and skills were not too successful. The 'on-the-go' design just based on a few sharply formulated overall aims provided wonderful flexibility up to a certain number of educational teams, but particularly the shift of the programme leader additionally becoming a full professor illustrated how thinly spread the competences in the programme team were. A different set-up would have made the programme much less flexible and much slower in providing developments across the university, but would potentially have made the changes more robust in the long run.

There are two relevant perspectives to the last factor of staff development. This factor should assist in providing people with the leadership and skills 'to more effectively communicate, make decisions, and provide input on the change initiative' (Kezar & Eckel, 2002, p. 312). First of all, staff development can be seen as similar to the awareness and desire stages of the ADKAR model. The Amsterdam programme focused on these two stages and was very successful in bringing leadership and skills in this regard to the stakeholders in the different educational teams. Towards the end of the strategic programme's five years, this success was even expanded to policy departments, research teams and participatory councils across the university. However, there is another perspective to this factor, which the ADKARs stages of knowledge and ability can capture. These stages were not part of the five-year plan.

The need for these next stages became more visible towards the end of the five-year term. The more stakeholders that were actively and willingly getting involved in changing research–education connections, the louder their request became for 'the right solutions', 'the best choices', and 'the most proper practices'. As explained throughout this book, these examples are lacking and one can wonder if they are conceptually possible due to the contextuality of research–education connections. Also, there was an increased request for full partnership in detailed curriculum changes, for which no sufficient funding or personnel was available. Optimistically, one can say that the university had been made ready for the next two ADKAR stages. However, the feeling of disappointment with the educational teams about limitations to the help offered also was very present. This disappointment might partly be countered by the newly created research group (project 5). Paradoxically, as long as the ability of those involved does not stretch to the awareness that research–education connections cannot be realised through quick fixes, likely the disappointment remains.

Not disregarding its potential for improvement, we can conclude that in the Amsterdam programme, origin, content, approach, phases, and factors were made interdependently fitting to its particular situation; an Amsterdam balance was created for its change programme for research–education connections. This makes the Amsterdam programme an important example for future change programmes to alter research–education connections. As Kezar and Eckel (2002, p. 304) state: 'What elements and strategies specifically need to be balanced and the ways in which balance occurs are defined within each organisation as dictated by institutional type, culture, and context'.

Therefore, the Amsterdam programme has been consistent with Buller's (2015) three more fluent guidelines that can be considered the most important ones: It has considered changing the university as a collective voyage of discovery and not a line of firm decisions; it has provided the time and energy to let change grow from within, even when the start of the change was top-down imposed; and the programmes' content, approach, phases, and factors were not only focused on the proposed changes, but also built further on its origin. To appreciate the current situation and to understand how the organisations' people might change from there, provided the foundation of an effective change programme.

The Monitored Changes across the University's Layers

Change agents can often provide the perspective of success as described above: they reflect on the successes and failures of change programmes. While these insights are valuable, they also lack a more objective insight that could follow from a more scientific, longitudinal approach that takes place during the change programme and is closely designed in reference to its mechanism for change.

As explained in the Introduction and in Chapters 1 and 2, the mechanism of a change programme consists of:

1. the combined direction for action that follows from a topic origin,
2. a clear definition of the proposed content connected to particular organisational layers,
3. insight into the change context that can influence its result,
4. an approach that is flexible and fits the content, and
5. some type of phases the stakeholders can be expected to go through in their development.

Finally, Chapter 3 has shown that hands-on tools are needed to put the mechanism into action; in the Amsterdam case to let the stakeholders start discussing research–education connections, with different discussions relevant for each of them.

The systematic, objective monitoring of changes was designed across the university and closely related to the mechanism of the Amsterdam change programme. The systematic monitoring of change over time was captured in four measurement instruments: in the changes in the lecturers' and students' perceptions (Chapter 4); changes in the rationales of bachelor's curricula (Chapter 5); changes in the learning goals of bachelor's curricula (Chapter 6); and changes in the job descriptions of searched-for employees nationally (Chapter 7). Including such systematic monitoring instruments, which clearly reach beyond the generally more superficial focus of instruments of policy monitoring, provided a more in-depth insight into the developments across Amsterdam UAS.

These measurements have shown that there was a difference between the increased excitement among the stakeholders who chose to be part of changing research–education connections – about 600 at the end of the programme of about 3,700 lecturers – less substantial changes can be seen among the larger group stakeholders in the university, through the monitoring instruments that addressed the wider university or national developments. Chapter 4 by Bruinsma and Griffioen has shown that the lecturers' perceptions did not change so much between 2016 and 2019; lecturers continued to worry about the disconnectedness of research in the curriculum with other parts of the curriculum, especially the professionalism into which students are trained. Students mirrored these perceptions in 2019 (they were not asked in 2016) and generally felt that research could and should be better connected to the professional they were expected to become. Further, if research was to be expected of them, the build-up across the curriculum should be improved to serve them better.

The focus on the students' professionalism found in the perception measurements resonates with one of the four foci found in the chapter by Van Ooijen-Van der Linden and colleagues who wondered: Why would research be included in a bachelor's programme? They discovered four reasons, of which the first is similar to the perceptions found among stakeholders: to serve the profession. Other reasons were: to serve the student, to serve the educational programme by raising its quality and the university or national frameworks expect it. The last reason was rather instrumental: to work within the requested frameworks. In the first-time frame, a few educational programmes did not mention any reason. In the second-time frame, all educational programmes had arguments about why they included research in their curricula, resulting in a relative increase of all four types of arguments. Based on that notion, one can say that at least the committees writing the quality enhancement self-reports of educational teams – the data unit of this study – increased in their language possibilities for research–education connections.

This again resonates with the findings of the chapter by Van Ooijen-Van der Linden and colleagues about changes in learning goals of bachelor's curricula. This rather time-consuming study provided a much more detailed insight into how the language educational programmes use in their own curriculum descriptions changed over time. The detailed findings per faculty can be found in the corresponding chapter. The overall conclusion of these colleagues is that the changes are subtle and can be mostly seen in learning goals changing from being rather fuzzy to being more focused. Similar to the changes in rationales, one could say that there is an increase in clarity of language to be used to argue about research in the curriculum, in this case about learning goals. Considering that learning goals are expected to capture the clear, testable content of an educational programme, clarity is highly beneficial. However, the authors argue that an increased clarity can result in a risk for the research's position in the curriculum when learning goals are formulated in a rather instrumental manner. Especially when the curriculum's rationale is more instrumental, and therefore the 'why' of what a student is expecting to learn is lacking, thus there is the risk of learning the student tricks instead of providing them with sensible and usable knowledge.

The final monitoring study by Daas and colleagues provides insight into whether changes at the national level can be seen in the type of lecturers that are hired to create teaching and learning arrangements together with their students that can connect research to professionalism. That study's findings are complex and yield how research competences are increasingly valued because fewer lecturers are sought after that have research tasks but no research competences. However, fewer lecturer-researchers are requested, and more teachers without research tasks or competences are requested. Thus, it seems that research competences are taken more seriously, but are less sought after, which most likely does not increase students' interactions with researchers. The authors argue that organisational characteristics – such as separated budgets and responsibilities for research and education – are likely limiting factors for hiring combined personnel. However, the presence of research ability in the wider organisation, especially at shop-floor level, is an important prerogative to further the developments in research–education connections. A larger ability among new personnel would make it easier to create the changes in the knowledge and ability stages of the ADKAR model.

The Relevance of Multi-layer Change

The multi-layers of changing research–education practices have been visible throughout this book, and were explicated in Chapter 1. As argued here, it is important to be aware of the possible negative and positive influences that can result from the multiplicity of perspectives across the university's multiple organisational layers, and sometimes beyond to regional and national policy. This goes beyond Jenkins and Healey's (2005) notion that the different organisational layers should be aligned to best benefit student learning. The additional argument made here is that the multiple organisational layers can influence each other's change processes and therefore provide opportunities for university change agents. The argument shown through this book is that change agents need to have their own specialism at the crossroads of knowing about organisational change, knowing about the topic at hand – here the research–education nexus – and how to bring these hands-on into a change programme in a university. This specialism, as well as the multi-layeredness of organisational change on a certain topic, also complicates conversations with stakeholders, lecturers, and central administrators alike. Generally, university stakeholders reason from their own perspective and it is up to change agents to be knowledgeable across layers, to follow in the lead of their collocutor and to bring other 'layers' into their perspective when beneficial. This requests change agents to have a deep insight into theory and practice of organisational change, as well as knowledge of the specific topic at hand. Further, as long as systematic studies that could bring these perspectives together remain mostly absent, change agents need to benefit from theory-embedded case studies, such as presented in this book.

One conclusion from this book is that organisational change that addresses the core of a university is complex and takes a lot of time and energy to achieve small-level changes, such as in lecturers' language usage. Many universities work along a five-year plan, as was done in the Amsterdam case. As this book has shown, the changes achieved in the awareness about the organisational direction, and the desire to contribute to this direction were accomplished among a substantial core group. Educational programmes were changed and debates about connections between research and professional practices took place in many educational teams. However, considering the changes found in the perceptions of the larger group of lecturers from a rather soft perspective, or in the job application texts from a more firm organisational perspective, then not so much has changed. This implies that administrators should perceive these types of changes in a much longer perspective, and should align different change programmes over time to achieve more substantial changes. Only very few are willing to do so at the national (Ministerie van Onderwijs, 2015) or local level (Fung, 2017), and generally, they are countered as soon as they are replaced in office.

A similar call can be formulated for higher-education research. Where substantial changes in a university can only be captured across a university, in its multiple layers, and over a longer duration, it is important that instruments are developed to capture these changes. Obviously, it is easier to capture change through analysing documents as the carrier of a particular narrative or time frame. However, as we have shown in this book, some changes can be captured through documents – such as changes in written curriculum rationales, written learning goals, or job openings – but others can only be captured by actively asking, such as in the lecturers' perceptions in this book. The different data carriers resulted in different insights on the changes at this university, which showed a different segment – or layer – of the change at that time. These are again other perspectives than instruments administrators used in the same university, such as the judgement of educational quality enhancement agencies, the number of lecturers or students working in research or the increasing number of PhD graduates among lecturers. This case study has shown that it is important to consider what indicators are rich enough to capture the changes that one intends to see. However, the case study also shows that reaching for these indicators is time consuming and takes a lot of effort, energy and patience. That said, to have a proper insight into the shop-floor changes, it is wise to make at least some effort.

Final Remark

The authors of this book have aimed to contribute to the integrated conceptual fields of organisational change, the research–education nexus, and a more hands-on perspective of changing research–education connections across the university. Our ambition is to present more research-informed practices on such a complex topic by providing a more integrated knowledge base between these fields. Hopefully, others follow in this lead to share practices positioned in the wider literature base. For the future, we hope for more instruments for systematic research, for more tools for changing practice, and that the conceptual connections between the three fields are deepened. This book's authors very much would like to invite others to share their own work to help achieve these goals.

References

Buller, J. L. (2015). *Change leadership in higher education*. San Francisco: Jossey-Bass.

Fung, D. (2017). *A connected curriculum for higher education*. London: UCL.

Jenkins, A., & Healey, M. (2005). *Institutional strategies to link teaching and research*. Retrieved from York: http://www.heacademy.ac.uk/assets/York/documents/resources/resourcedatabase/id585_institutional_strategies_to_link_teaching_and_research.pdf

Kezar, A., & Eckel, P. (2002). Examining the institutional transformation process. *Research in Higher Education, 43*(3), 295–328.

Ministerie Van Onderwijs, C. W. (2015). De waarde(n) van weten. Strategische Agenda Hoger Onderwijs en Onderzoek 2015–2025. Den Haag.

Index

4CID model (*four component instructional design*) 125

academics
   coping strategies regarding research 178, 180-2
   job profiles 175-97 (see also *job profiles of academics*)
   identities (*see identity*)
accountability 13, 127, 134, 138, 179
action 2, 4, 27, 31, 32, 34, 35, 43, 44, 50, 52-4, 56, 67, 68, 83, 85-8, 100, 108, 109, 126, 129, 131, 135, 138, 140-2, 163-4, 179, 200-1, 203-4
ADDIE model (*analysis, design, development, implementation, and evaluation*) 125
ADKAR model for change (*awareness, desire, knowledge, ability, reinforcement*) 54-6, 143, 200, 202, 206
assessment 22, 125, 131-2, 140, 182
awareness 28, 37, 53, 54, 56, 60, 63, 143, 169, 199, 200, 202, 206

backward design 125, 132
Bologna declaration 24, 149
Bologna process 128

capital
   embodied 5
   institutionalised 5, 6
change
   approach of 1-10, 21, 43-60
   intentional 23, 44
   multiple-layer perspective 2, 13, 14, 28-30, 37, 44, 50, 52, 63-4, 67, 88, 131, 143, 169, 199-207
   reasons for 4-9, 22, 75, 107, 111, 204-5, 206
change agents
   lecturers as 51, 128

university 5, 9, 13, 21, 22, 26-9, 33, 37, 43, 45-6, 51, 52-3, 54, 58, 63-5, 68-70, 72, 75, 88-90, 97, 128, 143, 171, 181, 194, 203, 206
change mechanism 4, 13, 21-2, 23, 27, 29-31, 34
change strategies
   emergent 44-5, 47, 48, 103
   planned 44-5, 47, 53, 201
   received 23, 57
collaborative leadership 200-1
collective language 80
constructive alignment 125
Covid-19 pandemic 8
creativity 11, 44, 136
critical thinking 108, 141, 154, 157, 159, 160, 165, 166, 168, 169
curiosity 80, 141, 157, 159, 160, 162, 163, 165, 166, 167
curriculum design 14, 15, 58, 95, 100, 104, 123-4, 125, 127, 129, 132, 141, 151, 156, 170
curriculum rationale 50, 123-44, 207

desire x, xiii, 1-16, 43, 54, 56, 60, 119, 125, 143, 169, 200, 202, 206

emergent change strategy 44-5, 47, 48, 103
empirical research cycle 77-8, 153
evidence based practice (EBP) 135, 139, 160-1, 162, 166-7

freedom of choice 114

hiring practices 177
hybrid organisation 1, 9-10, 29, 34, 57

ICT 5, 8, 22, 191
ideal research-education connection 11, 14, 97-8, 101, 114, 115, 117, 118, 128, 142, 151, 152

identity
- academics' 55, 56, 128, 176, 180-1
- dual 34-5, 180
- lecturers' 55, 55, 56, 128, 180-1
- lecturers' coping strategies 180-1
- professional 6, 124, 129, 176, 179, 180
- student 124, 126

inclusiveness 7
innovation 11, 25-6, 44, 50, 52, 85-7, 106-7, 139, 141, 142, 162, 175, 179, 181, 190
inquiry 11, 73-4, 79, 97, 126, 128, 149, 158
institution
- of education 46
- of science 46, 50

instrumental skills 108, 157, 158, 159-60, 161, 163, 164, 165, 166, 167, 168

job openings 15, 178, 183-8, 191-2

knowledge
- disciplinary 6, 8, 126, 129, 144, 189
- objectified 5, 7-8
- pedagogical content knowledge (PCK) 126-7
- professional 6, 8, 24, 25, 31, 85-6, 105, 131, 179

knowledge sharers (Dutch: *kennisdelers*) 49
knowledge structures 126, 179

landscape overview instrument 69-70
learning context 132
learning goals x, 15, 50, 80, 125, 131, 143, 149-71, 204-5, 207
learning outcomes 132, 143, 153
lecturers (*see also research integration, see also perceptions of research integration*)
- as change agents 51, 128 (see also change agents)
- identity (see *identity*)

levels of certainty and risk model 76
line-management responsibilities 25-6, 32, 47
logics 11-12, 34, 35

methodology 6, 51, 70, 72, 140, 157, 159-60, 161, 164, 165, 166, 167, 168, 169

multi-layer 2, 13, 14, 28-30, 37, 44, 50, 52, 63-4, 67, 88, 96, 98, 101, 131, 143, 169, 199-207 (*see change, multiple-layer perspective*)

new aspects of research tool (NAR-T) 80

organisational
- architecture 9, 29-31
- fixed elements 9-10, 27, 34-5, 52
- fluent elements 9-10, 27, 34, 52, 53
- legitimacy 11

pedagogical content knowledge (PCK) 126-7
perceptions of research integration 29, 32, 48, 50, 66, 194, 95-120 (*see also research integration, see also research-education connections*)
positive-normative view 29, 194
personnel's capacity 177-8
perspectives of research instrument 73
phases of research instrument (see also *research phases model*) 76-80
planned change strategy 44, 47
polytechnics 10, 24
practice-based research 78, 79, 136-7, 184, 188
professional
- innovation 85-6
- routine 85-6
professional higher education 14, 23, 24, 85, 88, 107, 180 (see also *research, role in professional higher education*)
professional identity 124, 129, 176
professional knowledge 6, 8, 24-5, 31, 85-6, 105, 131, 179
professional practice 32, 51, 55, 85, 103, 106, 110, 117-18, 119, 133-6, 137-43, 153-4, 157, 162, 165, 168, 170, 187, 188, 189, 190, 192, 207
- and education 119
- and research 110-12, 117-18, 135-6, 137-43, 153-4, 157, 162, 165, 168, 170, 187, 188, 207
professionalisation 70, 84, 177, 178
professionalism 32, 51, 59, 85-8, 116, 118, 143, 179, 204-5

professions
    design-oriented 88
    reflective 88
    research-dependent 88, 89

regulative research cycle 76-7
research
    conceptions of 65, 66, 71, 72, 95, 96
    in the curriculum 80, 84, 89, 102, 103-10, 114-15, 133-43, 152-6, 169, 170, 175, 204-5
    definition of 58
    practice-based 137, 184, 187
    and professional practice 103, 117-18, 153
    role in professional higher education 14, 23, 103, 104, 109, 113, 116, 117, 118, 129-33, 152, 170
research autonomy and complexity tool (RAC-T) 80-4
research capacity 141, 177
research competencies 15, 28, 36, 79, 87, 103, 105, 108-10, 116, 155, 156, 157, 159-60, 162, 165-6, 167, 168, 177, 180, 185-94
research-education connections (*see also research integration, see also perceptions of research integration*)
    ideal 14, 97-8, 102, 114-18, 128, 151
    success of change (see *success of change*)
    togetherness 119
    two-way traffic 95
researcher 88
research-informed practices 4, 50, 90, 207
research integration (*see also perceptions of research integration, see also research-education connections*)
    advocacy of academics 58, 106-8, 115-16, 130
    coping strategies of academics 178-81, 182
    reasons for 106-8, 115-16, 123-44
    resistance of academics 35, 45, 53, 58, 182, 106-8, 115-16
research level and content instrument (RLC-I) 80, 84
research phases model (see also *phases of research instrument*) 76-80
robust design 200, 201

scholarship 1, 73-4, 79
self-reports 131-3, 136, 137, 142, 143, 205
senior administrative support 200
sensemaking 56-60, 200, 201
social cognition theory 45-6, 51, 53
social constructionist assumptions 44
societal
    issues 141, 152, 154
    purpose 5
    responsibilities 5, 6-7, 22
spider-web model 125
staff development 202
strategy mapping instrument 66-7
string instrument 68-9
student-centred teaching 124, 126
student identity (see *identity*)
student perceptions (see *perceptions of research integration*)
success of change (programme) 12, 33, 34, 53, 200-3
sustainable development 154
synergy 12, 28-9, 31, 97

taste makers (Dutch: *smaakmakers*) 49
teaching competencies 183, 188

visible action 200-1

www.ingramcontent.com/pod-product-compliance
Lightning Source LLC
Chambersburg PA
CBHW062223300426
44115CB00012BA/2198